Remaking Media

What is the political significance and potential of democratic media activism in the Western world today?

Remaking Media rides on a wave of political and scholarly attention to opposit- ional communication, triggered by the rise in the 1990s of the Zapatistas, internet activism and IndyMedia. This attention has mostly focused on alternative media and the 'media strategies' of social movements – i.e., 'democratization through the media'. This book concerns democratization of the media themselves, efforts to transform the 'machinery of representation', as a distinctive field that is pivotal to other social struggles.

Remaking Media takes as its premise the existence of a massive 'democratic deficit' in the field of public communication. This deficit propels diverse struggles to reform and revitalize public communication in the North Atlantic heartland of globalization. It focuses on activism directed towards challenging and changing media content, practices and structures, as well as state policies on media.

Hackett and Carroll's approach is innovative in its attention to an emerging social movement that appears at the cutting edge of cultural and political conten- tion. The book is grounded in three scholarly traditions that provide interpretive resources for a study of democratic media activism: political theories of democracy, critical media scholarship and the sociology of social movements. By synthesizing insights from these sources they provide a unique and timely reading of the contemporary struggle to democratize communication.

Robert A. Hackett is Professor of Communication at Simon Fraser University in Canada.

William K. Carroll is Professor of Sociology at the University of Victoria in Canada.

Communication and society

Series Editor: James Curran

Remaking Media

The struggle to democratize
public communication

**Robert A. Hackett and
William K. Carroll**

Routledge
Taylor & Francis Group

NEW YORK AND LONDON

First published 2006 by
Routledge
270 Madison Avenue, New York, NY 10016

Simultaneously published in the UK
by Routledge
2 Park Square, Milton Park, Abingdon, Oxon OX14 4RN

Routledge is an imprint of the Taylor & Francis Group, an informa business

Typeset in Baskerville by
Bookcraft Ltd, Stroud, Gloucestershire
Printed and bound in Great Britain by
MPG Books Ltd, Bodmin

Library of Congress Cataloging in Publication Data
Hackett, Robert A.
    Remaking Media : the struggle to democratize public communication /
Robert A. Hackett, William K. Carroll.
        p. cm. – (Communication and society)
    Includes bibliographical reference and index.
1. Mass media – Political aspects.   2. Communication – Political aspects.
3. Democratization.   4. Democracy.   I. Carroll, William K.   II. Title.
III. Communication and society (Routledge (Firm))
    p95.8.H33 2006
    302.23–dc22   2005033106

British Library Cataloguing in Publication Data
A catalogue record for this book is available from the British Library

ISBN10: 0-415-39468-6 (hbk)
ISBN10: 0-415-39469-4 (pbk)
ISBN10: 0-203-96992-8 (ebk)

ISBN13: 978-0-415-39468-0 (hbk)
ISBN13: 978-0-415-39469-7 (pbk)
ISBN13: 978-0-203-96992-2 (ebk)

Contents

Illustrations

Figures

Tables

Foreword

This important book by Bob Hackett and Bill Carroll is premised on two important intellectual observations.

First, sociologists have developed the notion of 'critical junctures' to explain social change and the historical process. Although history proceeds one day at a time, and although humans make their own history under the heavy hand of conditions they inherit, social change tends to take place in condensed historical periods of intense activity. These periods are termed 'critical junctures', and it is during these periods when the options facing society are much greater than they are otherwise. Critical junctures tend to take place during profound social crises when the existing order is subject to intense scrutiny and criticism. So it was during the 1930s in the United States, when all sorts of social policies were debated and enacted that would have been difficult to imagine a decade earlier or a decade or two later.

Second, media scholars have in recent years stripped away the self-serving rhetoric of commercial news media and their ideologues that a profit-driven media system is the 'natural' system for a democratic society, or even a capitalist society. Increasingly, scholars have established that media systems are based primarily on a large number of significant government policies and subsidies, even in the most capitalist of nations, the United States. Even if one wished to establish a 'free market' media system, with competitive markets, it would require extensive government policymaking to bring it into play. Accordingly, considerable emphasis in recent times has examined the media policymaking process in nations around the world, and at the transnational level. Once largely overlooked, it is now understood that this is where one must go if one wishes to understand why media systems work the way they do.

In the United States, for example, the profit-driven, concentrated, hyper-commercialized, corporate-dominated media system is not the result of free markets or the wishes of the nation's Founders. It is the result of extremely corrupt policymaking, where lucrative subsidies and monopoly licence and regulations were enacted on behalf of powerful corporate lobbies. These policies have been made in the public's name but without the public's informed consent. In fact, until very recently, few Americans had any idea that media systems were the result of policies, and they certainly would know nothing of the matter from the news media.

When we combine these two observations we begin to see the potentially revolutionary nature of the current period. Media policies are now in the midst of a 'critical juncture', not just in the United States but worldwide. It is the result of three overlapping factors. First, the existing media system is in deep crisis. Due to corporate pursuit of profit and corrupt policymaking, the calibre of journalism and entertainment is well below the requirements of a democratic society. Public concern about media has risen, and the notion that this is a 'natural system' is increasingly less palatable. Second, the broader socioeconomic system is in a perilous condition. Global inequality and poverty, war and militarism, ecological crisis, public health calamities, and economic traumas mark this era as one where fundamental political decisions may determine the course of humanity for some time to come. The political environment is increasingly demanding a more open look at solutions to major social problems, as the status quo is not satisfactory. Third, technological developments in communication are both radically expanding what media systems are capable of doing and undermining the existing media structures.

All in all, this explains the vast increase of media activism in the past decade all across the planet. Millions of people who had never thought much about media are now actively working to make media and to change media policies to blast open the system. It is becoming an accepted observation that any effort to democratize society must include a campaign to change the media system or else the prospects for success will be far lower.

Remaking Media is a testament to this historical moment and a book of considerable importance to the politics of our times. This is no superficial exercise in buzzword lobbing. It is a rigorous historically based and politically sophisticated analysis of the media movement and its prospects for success. It is required reading.

Robert W. McChesney

Acknowledgements

Several hundred people have contributed directly to this book. Many informal conversations as well as structured interviews have informed it. With apologies in advance for those we have not named, we owe thanks to dozens of journalists, academics and activists (including several who preferred not to be identified) for generously sharing their time and insights. Most of them were expressing their own views, not necessarily those of their organizations.

From the Campaign for Press and Broadcasting Freedom, the World Association for Christian Communication, the National Union of Journalists, and other organizations based in the UK, these people included Stuart Allan, Cynthia Carter, Paddy Coulter, James Curran, Kathy Darby, Andy Egan, Maurice Frankel, Bob Franklin, Tim Gopsill, Jonathan Hardy, Sean Hawkey, Paul Holleran, Myriam Horngren, Christine Jardine, Mike Jempsen, Arun Kundnani, Philip Lee, Tony Lennon, Kathy Lowe, Gerry Morrissey, Randy Naylor, Tom O'Malley, Simon Paranini, Don Redding, Clive Soley, Damian Tambini, Pradip Thomas, Sean Tunney, Anna Turley, Barry White, and Granville Williams. Robert Hackett gratefully acknowledges Barry White's and James Curran's congenial hospitality during visits to London, and invaluable comments from them, Jonathan Hardy, Mike Jempsen, and Granville Williams on drafts of Chapter 6. At the international level, we spoke to Cees Hamelink, a driving force behind the People's Communication Charter, and Aidan White, general secretary of the International Federation of Journalists.

In the US, we thank Jeff Cohen, Peter Hart, Janine Jackson, Jim Naureckas and Steve Rendall at Fairness and Accuracy in Reporting (FAIR) in New York; and Larry Bensky, Andrea Buffa, Daniel Ben-Horin, Ben Clarke, Kim Deterline, Laura Fraser, Van Jones, Linda Jue, Jeff Perlstein, Jerry Roberts, Tracy Rosenburg and Fred Stout, past or present members or staffers with Media Alliance in San Francisco. Other respondents in the San Francisco Bay area – with the Independent Media Institute, Project Censored, the Independent Press Association, the Democratic Media Legal Project, the Institute for Public Accuracy, the Public Media Center, Berkeley Media Studies Group, Free Radio Berkeley, San Francisco Liberation Radio, the Gay & Lesbian Alliance Against Defamation, and other advocates for democratic communication – included John Anner, Bernadette Barker-Plummer, Robert Bray, Lori Dorfman, Stephen Dunifer, Richard

Edmondson, Peter Franck, Seeta Gangadharan, Herbert Chao Gunther, Don Hazen, Dorothy Kidd, Henry Kroll, Holly Minch, Peter Phillips, Fernando Quintero, Yvan Roman, Don Romesburg, Jeremy Smith, Norman Solomon and David Zupan (and with added thanks to Messieurs Kroll and Phillips for their hospitality). Elsewhere, we also spoke with Jeff Chester, Aliza Dichter, George Gerbner, Jonathan Lawson, Mark Lloyd, Bob McChesney, Kathryn Montgomery, Bob Neal, Greg Ruggiero, Danny Schechter, Nancy Snow, Jerry Starr, Makani Themba-Nixon, and Karen Toering. Their hard-won insights from a range of groups, including Free Press, the Cultural Environment Movement, Praxis Project, Community Media Alliance, Citizens for Independent Public Broadcasting, Media Channel, Civil Rights Forum on Communication Policy, Center for Digital Democracy, and others, benefited us greatly.

In our home country, we spoke with journalists David Beers, Kim Bolan, Christina Montgomery, Frances Russell, Michael Valpy and Mike Walsh, as well as folks from C-CAVE (Canadians concerned about violent entertainment), the Communications, Energy and Paperworkers Union, the Canadian CPBF, the Friends of Canadian Broadcasting, and the federal New Democratic Party – Rose Dyson, Gail Lem, Wendy Lill, Ian Morrison, Peter Murdoch, Marc Raboy, David Robinson, and Armand Roy.

We also acknowledge the panellists and speakers at the Media and Democracy Congress II (New York 16–19 October 1997), Reclaiming the Media (Seattle, September 2002), the ACME Summit (Albuquerque, October 2002), Disciplining Dissent (Ottawa, October 2002), the outstanding Free Press national conferences on media reform (Madison, November 2003, and St Louis, May 2005), and other such events – all arguably evidence of a movement in formation – that we have plumbed for publicly expressed insights. Robert Hackett also acknowledges the good cheer of his colleagues on the steering committee of Vancouver's Media Democracy Day, particularly interviews with Brant Cheetham and Tim Walker, and the students in his annual fourth year seminar on media democratization at Simon Fraser University.

In Vancouver, we interviewed Mary Ann Abbs, Megan Adam, Alicia Barcello, Joe Barrett, David Bieber, Ivan Bulic, Peter Coombes, Libby Davies, Shannon Daub, Elsie Dean, Murray Dobbin, Julius Fisher, Janine Fuller, Shari Graydon, Beau Gus Moniker, Donald Gutstein, Herschel Hardin, Ken Hiebert, Alan Jensen, Jean Kavanagh, Dan Keaton, Seth Klein, Larry Kuehn, Kalle Lasn, Louise Leclair, Jim Lipkovits, James MacKinnon, Emira Mears, Geoff Meggs, Kevin Millsip, Pedro Mora, Scott Nelson, Noam de Plume, Stewart Poyntz, Marco Procaccini, Andrea Reimer, Peter Royce, Tara Scurr, Nandita Sharma, Sid Shniad, Jillian Skeet, Dave Skinner, Catherine Stewart, Steve Stewart, Jean Swanson, Shauna Sylvester, Sid Tan, Sunera Thobani, Bill Tieleman, Oline Twiss, 'Drea Uzans, Scott Uzelman, Richard Ward, Joie Warnock and Edward Yuen, among others.

Hundreds of hours of interview and conference audiotapes were ably transcribed by Janet Laxton and Janet Lum, supplemented by some of our student assistants in the School of Communication at Simon Fraser University. For their research and clerical assistance over the six years of this project, we thank Megan Adam, Shawndra Beaton, Pablo Bose, Shiloh Bouvette, Alexandra Guemili, Angela Gunther, Mia MacDonald, Nawal Musleh, Cliff Rickard, Shannon Ross, Adam Schachhuber, and Tai Silvey. Coding and/or analysis of interview data was efficiently conducted by Vladan Pantic, Matt Powers, Kate Rafter, and Jackie Stewart. Rob Prey editorially trimmed our verbosity in Chapters 7 and 8 with professional aplomb. We have drawn upon excellent working research papers on several key organizations by Arthur-Martins Aginam and by Scott Uzelman, who also helped organize the dozens of Vancouver interviews. The School's office staff, especially administrative assistant Lucie Menkveld, provided indispensable and efficient administrative support. Michael Hayes, Pat Howard and Roger Howard provided welcome workspace for Hackett and his migrating laptop.

At the University of Victoria, research help was provided by Larry Borins, Chris Hurl and Blake Speers, who coped heroically with the copious transcripts from our Vancouver interviews.

We acknowledge financial support from the Social Sciences and Humanities Research Council of Canada, in the form of three small SSHRC Small Grants administered by Simon Fraser University, which helped initiate and conclude the project, and, especially, a three-year SSHRC Standard Research Grant on 'Democratic Media Reform as a Social Movement', awarded to the two co-authors in spring 2000. In the manuscript's final stage of production, which Shawndra Beaton navigated coolly under time pressure, important financial assistance came from SFU's University Publications Funds. At Routledge, we owe much to series editor James Curran for his support, and to Aileen Irwin for her patient advice.

For permission to incorporate modest sections from Hackett's previous publications, we thank University of Toronto Press (Hackett 2001, in Chapter 2); Open University Press/McGraw-Hill Education (Hackett 2005, in Chapter 4); and Rowman & Littlefield (Zhao and Hackett 2005, in Chapters 4 and 5). We also thank our friends at World Association for Christian Communication, whose version of the People's Communication Charter is discussed in Chapter 4.

We could not have steered this book through its lengthy journey without all the help mentioned above. It goes without saying that we as co-authors jointly share the responsibility for any errors or shortcomings in it. The book has been a productive collaboration from the start, and we have mutually benefited from our many conversations and the interchange of our respective disciplinary backgrounds. For the record, we can roughly specify a division of labour: Hackett had primary responsibility for Chapters 1, 2, 4, 5 and 6, and the overall structure of the book; Carroll for Chapters 9, 10 and 11, and most of the tables; Chapters 3, 7 and 8 were the most extensively co-written. But our collaboration has been wide-ranging, ongoing and congenial, and we jointly stand behind the arguments presented.

Finally, we have run out of words to express appreciation for our forbearing spouses and children, Angelika, Karina and Melanie Hackett, and Anne Preyde, Myles and Wesley Carroll-Preyde. Once again, they have accepted with (more or less!) good grace the unreasonable burdens that an author in the family imposes. We dedicate this book to the future of our respective children, soon to become relatively autonomous agents in a media-saturated world; and with gratitude to our parents, Joyce and Ambrose Hackett, and Mary Jane and John Millar Carroll.

Robert A. Hackett, Simon Fraser University
William K. Carroll, University of Victoria
October 2005

Abbreviations

ABC	American Broadcasting Company
ACLU	American Civil Liberties Union
ACME	Action Coalition for Media Education
AMARC	Association Mondiale des Radiodiffuseurs Communautaires (World Association of Community Radio Broadcasters)
AOL	America Online
APC	Association for Progressive Communications
APEC	Asia-Pacific Economic Cooperation
BBC	British Broadcasting Corporation
BCE	Bell Canada Enterprises
BECTU	Broadcasting, Entertainment, Cinematograph and Theatre Union (UK)
CBC	Canadian Broadcasting Corporation
C-CAVE	Canadians Concerned About Violence in Entertainment
CCPA	Canadian Centre for Policy Alternatives
CDC	Committee for Democratic Communications (of the National Lawyers Guild)
CEM	Cultural Environment Movement
CEP	Communications, Energy and Paperworkers Union of Canada
CIA	Central Intelligence Agency
CIDA	Canadian International Development Agency
CPBF	Campaign for Press and Broadcasting Freedom
CPF	Campaign for Press Freedom
CRIS	Campaign for Communication Rights in the Information Society
CRTC	Canadian Radio-television and Telecommunications Commission
CUPE	Canadian Union of Public Employees
DMA	democratic media activism
EZLN	Ejercito Zapatista de Liberacion Nacional (Zapatista Army of National Liberation)
ECHR	European Convention on Human Rights
FAIR	Fairness and Accuracy In Reporting
FBI	Federal Bureau of Investigation

FCC	Federal Communications Commission
FOI	Freedom of Information
GATS	General Agreement on Trade in Services
GCIU	Graphics Communication International Union
GLC	Greater London Council
GM	Guerrilla Media
ICT	information and communication technology
ICTV	Independent Community Television (Vancouver)
IMC	Independent Media Center
IMF	International Monetary Fund
IMPACS	Institute for Media, Policy and Civil Society
IPA	Independent Press Association
IRA	Irish Republican Army
ISP	internet service provider
ITN	Independent Television News (UK)
ITV	Independent Television (UK)
MA	Media Alliance (San Francisco)
MAI	Multilateral Agreement on Investment
MAMA	Media Alliance Meritorious Achievement awards
NAFTA	North American Free Trade Agreement
NDP	New Democratic Party (Canada)
NGO	non-governmental organization
NPR	National Public Radio
NSM	new social movement
NUJ	National Union of Journalists
NWICO	New World Information and Communication Order
OECD	Organization for Economic Cooperation and Development
Ofcom	Office of Communication (UK)
PBS	Public Broadcasting Service
PCAJ	Pacific Centre for Alternative Journalists (Vancouver)
PCC	Press Complaints Commission (UK)
PNS	Pacific News Service
PSB	public service broadcasting
PTA	Parent–Teacher Association
SMO	social movement organization
SMT	social movement theory
SOGAT	Society of Graphics and Allied Trades (UK)
SPIN	Strategic Progressive Information Network (San Francisco)
TUC	Trades Union Congress
UDHR	Universal Declaration of Human Rights
UNESCO	United Nations Educational, Scientific and Cultural Organization
WACC	World Association for Christian Communication
WSIS	World Summit on the Information Society
WTO	World Trade Organization

1 Introduction

Beyond the media's democratic deficit?

Struggles to shift the direction of human history, away from ecological destruction and resource depletion, imperial militarism and fundamentalist terrorism, authoritarian regimes and failed states, ethnic nationalism and growing inequality, entrenched hierarchies of gender and of race – in short, from barbarism towards more just and sustainable futures – are emerging and continuing on many fronts. One of the prime terrains of struggle is the politics and culture of the North Atlantic heartland of global capitalism – the United States, United Kingdom and Canada.[1] That is not to blame these countries for all the world's ills, nor to commit the hubris, characteristic of yesteryear's scholarship and today's political rhetoric, of equating these countries' governments with 'the international community', or asserting that only they are the subjects of history, or that societal trends in that corner of the world have universal purchase.[2] Rather, it is to recognize that even as other regions (Europe, China, India) sometimes contest their current hegemony, the culture, politics and policies of the North Atlantic Anglo-American democratic capitalist states are pivotal, both positively and negatively, to alternative global futures. Their global influence is evident in international institutions from the World Trade Organization (WTO) to the United Nations, and more broadly in the trajectory of economic globalization, reinforced by military interventions such as the 2003 invasion of Iraq and by the 'imperial commodities' of the Hollywood dream machine (Forsyth 2004).

If global futures are linked to the formation, reproduction and contestation of cultures, ideology and politics in the North Atlantic region, the latter in turn are inextricably interwoven with the exercise of power by and through the dominant institutions of public communication, the mass and electronic media, and particularly the corporate conglomerates which act as gatekeepers of the public sphere, that (conceptual) realm of social life where public opinion is formed. Through their concentration of society's symbolic power (Couldry 2003) and their capacity to define reality for huge audiences in a world of second-hand experience, media make some futures more likely and others less so. With their enormous potential for expanding communication, do the media cultivate intercultural dialogue and informed civic engagement, or fear, greed and ignorance? Is the world wired for humane, peaceful, democratic governance, or for violence, tyranny and environmental degradation?

In some quarters, British and American media are revered as exemplars of democratic practice. Their professional ideologies and policy frameworks are, in effect, being exported to the 'transition societies' of the supposedly democratizing, post-authoritarian states of the former Soviet bloc and parts of the global South. Yet there is, in their home base, a growing disillusionment with the performance and, increasingly, the structure of dominant media, when measured against the democratic expectations inherent both in official state documents (from Canada's Broadcasting Act to the US Constitution's First Amendment) and in everyday talk about the media, particularly journalism's 'regime of objectivity' (Hackett and Zhao 1998).

Indeed, in the past two decades American and British scholars and citizen-activists have compiled an impressive dossier of 'power and betrayal' (Taras 2001) on the part of the corporate media behemoths, and the governments and regulatory agencies which are supposed to regulate them in the public interest. Media, it is argued, have not only failed to actualize such democratic values as participation, equality, representative diversity, civic engagement, and genuine choice (Hackett and Zhao 1998: 226); media are themselves becoming significant threats to sustainable democracy. How so? From the countless critiques, we can identify eight main themes.

Media's democratic deficit: critical themes

Public sphere failure

Media are not only *failing to furnish citizens with ready access to relevant civic information* – 'democracy's oxygen', as Canadian professor James Winter (1997) put it – but also, and more broadly, they are *failing to help constitute a democratic public sphere*. As developed by social theorist Jürgen Habermas (1989), the public sphere is not necessarily a physical space, but a conceptualization of social and institutional interactions and venues, where:

> people openly and transparently debate on the basis that they can be convinced by reason, by the rationality of argumentation, and not by rhetorical appeals or through the suppression or distortion of information. A distorted public sphere, controlled by narrow interests, can obfuscate and conceal injustice, smother voices of dissent, and place insurmountable barriers in the path of would-be campaigns. The result is heightened social tensions and inequities, with all that they entail.
>
> (Ó Siochrú 2005a: 206)

The public sphere is not a mere 'pie in the sky' ideal; actual media systems have sometimes approximated or at least simulated a representative public sphere. The public service broadcasters of Britain, Canada and Western Europe, at their best, have attracted broad audiences with civic information, and enabled access for a wide range of relevant views. A crisp and diverse local newspaper, or an email forum on the internet (despite spam, pornography, pop-up ads and flame-outs), can function as a specialized or smaller-scale public sphere. But in a capitalist society, where media are businesses first, the capacity of dominant media to represent diverse interests, and to provide the space for democratic dialogue, is never secure. And whatever the democratic shortcomings of Anglo-American media may be, they have global significance, given trends such as these: the growth of transnational multi-media conglomerates, technological convergence between once separate media sectors, the development of global markets in most media industries, the spread and intensification of commercialization, the relative decline of public service broadcasting, the growth and consolidation of the advertising industry, the development of communication technology spurred by business demand for the best global communication networks possible, and dramatic corporate consolidation (Herman and McChesney 1997, Chapter 1; Hackett 2000: 62–3).

Particularly relevant to the public sphere is the sustained attack on journalism's ethos of public service. Since the 1990s, waves of mergers have yielded more and more media owned by transnational, bottom-line driven conglomerates. As media become part of corporate empires with multiple and far-reaching tentacles, conflicts of interest and organizational self-censorship risk becoming endemic. How vigorously can the American network NBC cover nuclear power, for example, when it is owned by the energy giant and military contractor General Electric? Conversely, cross-promotional marketing influences editorial decisions. One example: the once prestigious *Los Angeles Times*, using its pages in 1999 to promote the Staples Center, without declaring its own financial stake in that sports complex (McChesney and Nichols 2002a: 61).

Moreover, owned by profit-hungry investors (as distinct from the family firms of yesteryear) and often saddled with huge merger-induced debts, media conglomerates typically look for the fastest route to maximum returns (Bagdikian 1997: 201–2; Hallin 2000: 222). That structural imperative helps explain television's drift towards tabloidization and infotainment: offer audiences content which is relatively cheap and titillating, even outrageous (like 'true confession' talk shows, or 'reality' programmes featuring statuesque contestants gobbling horses' intestines) but avoids genuine, thoughtful and politically-relevant controversy.

In newsrooms meanwhile, a culture of conformity spreads and the public service ethos shrivels. Motivated by corporate strategies like 'total newspapering', management encourages journalists to think of themselves as company team players, as content providers meeting consumer demand and corporate priorities, rather than as independent professionals pursuing public truths (Underwood 1995). Dissidents learn to conform or drift to other occupations, as media concentration exerts a chilling effect. Following Conrad Black's takeover of the Southam newspaper chain, *Toronto Star* columnist Dalton Camp wrote in 1997 that the 'chaining' of Canadian newspapers 'limits employment opportunities and career mobility' for journalists; chain ownership produces 'less dissent, fewer questions and more Velveeta', a measurable 'lack of diversity of opinion in Canadian print media' (cited in Hackett and Gruneau *et al.* 2000: 64).

Such trends help engender a depoliticized culture of selfishness and consumerism, rather than civic engagement and a participatory public sphere, according to Robert McChesney (1997), one of North America's leading media critics.

If the proof of the pudding is in the eating, what are the implications of these structural tendencies for a news system which, according to liberal theory, is supposed to inform citizens? One useful approach to this question considers what is *not* in the news. Each year in the US, Project Censored lists important and seemingly newsworthy stories which are virtually ignored by the corporate media. Its top stories for 2003 included the hidden agendas behind the US government's attack on Iraq, the threat to civil liberties from homeland security measures, a Pentagon plan actually to provoke terrorist actions in order to enable a counterattack, the Bush administration's largely covert campaign to undermine labour unions and worker protections, and increasing monopoly control over the internet (Phillips & Project Censored 2004). Such stories bespeak a lack of investigative journalism in US media, and a failure of the 'watchdog' function vis-à-vis corporate and state power.[3]

Centralization of power

A second critical theme concerns *the centralization of political, civic and symbolic power* inherent in the political economy of media industries. To be sure, some centrifugal forces are at work: the fragmentation and segmentation of audiences, and a deconcentration of business into networks of flexible producers, suppliers and investors, which some theorists regard as a hallmark of a new 'post-Fordist' phase of capitalism (Mosco 1996: 109). Yet today's watchword is 'convergence' – in terms of both the digital technologies which are merging previously separate media industries, and the expansion and interlocking of corporate media behemoths, nationally and globally. When Pulitzer-prize-winning journalist and academic Ben Bagdikian (1997) began his analysis of 'media monopoly' in the 1980s, he estimated that 50 companies dominated America's media output, but he predicted that then current trends would reduce that number to about six. With a wave of massive mergers in the 1990s, history seems to have borne him out. Specific statistics on media concentration will be outdated by the time this book is published, and they need not detain us (but see e.g. McChesney 2004: 176–83). The key points are the continued dominance of a handful of firms over the media industries which comprise the means of public communication, and the expansion of these firms both transnationally and to different media forms, in the context of the general 'marketization' of communications industries internationally. Even a liberal Canadian media scholar concluded that global alliances among major corporations are 'virtually unprecedented in world history', and that 'a handful of gigantic corporations control almost all of the world's media' (Taras 2001: 24). And at the end of the day, owners and dominant shareholders still 'influence the ethos, direction and goals of [media] organizations through the setting of policy, the hiring and firing of key staff, and the allocation of rewards' (Curran 2002: 149) – however out-sourced and temporary much of the menial work may be.

While it takes on new wrinkles in today's globalizing capitalism, industrial concentration has been evident in the first modern mass medium, the daily newspaper, for nearly a century. Bigger media companies enjoy easier access to capital funds, administrative expertise, economies of scale, distribution networks and advertising revenues; and high entry costs protect dominant media firms, very effectively, from new competition. There is thus an understandable economic logic to media concentration, and in conventional policy and media discourse, it is often reduced to simply a business phenomenon.

Yet concentration has potentially profound political implications. Media owners have disproportionate influence over what political issues enter the public arena, and how they are framed; so their political interests and causes have an unfair advantage. Media owners do not necessarily use such power for specific political ends, but when the stakes are high enough (as in government policy towards the media themselves), there is often little to stop them. Some owners do not need much prompting. Global media magnate Rupert Murdoch has famously used his media properties, like the Fox News channel, to promote hard-right pro-corporate and militarist policies. Political science research credited Murdoch's aggressive use of his mass tabloid, the *Sun*, with swinging the 1992 British general election from Labour to the more corporate-congenial Conservatives (Hackett and Zhao 1998: 179). Even more dramatically, Silvio Berlusconi parlayed his control over swathes of Italian media into occupancy of that country's highest political office.

Apart from their own power, the corporate media's vested interests mean that they are hardly likely to act as 'watchdogs' on other centres of power. As Canadian sociologist Wallace Clement (1975) argued decades ago, interlocking directorships, shared social milieux and worldviews, and structural dependence on corporate advertising, combine to make the 'media elite' part of a broader 'corporate elite', arguably the dominant power bloc in the North Atlantic societies. And journalism's barking even at its traditional target, government, has become rather muted in an era of massive government–business symbiosis. Nowhere is media silence more deafening than with respect to the media themselves, particularly crucial changes to communications policy which serve corporate interests, like the 1996 Telecommunications Act in the US. Its overall import was to subject US communications policy more directly to the dictates of a market already dominated by a few huge oligopolistic companies, to allow massive increases in media concentration, and to essentially give away the future digital broadcasting spectrum, then valued at $70 billion, to the dominant commercial broadcasters. It was arguably 'one of the most important' pieces of US legislation in a generation, yet outside the business and trade press, media coverage was almost non-existent (McChesney 2004: 51–4, 213–14).

Inequality

When it is personalized in the shape of press barons like Conrad Black or Rupert Murdoch, such concentration of power is easy to grasp. But owners' foibles are less important influences on media performance than more general cultural and economic mechanisms, such as the commodification of information and the dependence of commercial media on advertising revenue.[4] These mechanisms generate violations of the democratic norm of equality more subtle than the ham-handed editorial interventions of a Conrad Black. For instance, there are no obvious formal or legal barriers to women or people of colour in the Anglo-American democracies, yet they are still under-represented in key media occupations, and often misrepresented in media texts – for example, news coverage that over-emphasizes African-Americans as criminals or welfare recipients, and whites as victims (McChesney 2004: 87, 107–8). Allan (2004: 143–70) finds similar patterns – stereotypes and language which normalize 'white' and marginalize others – in British news media. Even in Canada, that 'peaceable kingdom' which unlike the US and UK has avoided inner-city racial insurrections in recent decades, the press subtly embeds the language and assumptions of racial hierarchy (Henry and Tator 2002). And in increasingly multicultural societies in an interconnected world, media's marginalization or demonization of language and religious traditions – for example, the treatment of Islam in Canadian media (Karim 2000) – is a key component of the democratic deficit.

The much noted 'digital divide' points to another huge dimension of media-related inequality: that of social class. Under conditions of profit-oriented commercial development, access to media services and information which enable full political and economic participation is limited to those who can afford it. Just as privatized medicine produces a multi-tiered health system, commercialized media reinforce the gap between the information-rich and the information-poor. Even the 'free' advertising-supported media have a bias towards the cultural and political interests of the affluent, since that is whom advertisers most want to reach. Advertising, in effect, imposes a class-based structural censorship on media. To take one example: in Britain, the social democratic *Daily Herald* died in 1964, even though it had a much larger circulation than economically thriving conservative upmarket national dailies, because 'its readers constituted neither a sufficiently mass nor a sufficiently affluent market to be attractive to advertisers' (Curran 2002: 102). The *Herald*'s fate is just one reminder that while the logic of democracy is one person, one vote, the logic of capitalism – 'the market' – is one dollar (or pound), one vote.

Homogenization

The media's fourth democratic shortfall concerns *homogenization*: the diminution of the potential diversity of publicly articulated discourses. With millions of websites and dozens of TV channels available to the average North American media consumer, how can such a claim make sense? Singer Bruce Springsteen intuited the answer: '57 channels and nothin' on'. In commercial broadcasting, *proliferation* should not be confused with *diversity* – of perspective, aesthetic, values, and politics. Diversity is limited to what can be profitably produced – and that excludes a lot (Baker 2002). The explosion of 'alternative' websites has not altered the balance of communicative power between popular social movements, and the corporate behemoths that are coming to dominate the internet as well as traditional media.

Homogenization takes place in several ways, and at several levels. Multi-media corporate empires trim costs and enhance profits by rationalizing resources: the newspaper chain centralizing its national political reporting or its book reviews for all its member papers, at the expense of local writers, is one longstanding example. In an age of technological and ownership convergence between once separate media industries, the risks are multiplied. The same expensively produced content can be 're-purposed' and recycled in different forms: the film becomes the sports team becomes the merchandise becomes the TV series becomes the theme park. Their brand-name recognition, economies of scale, privileged access to distribution networks, and cross-promotional resources, reinforced by high entry costs in most media industries, enable large media corporations to marginalize, coopt or exclude potential rivals – and more important, to establish their profitable programming formulae as the taken-for-granted norm. Even more broadly, the economic and political interests of the media multinationals encourage them to systematically promote a 'monoculture' of narcissistic consumerism and the politics of free market fundamentalism, so that 'a fundamentally unsustainable way of life and worldview takes hold' (Ó Siochrú 2005a: 208).

Undermining community

The ways in which media *undermine a sense of community* and a healthy political culture, at local, national and global levels, comprise a fifth kind of deficit. This is a problem with several dimensions. One is the declining connection between media and local communities – the 'Wal-Martization' of media. With the spread of chain and conglomerate ownership in American radio, for instance, local programming is on the brink of extinction, to be replaced by centralized, syndicated material with computerized 'local flavour' inserts, much like the regional variations in a McDonald's fast food menu. ClearChannel, owner of over 1,200 US radio stations, is a leader in this community-sapping strategy. Its consequences were dramatically illustrated in 2002 in Minot, North Dakota (McKibben 2003: 49). Following a train accident which released toxic fumes, local authorities tried to contact the six local ClearChannel stations to broadcast an alarm – only to find that in fact the stations had no staff: they were simply relaying satellite feeds from central office in San Antonio!

A related problem is the fragmentation of media audiences, as advertisers seek ever more precise and specific markets to target. It has now become commonplace to observe geographical segregation and cultural conflict between urban, secular, liberal 'blue' regions of America, and their rural, religious, conservative 'red' counterparts. Some theorists relate such apparent intensification of cultural differences and antagonisms within American society to the 'slice and dice' strategies of contemporary marketing and the segmentation of the media system into specialized outlets designed for specified demographic groups (Turow 1997).

The 'mean world syndrome' is another way that media undermine community. In his documentary *Bowling for Columbine*, Michael Moore suggested that through exaggerated emphasis on violent crime, Hollywood films and commercial TV news help foster a climate of fear and thus a culture of violence in America. There is academic confirmation of this linkage. The career-long research of the late George Gerbner (2002) indicates that, cumulatively, media programming cultivates perceptions of the world. Heavy television viewers are more likely than others to see the world as a threatening place, to overestimate crime rates, and to favour authoritarian solutions to social problems. And much concern has rightly been expressed about the desensitizing impact of ongoing exposure to media representations of violence and mayhem, and its implications for the socialization of the young. What is less often noted is that the ceaseless barrage of formula-driven media violence is driven primarily not by audience demand but by the ease with which 'action films' can be translated and dumped onto foreign-language export markets – in other words, a commercial imperative (Gerbner 1999: 8–9).

The commercial media's similarly ceaseless promotion of consumerism, whether through advertising or related 'lifestyle' content, likewise undercuts community. American environmentalist Bill McKibben goes so far as to suggest that:

> The thing to fear from television is less the sight of [people] mowing each other down with machine guns than the sight of people having to have every desire that enters their mind gratified immediately … [T]hat kind of culture is going to be a violent one, no matter what images one shows. Television hasn't done this by itself, … but it's the anchor and central idol of this system of values that dominates us.
>
> (1999: 45–6)

Finally, what about community at the international level? The process of globalization has done little to mitigate the longstanding tendency of dominant media to side with their national governments at times of international tension, potentially fanning the flames of nationalism and even war. Understandably, in authoritarian countries, state-controlled media would side with their governments in international disputes. What about British and American media, with their formal political independence? Informal pressures, such as commercial dependence on domestic audiences and routine reliance on official sources for news, could work as effectively as formal censorship in times of crisis. To be sure, there are exceptions; Britain's public service broadcaster, the BBC, has justly acquired a reputation for professionalism and independence, and the mass circulation tabloid *Daily Mirror*, emboldened by public opinion, campaigned against the British and US governments' plans to invade Iraq in 2003. More typically though, Britain's tabloid press is infamous for its xenophobia, racism and jingoism. In the US, corporate media, particularly the television networks spearheaded by Rupert Murdoch's Fox Network, vigorously beat the drums for war in 2002–3. They amplified the Bush administration's now discredited claims about Saddam Hussein's weapons of mass destruction, and highlighted Saddam's atrocities against Kurds in the 1980s, while virtually ignoring US support for his regime at that time (Rampton and Stauber 2003). So, in the era of globalization, dominant media are a long way from helping to build a global civil society, and this comprises an increasingly urgent dimension of the democratic deficit.

Corporate enclosure of knowledge

A sixth critical theme identifies an increasingly crucial site in struggles over communication structures: the attempt by corporate capital and its state allies to radically expand 'intellectual property rights' (IPRs), threatening to transform *the public commons of knowledge* into a *private enclosure of corporate-controlled commodities*. A background paper for the recently formed Campaign for Communication Rights in the Information Society (CRIS) explains that intellectual property rights

> emerged in the industrialized world as a means to mediate and control the cir-
> culation of knowledge, as a means of balancing the conflicting rights of differ-
> ent groups involved in the generation and use of ideas of economic value. IPRs
> are premised on concerns that the creators or authors of ideas have an eco-
> nomic right to a fair return for their effort and a moral right not to have their
> ideas misrepresented.
>
> However, ideas are not simply the product of individuals and corporations.
> For the most part they incorporate and build upon the traditions, collected
> wisdom, and understanding of social groups and societies … Consequently,
> society in general has a social right to use ideas to the benefit of the public good
> – especially if they are key to social and physical well being.

The CRIS paper adds, however, that in recent decades, the balance between these moral, economic and social rights is being skewed by three distorting trends:

> corporations have emerged as the key owners of copyrighted material; the
> scope, depth and duration of copyright has grown hugely, to encompass not
> only intellectual work but also plant and life forms; and copyright owners
> wield a formidable set of instruments to enforce their rights nationally and
> internationally.
>
> (CRIS 2002: 6–7)

Policy behind closed doors

A seventh theme concerns the *elitist process of communication policymaking* in the US and UK – particularly the virtual exclusion of the public from awareness, let alone partic-ipation, in shaping the mandates of the cultural industries. In theory, government legislation (such as anti-trust law and broadcasting statutes) and regulatory agencies such as the US Federal Communications Commission (FCC) are supposed to protect the public interest in media industries. Historically, public interest mandates have been applied to broadcasting, which made use of the broadcast spectrum as a scarce public resource, and telecommunications carriers like the telephone system, which enjoyed a 'natural monopoly' over an important public service. In practice, however, critics argue that the symbiotic relationship between the state and big media corporations undermines public interest regulation to the point of corruption; crudely put, politicians want favourable publicity, media companies want regulatory and legislative favours, and neither side wants media attention to the resulting policy outcomes. Secrecy and back-room deals are the order of the day, manifested most clearly in the massive giveaway of public resources embodied in the 1996 Telecommunications Act noted above (McChesney and Nichols 2002: 29).

To be sure, there is more scope for public input in the UK and Canada, where there has at least been a certain tradition of public enquiries on the performance of media industries, and some parliamentary scrutiny of communication policies. Still, it remains the case in all three countries that communication policy and regulation is disproportionately shaped by the corporate media and telecommunications lobby groups.

Eroding communication rights

Finally, an eighth aspect of the democratic deficit is *the erosion of privacy and free expression rights in the media*, particularly cyberspace. Ó Siochrú (2005a: 209) notes the 'growing surveillance, censorship, and direct repression pursued by governments and corporate sector' since 9/11, as 'troubling legal frameworks originating in the US' are replicated elsewhere, enabling governments and their secretive agencies to monitor a full range of communication instruments. Critics fear that new purposes and implementation measures are extending such laws beyond even their original draconian intent, and that the 9/11 attacks provided a pretext for US and European governments to take control of electronic space (Ó Siochrú and Girard 2003: 5). In fall 2004, the FBI-initiated seizure of servers used by several European Independent Media Centres added fuel to such fears.

The deficit in perspective

The first six themes discussed above all implicate the economic logic of capitalism, particularly its 'deregulated' neoliberal version currently dominant in the US and UK. The last three more directly concern the repressive role of the state. Neoliberals typically present 'the market' as the realm of freedom and the state as a darkland of coercion. And yet state repression and capitalism are not necessarily separate, let alone opposing, forces. The Berlin Wall has been rubble for 15 years, and we can now see that the post-communist global order is more capitalist than democratic. Soviet-style 'closed' societies may have nearly vanished but authoritarian market regimes like China's flourish; they are 'open for business', but closed to effective dissent and democratic change – and capitalism seems to thrive in such circumstances (Zhao 2005). Arguably, the very inequalities generated by a neoliberal regime necessitate a 'strong state', one with powerful police and military forces, to contain the attendant social tensions (Gamble 1988). Even the post-9/11 domestic erosion of civil liberties and the expansion of military bases and 'pre-emptive strikes' overseas are not simply responses to the terrorist threat. The 'war on terror' serves other political agendas, including containment of global justice activism, and control over the supply and distribution of oil and other strategic resources globally.

So, the democratic deficit derives from fundamental facets of the North Atlantic social order. But as we argue in Chapter 4, the democratic deficit is a concept defined (or ignored) through the prism of political and normative perspectives. Indeed, while it implies a progressive critique of the media, the concept itself can be radically critiqued – as too conservative! According to Webster's online dictionary, the phrase refers to 'organizations which are democratic to some extent but are not as democratic as they "should be"'. But for some critics, the dominant media are not even somewhat democratic, and the 'deficit' is not a temporary and reformable shortfall, as the term may imply, but a structurally guaranteed subservience to elite consensus. Such we take to be the logic of Edward Herman's and Noam Chomsky's (1988) well-known 'propaganda model' of the media (Allan 2004: 52–3).

Other critics problematize the very concept of democracy as a normative benchmark. George W. Bush, after all, styles himself a crusader for democracy. For millions of non-white and aboriginal people, one media activist reminded us, American democracy has historically meant expropriation, slavery, even genocide. Thousands of American activists of colour, challenging the media and other institutional fields, accordingly prefer to frame their struggles as seeking 'justice' rather than 'democracy'.

Moreover, democratic theory has typically taken for granted the nation-state framework. Its legitimacy as the container of political rights and citizenship is increasingly suspect in a world of decidedly undemocratic supra-state governance machinery, on the one hand, and millions of stateless refugees, diasporic migrants and 'guest workers', on the other. Considered historically, political democracy 'is contingent upon relations of hegemony and subordination within the nation-state system and upon the nature of class and ethnic compromise within nation-states' (Zhao and Hackett 2005: 23). The historical emergence of Britain's and America's democracies may rest in part on the wealth deriving from their (profoundly undemocratic) privileged position in the world system.

Furthermore, the global reach of American and British media networks (a legacy of an imperial past and arguably neocolonial present?), mean that their democratic deficit is not simply internal to those countries. As Unesco's MacBride Report (discussed briefly in Chapter 5) argued over two decades ago, Western-based conglomerates' dominance over the transnational production and distribution of images, and of communication technologies and networks more broadly, contributes to inequality in the global information order. Considered on this scale, the democratic deficit touches people's lives in vastly different ways, from the white middle-class American liberal who supports public service broadcasting in hopes of enjoying commercial-free opera, to the African woman dying of AIDS for lack of information and self-determination vis-à-vis sexual health. Multiple and overlapping axes of exclusion and repression – including gender, poverty, race, nation and language – would need to be redressed before the world's people can be said collectively and fully to enjoy self-governance.

We recognize and acknowledge the force of such perspectives. Some of them we take up again, especially in Chapters 4 and 5, but mostly, the focus of this book forces us to leave them aside. The democratic reform and/or transformation of

North Atlantic-based public communications media, and of their relationship to state, economy and civil society, are a small – but crucial – component of the global picture. And the 'democratic deficit' can be a useful benchmark, so long as we are mindful of democracy's contested and shifting nature, the need to expand and radicalize its implications, and the possibility that some uses of the term may erect new hierarchies and exclusions.

Challenging the democratic deficit

This book, however, is not about the media's well-documented democratic deficit as such, but rather citizens' mobilizations against it. The analysis above suggests that such a project, one of media democratization, is very broad indeed, entailing challenges to both capital (particularly corporate ownership and commercialization of media and information), and to the state (particularly its neoliberal policies as they apply to communication). Put that way, the task seems forbiddingly daunting.

This book, however, explores potential sources for change and for optimism. Democracy is neither a final and permanent state of affairs, nor a gift handed down from elites; it requires continual renewal from below and from the margins. With their capacity to bring new voices and issues to the public sphere, and indeed to broaden the enfranchised public and the scope of democratic decision-making, social movements are key to such revitalization (Angus 2001). Their ability to undertake this task is now refracted through a shifting mediascape – the mass dissemination of images and frames, supplemented by the networks and flows of electronic communication. On the one hand, new media and the internet have opened tremendous new possibilities for organizing and mobilizing, and diffusing critiques to broader constituencies. On the other hand, the increasingly tight integration of major public communication institutions into the logics and circuits of global capital – of which media concentration, convergence and commercialization are symptoms – poses new problems and blockages for the trajectory of social movements. The openings in dominant media for oppositional movements, especially those which challenge core corporate and state interests, are arguably fewer and narrower compared to the 1960s, when the US television networks helped catapult the civil rights movement into the national political agenda.

That dark side of the new mediascape means that most movements can no longer afford to regard media merely instrumentally, as neutral conduits for their messages. From the viewpoints of movements requiring access to the public sphere, and citizens seeking to redress the increasingly recognized democratic deficit in the North Atlantic political systems, media now loom as necessary sites of intervention and struggle. Elite-driven movements of the Right, especially in the US, have understood the media's strategic position for thirty years; their 'ideological mobilization' against the 'liberal' media has been remarkably successful in shifting the goalposts of public language (Dreier 1982).

Progressive movements have been slow to respond with a media-oriented politics of their own. But there are growing signs that media democratization may be becoming a movement in its own right. In the US, nascent national coalitions for more humane and democratic media – the Cultural Environment Movement (CEM), the Telecommunications Policy Roundtable, two national Media and Democracy Congresses – emerged in the 1990s. Though short-lived and perhaps premature, these organizations laid important groundwork for later media reform coalitions, such as Free Press. The late 1990s saw the climax of a movement to recognize and institutionalize low-power FM radio, using tactics ranging from illegal clandestine broadcasting to court challenges against the FCC (Ruggiero 1999). It enjoyed good legislative prospects until the Republican sweep of Congress and (with the Supreme Court's help) presidency in 2000. Alternative and do-it-yourself media have also flourished on the internet; most celebrated are the IndyMedia Centres which have mushroomed around the world since their dramatic emergence at the anti-WTO Battle of Seattle in 1999. Critical media education gained momentum with the formation of the Action Coalition for Media Education (ACME) in 2002. Most dramatically, FCC proposals to liberalize media ownership ceilings sparked an unprecedented and successful upsurge of citizen protest across the political spectrum in 2003, with millions signing petitions to Congress against media concentration.

In Canada, media activism has proceeded at a lower pitch, but the spread of press concentration combined with government cutbacks to public broadcasting during the 1990s catalysed coalitions with a broad range of partners, including media unions. In the UK, progressive media activism reached a peak in the 1980s, when militant trade unions were battling both the radically right-wing Thatcher government and its allies in the daily press. These struggles gave birth to one of the longest-surviving media reform groups in the Western world, the Campaign for Press and Broadcasting Freedom (CPBF), which continues to contest the neoliberal drift of the current 'New Labour' government's communication policies.

And in all three countries, non-governmental organizations (NGOs) focused on communication and information rights and strategies have proliferated. At the international level too, NGOs like the London-based World Association for Christian Communication (WACC) have begun to mobilize around 'global media governance' (Ó Siochrú 2005a). Conceptualizing themselves as representatives of an emergent global civil society, NGOs are forming coalitions like CRIS, and intervening on communication issues in elite fora like the WTO and particularly the World Summit on the Information Society (WSIS).

Such struggles are not only defensive, an attempt to 'fix' the democratic deficit and force media to function as they are supposed to in liberal theory. Media activism implies a redefinition of the very idea of democracy to include new rights – the right to communicate – and a broader and deeper vision of democracy as entailing not simply elections and individual liberties, but also popular participation and social equality. So, the struggle for media reform is both defensive and pro-active; this nascent movement (if that it be) occupies a key location in the field of progressive-democratic politics, since it is forwarding new, enhanced visions of what democracy could come to mean.

At the same time, apart perhaps from some academics or policy specialists, media activism is not typically driven by abstract principles of democracy, but by the very real impact of the democratic deficit on people's lives. Malkia Cyril, a young activist of colour with the Oakland-based Youth Media Council, speaks compellingly of media invisibility and misrepresentation as literally a 'life-or-death' issue: the media demonization of black youth as criminals makes it easier for police to get away with shooting unarmed African Americans. The corporate practice of 'infrastructure redlining' – refusing to provide telecommunications service to non-profitable areas, such as Native American lands, or low-income neighbourhoods – tangibly constrains people's right to communicate and to be informed (Dichter 2005: 14). Even if they are not framed as such, struggles over these issues are at the heart of meaningful democratization.

After years of ignoring oppositional communication practices, North Atlantic scholars are beginning to take notice. There has been a welcome and overdue flurry of attention to alternative media (Downing *et al.* 2001; Atton 2002; Couldry and Curran 2003a), and as we discuss in Chapter 3, 'new social movements' in general have been identified as an object of analysis since the 1980s. But to date, there has been less attention to organized collective action which seeks not simply to create 'alternative' and/or autonomous spaces, but directly to challenge and remake the hegemonic public communication system and its nexus with political governance – and thereby, to transform the terrain on which all movements contest established power.

Whether such collective action constitutes an emerging social movement, and what its political character and its conditions of survival and success might be, are the broad questions informing this book. Our concerns are practical as well as political:

- What strategic action repertoire and cultural-ideological frames does the movement employ, and how does it deal with the openings and opportunities, as well as blockages and opponents, that make up its political and cultural environment?
- Where is democratic media activism situated historically and ideologically? Does it contest only the application of hegemonic codes, or has it developed fundamentally alternative conceptions of communication and democracy? Or, does the movement contain both reformist and counterhegemonic currents?
- Does such activism constitute the nucleus of a new movement, similar to environmentalism thirty years ago; or is it destined to be (at best) a bridge-builder between existing movements?

We do not claim definitive answers to any of these questions, but by posing them, we hope to help stimulate further scholarship as well as political practice.

Organization and scope of the book

Methodologically, this book is based on a combination of empirical research (primarily interviews with activists and case studies of organizations and campaigns) and selective use of secondary literature. The context is mainly American, but also includes an important British media reform group (the CPBF), and media and social movement activism in Vancouver, Canada, as well as some attention to transnational media activism (notably the WACC and the People's Communication Charter). We thus have some basis for making comparative observations. Our interviews were conducted between 1998 and 2004 with about 150 media activists in the US, UK and Canada. One subset of some 54 respondents comprised media activists, as well as activists from other movements, whose political work brings them into frequent contention with media power in Vancouver. In selecting the remaining respondents, we focused on particularly important social movement organizations (SMOs) in the communication field, and three cities with a history and density of media activism – San Francisco, New York and London.

Respondents were asked questions concerning their personal background and political vision, their organization's history, politics, structure and strategies, their views and experiences vis-à-vis the media, their view of the relationship between media democratization and other movements, and other queries. We also attended or obtained transcripts of public talks and conferences on media activism, and analysed movement documents, including organizational newsletters or magazines, and several important manifestos. As well, we compiled brief case histories of three key groups: the British CPBF, Media Alliance in San Francisco, and Fairness and Accuracy in Reporting (FAIR) in New York.

With respect to theory, we have been shamelessly eclectic. We have selectively pilfered from critical media studies, social movement theory, and to some extent normative theories of democracy. Within each of these fields, we have rummaged around for concepts and frameworks useful to our purpose, even dusting off some ideas (like aspects of Smelser's (1962) functionalist approach to social movements in Chapter 8) from academia's attic of unfashionable antiques. Throughout the book though, we have maintained a focus on the questions posed above, and we have repeatedly deployed a handful of key concepts, notably these: the media's democratic deficit (discussed above); the distinction between democratization through the media, and democratization of the media; contending perspectives on media and democracy (market liberal, public sphere liberal, radical democratic); Pierre Bourdieu's notion of media (and journalism) as an institutional 'field'; Antonio Gramsci's concepts of hegemony, and counterhegemony; Jürgen Habermas's distinction between the logics of system and lifeworld in contemporary society; and of course, Habermas's irreplaceable (however idealized and historically unfulfilled) notion of public sphere as a normative benchmark, albeit one amended by Nancy Fraser's attention to subaltern spheres and counterpublics.

While the scope of the book is rather broad, we are certainly not attempting to offer *the* map of media democratization. Generously defined, that vast field includes not only media reform campaigns in advanced capitalist democracies but also contestations of cultural power in the capillaries of everyday life, the tactical media interventions of insurgent groups like the Zapatistas, other forms of cultural activism in the neo-colonies of the global South, and the resistances of subaltern communities of colour, women and labour. Add to this diversity the fact that contemporary media activism is a fast-changing field – especially in the US – and it becomes obvious that all any one book can reasonably offer are blurred snapshots, unavoidably taken from only some of many possible vantage points, and focusing imperfectly on certain themes. As noted above, the book focuses on the North Atlantic heartland of global capitalism, and on struggles against the concentration of symbolic power in the means of public communication – the 'agenda-setting' media (which now include parts of the internet) or, in Stuart Hall's (1986) notable phrase, 'the machinery of representation'. While issues of telecommunications access and regulation, intellectual property and cyber-rights have risen alongside longstanding concerns about media control and practices, it is the latter – the pressing need to challenge invisibility or misrepresentation in the public sphere – that continues to drive much grassroots media activism. As one African American organizer told us, it's all about content. Moreover, while our interviews and case studies sample different forms of media activism, we give particular emphasis to those that directly and consciously challenge the media's democratic deficit, as discussed above, and that aim, from a radical democratic perspective, to build coalitions to change the 'rules of the game' institutionalized in the state and dominant corporate media. Such media reform is hardly the only relevant type of media democratization; such a narrow view would in effect allow hegemonic institutions like the FCC to define the field of media activism for us. As noted above, that field takes in a great range of cultural and political formations, and as some of our respondents pointed out, media reform has been insufficiently responsive to subaltern communities. But rather than widen our lens at the risk of attempting too much, by focusing on media reform we can diagnose both its promise and problems as a democratizing strategy. Our extensive interviews within and around flagship SMOs provide the thick descriptions needed to assess media reform's limitations and to explore its relations with other movements, including those representing marginalized/ subaltern groups. Our case study of media activism in Vancouver, presented in Chapters 9 and 10, allows us to map media reform in depth, in relation to social networks and a broader organizational ecology that includes not only independent media producers but also relevant movements, such as organized labour. Finally, as noted, this book complements and helps offset a recent scholarly emphasis on autonomist and alternative media practices.

    What of our own political and normative vantage point? As with any other author, even in disciplines loudly proclaiming their objectivity, our analysis is informed, but we hope not trapped, by our own political and social location – in our case, as progressive, white, male, Canadian academics. We broadly share the commitment of most of the activists we interviewed, to build coalitions and campaigns to engage with and transform the dominant machinery of representation, in both the media and political fields. That puts us in a different camp from those who regard the state and/or hegemonic media as so incorrigibly unreform-able that the *only* option is to create parallel, autonomous alternatives. Or, conversely, from those who exaggerate and celebrate the ability of audiences to ignore, re-interpret or contest the 'preferred readings' embedded in dominant media to such an extent that the need for institutional change disappears – a tendency strongly evident in some strands of cultural studies (e.g. Fiske 1987). We believe (as briefly argued in Chapter 2) that the media's entrenched democratic deficit matters, that it influences social and political life profoundly, and that it is not self-correcting through established political or market logics: that task requires concerted, coherent collective action.

However, we recognize and welcome the legitimacy of a plurality of perspectives within media democratization. We also recognize that as with any social move-ment, media democratization could unwittingly reproduce social inequalities or create new ones. That is one reason that subaltern and radical critiques of the liberal terms in which media reform is often framed – citizenship, public sphere, even democracy – need to be taken seriously.

The book's chapters are organized as follows. In Chapter 2, we explore why the democratic deficit matters, by considering both power *through* the media – the ways that dominant groups, logics, and institutions influence media – as well as power *of* the media, their impacts on other social institutions and processes. Pierre Bourdieu's concept of media and journalism as a 'field' helps both to make and to transcend this distinction, and to map institutional relations and political strategies.

Chapter 3 mines social movement theory (SMT) for insights into movements as agents for democratizing communication and society more broadly. New social movements since 1968 have broadened the definition of the political to include culture, and have themselves become more reflexive concerning the nexus of power and knowledge, pointing towards the media field. Yet surprisingly, neither movement praxis nor theory has until recently entertained the possibility of a movement aiming to democratize the media field itself. Instead, the media field has been taken for granted as part of the political environment, to be used instrumen-tally. Different strands from social theory offer useful insights regarding the possible nature, tasks and contributions of such a movement. Building on these concepts and the analysis in Chapter 2, we offer a two-dimensional typology of democratic media activism (DMA).

Given the diversity of *strategies* of media democratization, Chapter 4 explores where contemporary activism fits on an *ideological* grid. We map DMA in relation to some broader narratives about democracy and the media in the North Atlantic – market liberalism, public sphere liberalism and radical democracy. We also ask whether media activism shares a sufficiently coherent moral or political vision to generate a viable social movement – and here we part company with the view that transformative collective action needs no more than networks built around shared actions and emotional or aesthetic sensibilities rather than coherent programmes. Using the People's Communication Charter as a documentary touchstone, we ask what kinds of political commitments and tensions are evident in a nascent media democracy movement.

Chapters 5 and 6 situate contemporary media activism in the North Atlantic historically as well as politically. We identify several 'waves' of media democratization in recent global history and add detail to this narrative through historical sketches of two highly significant media reform organizations in the US and UK – San Francisco's Media Alliance and Britain's CPBF.

Chapters 7 and 8 fast-forward to the present period. Based largely on interviews with media activists, we sketch the obstacles, challenges and opponents that DMA faces, as well as the resources, opportunities and strategies upon which it can draw. If these two chapters enquire into conditions of success, Chapters 9 and 10 asks about the *distinctiveness* and the political character of a media democracy movement. Here, we draw upon our interviews in Vancouver, a self-consciously global city, to analyse relationships between media-oriented and other activism, and to situate media activism within a larger field. This enables us to assess whether a distinct media democracy movement has emerged and the extent to which DMA remains an adjunct or supplement to other movements. We also speculate on the extent and ways in which DMA can be considered counterhegemonic. Finally, Chapter 11 considers what this study suggests about the specificity of DMA as an emergent form of politics, its possible relations with other contemporary movements, and the prospects for a democratic media system.

2   What is at stake?

Power and the media field

Why do the media's democratic deficit – and struggles over it – matter? What is at stake?

In this chapter, we consider media and power as 'prismatic' concepts, ones that we can look at from different angles, each revealing new aspects (Dahlgren 1995: 25). We then turn to perspectives on the relationship of media institutions to other centres of power, and the question of the media's own social power. We propose thinking of media as an institutional 'field', to use Bourdieu's concept, albeit one which takes distinct shape within differing national contexts. Finally, we sketch some of its implications for conceptualizing the project of media democratization.

Media and power

To chart this vast terrain, we need to do some conceptual brush-clearing. Neither 'media' nor 'power' are straightforward terms. A 'medium' can be literally any means or channel for conveying messages or meanings. In their sweeping historical panorama of radical media, Downing *et al.* (2001) show that graffiti, street theatre, dance, jokes, song, posters, murals, dress and quilts have all been used in building subaltern public spheres and amplifying counterhegemonic messages. Similarly, Bennett problematizes

> the core question of just what we mean by 'media' these days. With the frag-
> mentation of mass media channels and audiences, and the proliferation of new
> digital communication formats, it is difficult to draw sharp boundaries around
> discrete media spheres. As various media become interactively connected, in-
> formation flows more easily across technological, social, and geographical
> boundaries.
>
> (2003: 18)

How then, do we avoid analytical paralysis in the face of such apparent complexity and pluralism? Our solution is to avoid being mesmerized by technological forms, and to look beyond them to the few dominant and globalizing logics and institutions that comprise the commanding heights of the mediascape. Our focus is activism oriented towards challenging the democratic deficit of dominant means of public communication, especially journalism as a genre most directly relevant to the formation, contestation and circulation of political discourse.

To be sure, mass media are multifaceted creatures, at once technologies, industries, organizations and cultural practices. They generate meanings as well as profits, and thus we need the tools of both political economy and cultural studies to fully assess what is at stake: both control over the institutional means of public communication, as well as the practices and codes of signification, with their cultural and political effectivity. As Couldry puts it:

> This is why, in considering possible sites of resistance to media power, we must look not only at the distribution of economic and organizational resources and at contests over specific media representations of reality, but also at the sites from which alternative general frames for understanding social reality are offered. Beliefs in the media's central place in social life can be effectively challenged by *alternative* frames.
>
> (2003: 41)

Couldry's search for alternative frames leads him, understandably, to the alternative media. We choose instead to highlight the relatively neglected question of social movements as potential challengers to both the media's frames, and their concentration of symbolic power, particularly as manifested in media's institutional architecture and policy frameworks.

Like media, power is a multifaceted concept. Power has a positive and productive face: the individual and collective capacity to develop potentialities and achieve goals. Over the past century, technologies have exponentially multiplied two human capacities: to destroy, and to communicate. Individual communicative empowerment through digital technology is hyped by its commercial promoters, but it is no mere illusion. It forms a key part of the context of media democratization, positively by creating new channels for activism of all types, and negatively in tending to occlude the second, negative face of power: power over or against others. Often, power approximates a zero-sum game. Wasteful consumerism versus environmental well-being, workers' wages versus corporate profits, reproductive choice or gay rights versus religious conservatism – these are situations where the success of one side in setting socially binding rules may be at the expense of the other.

This 'negative' face of power is three-dimensional (Hall 1982: 64–5; following Lukes 1974). The first dimension concerns the ability of Group A to persuade or defeat Group B in order to achieve Outcome X, in a situation of overtly contrary preferences (for example, a student challenging a professor's grade award). The second dimension is a 'non-decision' resulting when institutional practices limit the scope of decision-making to issues that are innocuous to the more powerful party (for example, the professor is never in her office and there's no appeal procedure). The third dimension references *ideology*: the power to shape the very perceptions and desires of subordinate groups, so they do not think to challenge existing social relations because they are taken as natural, beyond history or politics (the student does not question an unjust grade because she accepts the infallibility of professors!). Ideology, of course, blends into the broader concept of *hegemony*, a process (always contested and negotiated, never guaranteed in advance) whereby the dominant classes win the consent of subaltern groups to their social and cultural leadership, 'and by these means – rather than by direct coercion … maintain their power over the economic, political and cultural direction of the nation' (O'Sullivan *et al.* 1994: 133).

The media are relevant to all three dimensions of power. Media can editorialize for a course of action. But more importantly, media help set the agenda of public discussion and political decision-making, and help shape the whole ideological environment towards 'the winning of a universal validity and legitimacy for accounts of the world which are partial and particular, and towards the grounding of these particular constructions in the taken-for-grantedness of "the real"' (Hall 1982: 65).

Here, we shall largely bypass debates about how such coercive, agenda-setting and ideological power is distributed in North Atlantic societies in general. We simply note a liberal-pluralist tradition which emphasizes the diffusion and counterbalancing distribution of power; a radical and neo-Marxist critical paradigm which peaked during the 1970s, highlighting structured inequality and conflicting interests, particularly between capital and labour; and a 'revisionist' strand emerging from the critical paradigm in the 1980s, questioning the Marxist class conflict model, asserting the plurality of forms of domination, but ultimately (and very problematically) avowing the disaggregation of power and of social relations in general (Hall 1982; Curran 2002, Chapter 4). Each of these very broad paradigms carried implications for the media/power relationship. But here, following Couldry and Curran (2003b: 3–4), we simply distinguish between power *through* the media, and power *of* the media. Paralleling the distinction between democratization through and of the media, the first concept references how power, cohering in other social spheres, is exerted through media practices and texts; the second, the impact of media organizations on other social spheres. In the sections below, we discuss each of these respectively.

Power through the media

How are media institutions, particularly journalism as their most politically visible practice, related to political and economic power? Are media subordinate, independent, or antagonistic vis-à-vis governing elites?

Not so long ago, the answer seemed straightforward. Embedded in popular folklore and journalism's self-understanding, the standard view presented journalism as a watchdog against the abuse of power, a righter of wrongs, a humbler of hubris and arrogance, a promoter of positive social change, an agent to comfort the afflicted and afflict the comfortable (Hackett 2001: 197).[1] This once common view of media's relation to power was broadly supported by the then predominant liberal-pluralist scholarship that portrayed the media as an institution autonomous from others, in a society where power is diffused, shared among contending and overlapping interests, whose competition is bounded and kept manageable by an overriding consensus around basic social values. In this perspective, media serve generally positive social and political functions, and are held accountable and responsible to audiences and to the social system as a whole, through the mechanisms of the marketplace, the legal framework established by the state, and journalists' own sense of professionalism (Hackett 1991: 53; Hall 1982; and Curran 2002: chapter 5).

That rosy view is at the heart of orthodox British and American liberal histories of the press, from its role in undermining aristocratic and colonial privilege in the eighteenth century, to the Watergate exposé of Richard Nixon's corrupt presidency in 1973. Since the 1960s and 1970s, however, the 'watchdog' image has given way to other canine metaphors. One critique sees journalism as a mad dog, mindlessly attacking authority, especially government, focusing on scandals, celebrities and infotainment, rather than on serious public affairs news. In academia, political scientists like Larry Sabato (1991) have critiqued the 'feeding frenzy' of 'attack journalism'. In Hollywood films, the heroic journalists of the 1970s – Watergate heroes Bob Woodward and Carl Bernstein in *All the President's Men*, or Jane Fonda defying a sinister nuclear power corporation in *The China Syndrome* – gave way to airheads and scumbags. Ignoring ethical principles, onscreen journalists by the mid 1990s revelled in glitz and sensationalism, or even committed murder (in *Natural Born Killers* and *To Die For*) in their pursuit of career advancement or psychological thrills (Hackett and Zhao 1998: 163). Instances of 'mad dog' media behaviour arguably include the pursuit of former president Bill Clinton over his affair with intern Monica Lewinsky, American talk radio's and television punditry's relentlessly cynical focus on the foibles and strategies of politicians, and nearly any edition of a British tabloid daily, with its tales of royal and establishment icons with feet of clay.

It is, however, another canine analogy that motivates a good deal of media reform activism: media as 'lapdogs', subservient to the economic and political elite. An outgrowth of the critical paradigm, the media are seen to legitimize the unjust and/or repressive policies and privileges of the state and corporations, while marginalizing dissenters and ordinary citizens from public debate. In Herman and Chomsky's well-known propaganda model (1988), five 'filters' lock the US media into their lapdog role, ensuring that media 'manufacture' the subordinate population's consent to elite domination: concentrated corporate media ownership; dependence on advertising revenue; reliance on elite news sources; 'flak' from right-wing institutes; and the 'national religion' of anti-Communism during the Cold War, and more recently, free market fundamentalism.

At first sight, the lapdog and mad dog metaphors seem diametrically opposed. But perhaps not: if the media hounds bay selectively, they can be lapdogs to some, attack dogs against others. Arguably, in the US at least, with the domination of the airwaves by right-wing demagogues like Rush Limbaugh and Bill O'Reilly, the media's alleged hostility to authority is disproportionately directed not against the private sector but against governments and elected office-holders – and moreover, not right-wingers, but against those perceived as (horrors!)

'liberals' (Franken 2003; Alterman 2003). In that case, the media's impact would be largely consistent with the lapdog theory: coherent left/progressive alternatives are marginalized; political ignorance, passivity or cynicism amongst the public is reinforced; and unaccountable corporate power and economic inequalities are ignored and implicitly legitimized at the expense of a positive economic role for democratically elected governments.

A hierarchy of influences

Each of the above metaphors ('dogmas'?) arguably overemphasizes particular links between social/political structure and the media. Two American scholars, Pamela Shoemaker and Stephen Reese (1996), offer a more comprehensive framework for analysing the influences on media production, and thereby its relations to power. As summarized in Table 2.1, their model identifies five layers of influences, starting with the most immediate workaday level and moving 'downward' to deeper levels of structural determination (Hackett 2004: 145).

As it applies to journalism, the first level comprises the media workers who actually produce the news. This level of influence includes the demographic characteristics of journalists (race, gender, socioeconomic status, educational level), their political and religious views, and their occupational training and role conceptions. Some media research suggests that Canadian and American journalists have 'liberal' or 'post-materialist' values which influence the news (Lichter, Rothman and Lichter 1986; Miljan and Cooper 2003). A survey of Washington DC journalists concludes, however, that while they may be 'liberal' on social issues like abortion, journalists are actually to the right of the American public on economic issues like taxation or 'free' trade (Croteau 1998).

Of arguably greater import than personal views, however, are journalists' conceptions of their professional roles, such as notions of public service or objectivity, and 'news values' – the criteria of relevance that guide journalists in their choice and construction of newsworthy stories. A recent study suggests this 'top ten' list of news values in the British press: powerful people or organizations; celebrities; entertainment or human interest; surprise and/or contrast; bad news; good news; magnitude or scope; perceived relevance to the audience; follow-up to stories already in the news; and congruence with the news organization's own promotional or political agenda (Harcup and O'Neill 2001).

Such conceptions of what it takes to do 'professional' work are less the product of journalists' individual biographies, and more the result of their socialization on the job, and the constraints of their daily work routines (the second level of influence) and the institutional needs of the media organizations they work for (the third level). News routines typically include regularized 'beats', often focused on institutions able to generate an efficient and predictably newsworthy supply of material – the White House, city hall, the courts, and so on. Other aspects of news routinization include standardized genres (soft vs. hard news, documentaries, editorials, columns, etc.) and the key news agencies like Associated Press, which local editors use to guide the selection process. Small wonder that Canadian TV

Table 2.1 Power through the media: a hierarchy of influences

Level of influence	Openings for media pluralism, progressive social change	'Conservatizing' pressures
Journalists	<ul><li>'liberal' views on social issues</li><li>news values: scandal, human interest, spectacle (e.g. Greenpeace)</li><li>professional concepts of balance, fairness</li></ul>	<ul><li>'conservative' views on economic issues</li><li>over-representation of affluent white males in decision-making positions</li><li>some practices of 'objectivity' – e.g. orientation to elite sources</li></ul>
Media work routines	<ul><li>'both sides' to a story</li></ul>	<ul><li>institutional beats, prioritizing established institutions over the 'weak and unorganized'</li></ul>
Media organizations' structures and logics	<ul><li>legitimation and commercial needs of media corporations</li><li>alternative media of challenger groups</li></ul>	<ul><li>high entry costs limit ownership</li><li>large corporations' political interests</li><li>ownership power within media organizations over policy, hiring, resource allocation</li><li>concentrated ownership</li><li>economies of scale lead to middle-of-the-road content</li><li>'intimate relations' with governments, regulators</li></ul>
Environing conditions: extra-media factors (sources, advertisers, governments, laws, technology, audience, markets)	<ul><li>strategic communication, development of expertise, by progressive advocacy groups, earning source status</li><li>political mobilization by subordinate but large groups</li><li>market competition, consumer choice</li><li>democratic state policies (e.g. public broadcasting, ownership limits, regulation of private sector, subsidized diversity)</li><li>popular mobilization through the internet</li></ul>	<ul><li>state censorship or influence over information flows, especially since 9/11</li><li>bias to affluent consumers; market censorship due to advertising</li><li>public relations, information subsidies</li><li>corporate 'colonization' of the internet</li></ul>
Environing conditions: ideology (hegemonic, subcultural and oppositional discourses)	<ul><li>openings in dominant narratives (e.g. Canada as peacekeeper; US as land of freedom)</li><li>democratic values in general</li></ul>	<ul><li>journalists internalize hegemonic discourses, e.g. anti-communism</li><li>resource inequality influences the circulation of discourses</li></ul>

Sources: Croteau 1998; Curran 2002: 148–55; Gandy 1982; Hackett 1991; Hackett 2004: 147–52; Hackett and Uzelman 2003; McChesney 1999: 49–50; Shoemaker and Reese 1996; A. White 2004

actor Don Herron once said in one of his comedy skits, 'The news today is the same as it was yesterday, it just happened to different people' (Hackett 2004: 146).

The third layer comprises the broader organizational imperatives of media institutions. Considerations of supply, production, and consumption translate into maintaining a steady and manageable supply of news, efficiently producing it, and presenting it in formats that attract profitable audiences (Shoemaker and Reese 1996: 105–37; Hackett 2004: 146). This level of analysis concerns the internal hierarchies and division of labour, the ownership and control, the editorial and other policies, and the intended audience or markets of each media organization.

The fourth layer comprises 'extra-media influences' or environing conditions, discussed in Chapter 1 and again below. These include technology, the institutions that supply information to journalists, the advertisers who supply revenues, the governments that can set regulatory and legal frameworks as well as supply or withhold information, and audiences – or more strictly speaking for commercial media, markets.

Finally, and most broadly, there is the influence of 'ideology', which in the Shoemaker/Reese model includes the interplay of social relations, cultural narratives and power structures at the societal level – 'how media symbolic content is connected with larger social interests, how meaning is constructed in the service of power' (Reese 2001: 183). This notion meshes well with the concept of hegemony, noted above.

Going through these influences systematically, one could argue that 'conservatizing' forces which encourage the media 'to gravitate towards the central orbit of power' operate at every level (Curran 2002: 148–55; Hackett 2004: 147–52; Hackett and Uzelman 2003). While far from exhaustive, the right-hand column in Table 2.1 summarizes many of the main pressures on journalism which constrain the influence of consumers and progressive groups, and/or which conversely embed media institutions ideologically and economically not only in a capitalist social order but more specifically in neoliberal policies. Many of the listed factors are more or less self-explanatory, but several deserve further comment, particularly at the level of extra-media influences. In the post-9/11 era, censorship and surveillance by the state are increasingly important as a dimension of the democratic deficit, as we argued in Chapter 1. But contrary to conventional wisdom the state has no monopoly on censorship; market forces too can systematically narrow the flow of readily available public information. Thus, in a commercial media system, the interests and needs of affluent consumers are disproportionately served because their high disposable income makes them a prime market for specialized media services and a preferred target audience for advertisers (Curran 2002: 149). The needs of the less well-heeled, as well as media fare at odds with the consumerist ethos, tend to be filtered out; and indeed, advertising functions as a kind of licensing system, determining which media will survive, and which will go to the wall. Meanwhile, the expansion of the public relations industry provides a further tool for governments, corporations and well-funded policy institutes: information subsidies, whereby expensively produced and newsworthy (but self-serving) information is distributed at virtually no cost to media (Gandy 1982).

One of the most discussed 'external' influences on media, but one which is also constitutive of media, is technology. Arguably, the very definition of 'media' is shifting with the advent of interactive, point-to-point digital networks, and some feel that the power of the media needs to be rethought in the age of the internet. They argue that the internet is eroding the dominance of mass media, as well as blurring the boundaries between media consumers and producers (Bennett 2003). On the other hand, so long as the internet's development is governed by the logic of commercialization, the corporate giants who dominate the traditional mass media may well be able to shape the internet to their own advantage (McChesney 1999). Two leading progressive experts on internet policy debunk the naive optimism about the 'new' digital media's revolutionary and 'wildly democratic' character:

> First, the old media aren't going anywhere, and their dominance in our lives – radio and TV usage still outstrip the Internet by a factor of 20–1 – will continue for years. Second, the old media giants have made their presence felt online, too, establishing digital beachheads that might not be making much money (yet) but that are certainly attracting their share of online traffic … Thus, even if the long-touted media convergence has been slow in arriving, the distinction between old media and new – particularly with regard to the impact of conglomerate culture – is largely a false one.
>
> (Chester and Larson 2002)

So far, our summary of influences on the media parallels the propaganda model or lapdog metaphor. But of course it is not the whole story. Three implications of our analysis are worth highlighting.

First, we recognize that far from being predictably obedient lapdogs, the media are sites of struggle. Countervailing forces provide openings for media pluralism, for popular voices, and for progressive social change. These are summarized in the centre column of Table 2.1. Some 'pluralizing' factors derive from structural contradictions in the political economy of communications industries.[2] But such openings do not automatically create resistance; that integrally depends upon the agency of subaltern groups, including alternative media and social movements. In the 1970s, Greenpeace brilliantly exploited news values like human interest and spectacle to put environmentalism on the global agenda. Non-elite groups can establish organizations and develop expertise in strategies to gain the status of news sources, and they

> can develop alternative understandings of society, engender a strong sense of collective identity, and transmit collective allegiances and radical commitments from one generation to the next, through personal interaction, social rituals and the institutions under their control or influence. Through *collective action* in the workplace and civil society, and through *participation in the collective dialogue of society*, they can seek to change prevailing attitudes. Above all, their numerical strength means that potentially they can secure, through the

electoral process, political influence over the state and use its power to mod-
ify the organization and culture of society …

(Curran 2002: 151, emphasis added)

A second noteworthy feature of the analysis is the Janus-face of the state. Like technology, it can serve both repressive and democratic purposes. On the one hand, the state has justifiably earned suspicion for its historical role in repressing progressive forces and subaltern groups. On the other hand, much media activism is devoted precisely to pushing the state to adopt democratic policies to promote media pluralism. Such policies as investment in public broadcasting, regulation of private broadcasters, regulatory ceilings on cross-media and concentrated ownership, and arm's length subsidies for minority media have had at least partial success in western Europe. Even in the US, media reformers like those at the Free Press conferences advocate state regulation (most recently, ownership ceilings on broadcasting media) as a necessary counterweight to corporate power.

And third, while both state and media are sites of struggle, they are not a level playing field. Rather, they are 'structured in dominance', their routine opera-tions and institutional inertia tending to favour those who already enjoy the most economic and cultural capital. The right-hand column of Table 2.1 shows the weight of such 'conservatizing' forces. The democratic deficit resulting from such forces is precisely what creates the incentive and necessity for media democratization as a project. And interestingly, Table 2.1 suggests the scope and tasks of this project – namely, to amplify or utilize the factors identified in the middle column, and to challenge, counterbalance or even eliminate those in the right column.

Power of the media

Do media reinforce hierarchies and social inequalities, or challenge them? Do media solidify the status quo, or catalyse progressive social change? Or both, depending on context?

Remarkably, after decades of media research, these are still open questions. They require us to consider whether and how the media exert power in their own right, rather than simply reflect the power of other institutions. If we overempha-size the impact of external power on media, we risk losing sight of what happens inside the black box of the media – how they process and create meanings – and what difference they make in the world. Thus, to assess what is at stake in struggles over media power, we also need to reverse the causal arrow. and enquire into the media's own power. If media have no autonomy, no power of their own, there is little point to a social movement aimed specifically at democratically transforming them. As Couldry appropriately asks:

> Can 'media' possess a power that is contestable separately from the state or corporate sector's representations of itself through media? Certainly there are

overlaps between the contestation of media power and other forms of power, but this is not to say that distinctive social issues don't arise about 'media power' ...

(2003: 39)

At heart, Couldry adds, that power is the 'overwhelming concentration' of most of society's symbolic resources in the institutional space of the media. It comprises, in effect, Stuart Hall's (1982) third dimension of power – the ability to construct, define or name social reality, and thereby to shape a very important component of the terrain on which all political struggles are conducted.

To enquire into media power is not necessarily to accept the position, most famously associated with Marshall McLuhan, that media technologies, formats and texts are so constitutive of contemporary culture and politics that it makes no sense to isolate media 'effects' on other phenomena (Hackett 1991: 16–18). Such a position unduly dismisses the influences discussed in the section above, and is prone to technological determinism, forgetting that the development and uses of communications technology have themselves been strongly influenced by other processes, institutions and groups (Smythe 1981: 217–48). Still, it is admittedly difficult to isolate specific media 'effects' on other slices of social reality, in billiard-ball fashion. Fiske (1987) suggests instead the concept of 'effectivity', to denote the media's pervasive but indeterminate influence. The 'effects' literature is vast, but given our concern with media democratization, we simply sketch key concepts in two areas: popular political consciousness, and the trajectory of social movements as potential agents of democratic renewal.

Media, social movements and other political processes

Through their news coverage, their institutional dynamics, and their interaction with other social forces, mass media can help to make or 'unmake' movements for social change (Hackett 1991: 20). Protest movements need forms of communication beyond interpersonal discussion in order to articulate and develop their perspectives, coordinate their activities, maintain cohesion, and expand their base of support (Kielbowicz and Scherer 1986). The historical moment when radical movements in the US or UK could build a mass base through their internal media alone passed with the emergence of the mass commercial press in the nineteenth century (Curran 2002: Chapter 3). Since then, notwithstanding the internet's reduction of mobilization costs, movements seeking to garner wide-spread support for political change have not been able to ignore the mass media that affect every stage of their trajectory: their emergence, maintenance and success (Hackett 1991: 21).

Dominant media potentially play contradictory roles at each of these phases. Media may facilitate the emergence of protest movements simply by publicizing issues and events that may stimulate discontent and its mobilization – such as the American and British build-up to the invasion of Iraq, resulting in the largest global peace protests in history. And as Greenpeace showed dramatically, activists can learn to stage events and dramatize their concerns to gain media attention (Kielbowicz and Scherer 1986: 80–1). But media representations can also fragment processes that activists see as connected (for example, free trade agreements, and environmental degradation), or ignore them altogether, and thereby constrain the development and popularization of wide-ranging, coherent critiques of the status quo. It is difficult to criticize what you cannot name (Hackett 1991: 22).

Once a movement has emerged, media also play contradictory roles in its organizational consolidation, self-maintenance and cohesion. Thus, news coverage can confer status and legitimacy on a movement's efforts and issues, thereby reinforcing the commitment of activists, helping to recruit new members, and broadening its base. On the other hand, the kind of denigrative coverage that was applied to the American student New Left of the 1960s (Gitlin 1980), or to the anti-corporate globalization movement of the current decade, have helped to shape a public image of deviance, confrontation and radicalism, and to confine each to the margins of legitimate political debate.

Likewise, media inattention or negative framing has much bearing on a movement's success, whether this be defined as the maintenance of organizational continuity, the diffusion of its perspectives amongst the population, the achievement of recognition by policymakers, or actual influences on policy outcomes (Hackett 1991: 22). Without the ability to engage in public communication, movements typically are confined to marginalized ghettos, however much these be romanticized as 'prefigurative politics' or 'temporary zones' of emancipation from corporate and state control. On the whole, the North Atlantic media currently appear to play a 'conservatizing' role, delegitimizing and marginalizing radical protest, or inducing it to adopt bureaucratic structures and more moderate stands and tactics focusing on single issues rather than wholesale critiques (Hackett 1991: 23).

Media are centrally implicated in other social, political and cultural processes – such as war and peace. Media can affect decision-making and interaction between policymakers, for example, by reducing reaction time to events, thus escalating crises compared to earlier and slower forms of communication. Perhaps most crucially, news reportage can too often fan the flames of war through defining threats, victims and enemies in ways consistent with the politics of respective national governments. Notwithstanding the globalization of production and markets in media fiction and music, most media audiences are still exposed to daily news that is nationally produced. Thus, even within the 'free press' of liberal-democracies like the US and UK, the domination of local and national news media 'continues to stunt the development of global politics, and promotes a nationalist and localist perspective of human affairs' (Curran 2002: 180) – including war and peace. Consider the role of hegemonic American media in mobilizing public acquiescence in the US-led invasion of Iraq in 2003, noted in Chapter 1 (McChesney 2002; McChesney and Hackett 2005: 231–2; Oberg 2005).

Media power is not only negative. It is also integral in processes of democratization in formerly authoritarian countries (discussed in Chapter 5), though to what extent media act as independent catalysts is open to debate. In their overview of case studies, Price and Rozumilowicz (2002: 260) find relatively little evidence for 'an active and involved media system' directly leading to change in political structures. On the other hand, when they are organically linked to oppositional movements prying open the cracks in a decaying social order, even small-scale radical media can actively contribute to bringing it down (Downing *et al.* 2001).

Media and public consciousness

Media influence on popular consciousness is too often conceptualized through concepts like propaganda and indoctrination, which imply intentional efforts to manipulate and persuade. Such efforts do of course exist; they are at the core of the massive advertising and public relations industries. But such general notions ignore the complexity of media production and audience interpretation; they also lead progressives too readily to scapegoat the media for political failures whose roots lie elsewhere.

On the other hand, the fashionable celebration of the internal tensions in media texts, and of media audiences as active producers of meaning, is equally one-sided. By implying that media power is limited because audiences make of media what they will, some strands of 'new revisionist' and 'cultural populist' scholarship in effect dismiss the need for structural media reform, and come close to colluding with the neoliberal position that existing commercial media 'give people what they want' (Curran 2002: 115–24; McGuigan 1992: 173).

Well, not quite. Audiences actively interpret media texts, but not under conditions of their own choosing. Unless they have access to contrary experiences or discursive resources, they tend to work with the raw material provided. Moreover, while commercial media certainly must attract audiences to succeed, this does not mean they merely reflect popular values or politics. Rather, the structural pressures summarized above mean that commercial media

> give some of the people part of what they think they want – programming that media corporations find economical and convenient to offer, that is generally compatible with a consumerist stance, and that affluent and/or mass consumers (who lack ready access to the full range of potential alternatives) are prepared to accept as a reward for joining the audience.
>
> (Hackett and Zhao 1998: 188)[3]

Rather than either propaganda or consumer sovereignty, concepts like agenda-setting, spiral of silence, cultivation and ideology offer more useful ways to think about the media's impact on public orientations towards political issues (Hackett 2001: 199).

The media's *agenda-setting* role is a by-product of our collective dependence on mass media for information beyond our direct experience. Through their ability to focus public attention on some events and issues, and away from others, the media influence public perceptions of what exists, what is important, what is good and valuable, what is bad and threatening, and what is related to what (Gerbner 1969). Media-inspired *perceptions* (for example, that welfare fraud is pervasive) can in turn affect *attitudes* – especially when such representations mobilize longstanding dispositions, such as hostility towards the 'undeserving poor' (Curran 2002: 161).

The flip side of agenda-setting is the *spiral of silence*, a concept pioneered by Elizabeth Noelle-Neumann (McQuail 1994: 361–3). People who hold views which they feel are those of a minority and which are seldom expressed in public become reluctant to express them for fear of social isolation; without social reinforcement, their own adherence to these views declines. Thus, if they persistently ignore a certain viewpoint, media may actively contribute to its erosion.

The process of *cultivation* is similarly cumulative and long-term: TV viewing 'gradually leads to the adoption of beliefs about the nature of the social world which conform to the stereotyped, distorted and very selective view of reality as portrayed in a systematic way in television fiction and news' (McQuail 1994: 364–5). As developed by Gerbner (2002), the theory also holds that within its current industrial, commercial framework, television (at least in the US) serves primarily to reinforce rather than alter or threaten hegemonic beliefs and behaviours (McQuail 1994: 364).

Taken together, these concepts point to the *ideological* role of news media, in the sense of Stuart Hall's third dimension of power, discussed above. If ideology is the production of meaning in the service of domination (Thompson 1984: 130–1), then news and other media genres are ideological to the extent that they construct symbolic maps of the world which favour dominant values, institutions, elites, or social relations – at the expense of alternative mappings of social reality. But unlike propaganda, ideology is not necessarily produced with the *intention* to dominate, manipulate or persuade. Rather, it typically involves taken-for-granted value commitments and reality judgements, assumptions which are naturalized, transformed into common sense, through the process of hegemony.

Crucially, such ideological work takes place not despite but *because* journalism claims to be objective, and commercial television purports to entertain rather than persuade. Even at its most objective and professional, journalism cannot escape the need for 'frames' (Gitlin 1980: 7) – judgements about what counts as a newsworthy 'story', what are the pertinent issues, who constitutes a relevant and credible source, what is the appropriate (even if implicit) context in which to place 'the story', and so on. Likewise, even the most apparently apolitical forms of TV entertainment must make assumptions about its audience, in order to adopt an appropriate form of address, relevant topics, and value positions. Those assumptions, about gender relations for example, have consequences. Thus, an analysis of Hollywood's top grossing films during the 1990s suggests that despite certain advances, women are still subjected to the kind of 'symbolic annihilation' characteristic of 1970s US network television (Press and Liebes 2003: 140–1). It's never 'just entertainment'.

Media as a field?

So far, we have framed the question of media power in terms consistent with much of the Anglo-American scholarship on media power, informed as it often is by empiricist notions of linear causality. Where scholars differ concerns the causal arrow's direction – from society to media, or vice versa. Stuart Allan (2004: 3) questions this media–society dichotomy, calling instead for attention to 'how the news media are embedded in specific relations of power and control while, at the same time, recognizing the ways in which they are working to reinflect, transform and, if only infrequently, challenge these same relations over time' – and, we might add, media may sometimes generate *new* relations of power, such as that of the celebrity.

Perhaps we can improve upon the Anglo-American paradigm of media power by cherry-picking some concepts from French structuralist and post-structuralist thinkers as diverse as Louis Althusser, Michel Foucault and Pierre Bourdieu. Taken together, their work implies an analysis of media as a relatively autonomous institutional sphere, one which articulates with relations of power, knowledge and production more broadly, but which also has a certain logic of its own. Foucault spoke of 'discursive regimes' – of how power is imbricated with knowledge, not by directly imposing censorship or coercion from outside, but indirectly and internally, through the criteria and practices that 'govern' the production of statements (Foucault 1984: 54–5; Hackett and Zhao 1998: 6). Thus, power relations may be manifested or even constituted, within the everyday routines and ethos of workaday journalism. Critics sometimes suggest that because Foucault sees power as diffused, operative everywhere, it is located nowhere in particular, thus blunting recognition of the inequalities sustained through state and capital (though Downing (2003: 250) suggests this may be a misreading of his work).

Perhaps Bourdieu's concept of 'fields' is more useful still, since it pays fuller attention to the relation between fields. In his view,

> any social formation is structured by way of a hierarchically organized series of fields (the economic field, the educational field, the political field, the cultural field, etc.), each defined as a structured space with its own laws of functioning and its own relations of force independent of those of politics and the economy … Each field is relatively autonomous but structurally homologous with the others. Its structure, at any given moment, is determined by the relations between the positions agents occupy in the field.
>
> (Johnson, in Bourdieu 1993: 6)

Each field is 'a social universe with its own laws of functioning' (ibid.: 14). Typically, each field is characterized by its own ethos, its own formal and informal rules and logics, its own set of status and power positions for individual agents (such as journalists) to occupy, its own forms of interests or resources – capital – for which agents compete. In the economic sphere, agents presumably compete for economic capital through investment strategies; in the political sphere, they compete for governmental power. If we regard cultural production in general, and mass media or journalism specifically, as distinct fields, two forms of capital are particularly relevant: symbolic capital, the accumulation of prestige or celebrity; and cultural capital, forms of cultural knowledge or dispositions (ibid.: 7). Indeed, this insight suggests that journalism and related forms of large-scale cultural production (the 'media'), have the distinct feature of combining economic power (the production of profit) and symbolic power, which is ultimately the capacity to define social reality. As suggested above, the 'media' are powerful in so far as they comprise a concentration of society's symbolic power (Couldry 2003: 39), thus imposing 'a structural constraint upon other fields', but at the same time, being 'considerably influenced by commercial or economic constraints' (Marliere 1998: 220).

This approach invites us to consider journalism and mass media as relatively autonomous fields within a broader field of power, which is itself structured in dominance: some fields exert more gravitational force than others, over the whole social formation.[4] This metaphor takes us beyond linear, billiard-ball causality to suggest a better way of conceptualizing how journalism interacts with economic forces, the political system, science, or other institutional spheres, and also with capitalism, patriarchy, racism, or other axes of domination. Without denying that individuals are active agents pursuing strategies, often creatively, it turns our attention to structured roles and relationships – including interactions between institutional fields. Thus:

> External determinants can have an effect only through transformations in the structure of the field itself. In other words, the field's structure *refracts*, much like a prism, external determinants in terms of its own logic, and it is only through such refraction that external factors can have an effect on the field. The degree of autonomy of a particular field is measured precisely by its ability to refract external demands into its own logic.
>
> (Johnson, in Bourdieu 1993: 14)

This is a very rich passage. It suggests that the most important form of external influence upon journalism is not explicit and occasional interventions (like an advertiser trying to kill a story, or a source pressing for favourable spin), but rather the long-term re-structuring of the ground rules and routines which shape (relatively autonomous) journalism on a workaday basis.

As a concrete example of the relative autonomy of the journalism field (and one incidentally very different from Bourdieu's own arguably polemical analysis: Marliere 1998), Hackett and Zhao (1998: 86) suggest that in the US and Canada, journalism has been characterized for most of the twentieth century, by a 'regime of objectivity'. By this, they mean an interrelated complex of ideas and practices which provide 'a general model for conceiving, defining, arranging, and evaluating news texts, news practices, and news institutions'. The regime comprises five dimensions: a *normative ideal* (factualness, detachment, accuracy, etc.); an *epistemology* (assumptions about knowledge and reality, like the possibility of separating values from facts); a set of *newsgathering and presentational practices* (like the use of appropriate sources); a set of *institutional relations* (complex, specialized news organizations, staffed by professionals and enjoying autonomy from the state); and an *active ingredient in public discourse*, providing the language ('bias', 'fairness', 'balance') for everyday talk about the news (Hackett and Zhao 1998: 83–6).

While journalism's regime of objectivity is no mere expression of external forces, however, neither is it free-floating. It has social, political and historical conditions of existence. One might say that journalism's objectivity regime, and the institutional environment of other fields, were mutually constituting. Factors which have shaped and solidified the objectivity regime included the emerging commercial press's economic interests in reaching large multi-partisan reader-ships, the rising status of science and empirical research in the nineteenth century, the increasing educational level and professional-status claims of jour-nalists, and the political legitimation needs of monopoly newspaper owners in the twentieth century (Hackett and Zhao 1998: 36–81).

Historically, the characteristics of the objectivity regime have not been fixed in stone. Both journalism, and its articulation with other institutional fields, have evolved over time. Thus, while the notion of objectivity as truth-telling in the public interest has been a remarkably persistent touchstone of North American journalism, both its practices and conceptualization have shifted. For instance, the 'naive realism' of late-nineteenth-century faith in the ability of facts to speak for themselves gave way after the carnage and propaganda of World War I to a narrower definition of objectivity as 'a method designed for a world in which even facts could not be trusted' (Schudson 1978: 122). Later, the upheavals in 1960s popular culture, and the 'credibility gap' between American government and public resulting from the Vietnam war and the Watergate scandal, paved the way for a more critical or adversarial style of journalism.

So, an interacting set of fields has generated journalism's regime of objectivity, which in turn has ideological consequences – largely unintended, but in a generally conservative direction. Take, for example, one of the hallmarks of 'objective' reporting – the use of 'appropriate sources' to provide relevant and credible 'facts'. It just so happens that the sources who are available, articulate, convenient and apparently authoritative, are frequently representatives of powerful institutions (Hackett and Zhao 1998: 142). While it may provide openings for change and dissent, journalism's objectivity regime on the whole

> provides a legitimation for established ideological optics and power relations. It systematically produces partial representations of the world, skewed to-wards dominant institutions and values, while at the same time it disguises that ideological role from its audiences. It thereby wins consent for 'preferred read-ings' … embedded in the news.
>
> (Hackett and Zhao 1998: 161)

Such 'conservatizing' consequences of objectivity are not necessarily intended, but, given the position of journalism within a structured field of power, neither are they purely accidental: journalism (and media) may be a relatively autonomous field, but it is not a level one on which to play. In this structuralist view, the field itself continually generates and reproduces inequalities, which can also, however, be creatively contested and adapted by journalists and others.

Moreover, the analysis of influences on the media, discussed above, suggests that journalism is a relatively 'weak' field, in two related senses. First, its boundaries are permeable, its autonomy more limited. Compared to fields like 'high' culture (art, literature, poetry), science and technology, or (though now in retreat) academia, the logics and resources of journalism/mass media are less self-determining. Second, while journalism/mass media is a field vastly more influential than high culture and academia, and while its concentration of symbolic power can constrain other fields, it does not perch atop the social formation. In the era of market liberal hegemony and state- and corporate-driven globalization, all fields have become more subject to direct determination by the economic field, and more specifically the untrammelled logic of capital accumulation. But journalism/mass media are especially vulnerable, because they are so heavily integrated into processes of generating political and economic capital. (Speculatively, in an era of corporate and political 'branding' (Klein 2000), the very distinctions between symbolic, economic and political capital are themselves eroding.)

Journalism's weakness as a distinct field is evident in the significant erosion of the regime of objectivity, the emblem of autonomy and professionalism, during the past two decades. The Reagan government's abandonment in the 1980s of the Fairness Doctrine, mandating opportunity for counterbalancing commentary in broadcasting of controversial issues, narrowed the range of views and paved the way for partisan (mostly right-wing) networks like Fox. The 1996 Telecommunications Act enabled massive growth in media concentration, and further encouraged the ethos of broadcasting as a property right rather than a public service. In 2001, the 9/11 attacks led many media pundits to disavow 'objectivity' as even an appropriate stance to take in reporting the Bush administration's 'war on terror' (Navasky 2002). Shifts in the economic field (e.g. the rise of conglomerates driven by shareholders seeking short-term profits) have contributed to the prevalence of 'infotainment'.

The eradication of objectivity finds its pinnacle in Rupert Murdoch's Fox News Channel. The fusion of news and commentary, the close political ties of its decision-makers with the Republican Party, the daily memos to set editorial agendas on blatantly political grounds, the political screening of its pundits, the musical and graphical tributes to American nationalism during news programmes, are all clear violations of even the cautious, conservatizing versions of objectivity that have marked US journalism in recent decades. The only vestiges of objectivity are window-dressing: point-counterpoint talk shows setting right-wing pitbulls against faux liberal poodles (such as Hannity and Colmes), and the network's marketing slogan 'fair and balanced' (Franken 2003). What is most revealing is not only that Fox has encountered little organized opposition within the ranks of journalism, but that its style is influencing other networks, impressed by Fox's ratings success (Knightley 2002).

National contexts

Fox TV's eccentricities remind us that media and activism take shape in real historical and cultural contexts, which differ even between the three globally similar North Atlantic states. Consider first Britain's media system. Unlike the US, the UK has a strong tradition of public service broadcasting, embodied by the world-renowned BBC, and stronger public service regulatory mandates for private broadcasters. By contrast with the US, Britain's newspaper press has a more openly partisan (rather than 'objective') tradition, a number of genuinely national newspapers with distinct editorial personalities, and a historical split between upscale 'quality' dailies, and the mass-market 'popular' tabloids. More than in the US, British public debate over the media has highlighted the sensationalist excesses of the tabloids, and among trade unionists and social democrats, the perceived right-wing bias of the press.

Politically, the UK has both libertarian and collectivist strands in its culture. While a globalizing culture of consumer capitalism is doubtless lapping at its foundations, collectivism was nurtured by a robust working-class culture and trade union movement, and found legislative expression in Britain's postwar welfare state. Even today, British workers are twice as likely as their American counterparts to belong to a union (28 to 14 per cent). The British Left has had a 'mainstream' political vehicle in the social democratic Labour Party, which has formed either the government or the main opposition party for many decades. Even for radicals who challenged its cautious reformism, Labour provided a horizon to which to orient, and confidence that progressive and socialist ideas could take root in 'mainstream' culture – at least until the extended hegemony of Thatcherism provoked a rightward turn in Labour itself during the 1990s. Until then, the British Left enjoyed confidence in the possibility both of majority support, and of achieving significant social reform through state regulation and legislation.

The American mediascape offers a different context for contestation. Based in distinct urban markets, newspapers and radio historically have been more locally oriented than Britain's; along with America's geographical spread and its feder- ated political structure, these factors have reinforced a localist organization of media activism as well. That localist base has perhaps handicapped public interest media reformers trying to intervene in national politics; they have tended to operate inside the Beltway (Washington DC) without an active mass base.

The regime of objectivity, the emblem of American print journalism for much of the past century, contrasts with the British and European tradition of partisanship. Whatever its subtle ideological biases, noted above, objectivity has cushioned the US press from political attack. Liberal press reformers, most famously the 1947 Hutchins Commission, have regarded monopoly and concentration as acceptable, so long as newspapers conduct themselves with 'social responsibility' (Baker 2002: 155–6). Instead, at the national level, American media reformers in the 1970s and 1980s focused on the then-dominant media, the three television networks – ABC, CBS and NBC. Here, the contestation was more over cultural values and their associated media representations – sex, violence, race relations – than over partisan politics as such.

Another contrast with the UK is the weakness of American public service broad- casting, and conversely, the unchallenged hegemony of commercialism – a bane to media activism in that there is no strong public broadcaster whose achievements and challenges have stimulated media reformers in Canada and the UK; but a boon, in that the excesses of hyper-commercialism – from saturation advertising and prime-time schlock to the recent decline of localism in radio – have angered many people across the political spectrum.

What about the political context? An adequate diagnosis of the American Left, as a 'natural' constituency for media democratization, would require a separate book (e.g. Gitlin 1995; Sanbonmatsu 2004, Chapter 1). We can simply highlight several points. First, progressive politics in the US is shaped by the intersection of class and race, and the historically long shadow of institutionalized racism. The struggle by communities of colour for racial justice provides much of the potential energy for radical politics in America. Yet the racial 'grand canyon' of American society influences the Left also, and the emerging media reform movement is still struggling to reconcile perspectives and priorities across this divide.

Second, compared to the UK, the American Left is more marginalized from political institutions and 'mainstream' culture. To be sure, socialist presidential candidates garnered nearly a million votes in 1920 (after the carnage of World War I) and 1932 (during the Great Depression); but since the anti-Communist McCarthyite repression of the late 1940s, the radical Left has had little influence within major unions or political parties. The student-based anti-war, anti-racist 'New Left' emerging in the 1960s arguably deepened that marginalization through its own practices and style. The New Left 'decisively privileged emotive and aesthetic expression of an inner, "radical" nature over considerations of strategy, theoretical coherence, or the patient construction of a counterhegemonic move-ment' (Sanbonmatsu 2004: 23). All told, the politics of expressivism, the historical experience of repression, the lack of an institutionalized presence in the political system, and the libertarianism which many on the Left share with many other Americans, have made progressives more distrustful of the state and less inclined to work for specific policy reforms, compared to their British counterparts.

As in many other ways, Canada lies between its two cultural neighbours. Canada has a public broadcasting and social democratic tradition stronger than the US, but weaker than the UK. And it has some characteristics distinct from both of them. Given its smaller population, Canada has a higher degree of media concentration, with fewer dominant companies. The regionalism of its political and media systems, and their bifurcation between the anglophone majority and the Quebec-centred francophone minority have implications for cultural identi-ties, which are less monolithically nationalist than in the US; and for media policy, where regional cross-media ownership looms as a more salient problem. Canadian communications policy, though now being transformed by neoliberal interna-tional trade deals, has sought to bolster some measure of cultural sovereignty vis-à-vis the powerful pull of American cultural industries.

Implications for media democratization

Insofar as journalism and mass media wield a distinctive and concentrated form of power, and constitute a field (with internally generated ethics, specialized skills and agent-positions, institutionalized practices and resources, and so on), it invites recognition, and mobilization, as a specific site of struggle. That is *not* to claim that every institutional field calls forth or requires a corresponding social movement. Probably most new social movements span different fields; peace activists, for example, may seek to transform not only strictly military institutions, but also public education, foreign policy, children's toys, or blockbuster films. Indeed, the militarization of popular culture has sometimes led the peace movement into media activism. One dramatic case was the coalition against *Amerika*, a 1986 ABC network television mini-series portraying the occupation of the US by the late Soviet Union. Regarding the programme as a sop to right-wing Cold War paranoia, peace groups joined forces with an emerging generation of media activists. Indeed, the campaign helped publicly launch FAIR as the country's leading progressive media monitor.

Still, the *specificity* of the media field does suggest the need to develop capacities specifically suited to challenging and changing media power: issue expertise; networks; archives of information and experience; leadership and spokespeople; coordination; critical analysis, mobilizing information, normative principles and models of democratic alternatives; platforms and venues; the ability to build coalitions, however temporary, and to develop issue-focused campaigns.

On the other hand, the *diversity* of influences on media, and the ways in which power is embedded in multifaceted workaday 'regimes' (not just individual agents, sites or acts), imply that a full-ranging project of media democratization would be vast. As can be surmised from Table 2.1, it would encompass not only the control, financing, practices and occupational ideologies of media institutions but also 'external' conditions: the democratization of economy and state, the equalization of communicative (and perhaps material) resources available to citizens. To take up this whole agenda would not only democratize the media system. It would transform the world. Does that imply that media democratization is an impossibly daunting task? Not at all. A movement to challenge corporate power is likely to find common cause with other social movements. Moreover, no campaign or movement organization needs to take on the entire agenda simultaneously. Dominant media institutions are still more diverse and fragmented than, say, the political or military spheres; that means that it is possible to decompose media democratization into discrete and manageable issues and sites, such as a struggle to win access television programming in a single community. Unlike election campaign finance reform, for example, it is not an all-or-nothing issue (McChesney and Hackett 2005: 238).

Provisionally, we suggest that the media field evinces a combination of (a) a high capacity to intrude upon the functioning of other fields (power of the media); (b) vulnerability to influence from political and economic fields, and structured subordination to them (power through the media); and (c) boundaries which are relatively porous and ill-defined. These factors have several implications. The weakness of journalism's autonomy from state and capital places severe limits on the strategy of reform from within, in the absence of strong allies without. The strategic importance of media to the legitimation, publicity and marketing needs of corporations and governments mean that effective media reform campaigns are likely quickly to provoke reaction from capital and state. Conversely though, struggles against the power of capital and/or state on non-media fronts will likely overlap with the 'contestation of media power' (Couldry 2003: 39), and a media democracy project has beneficiaries, and potential allies, outside the media field. That field, in other words, is a pivotal site for broader political and cultural struggles, the terrain of social movements. In the next chapter, we consider the possible contribution of social movements to democratization of and through the media.

3   Democratizing society
Social movements and public communication

If the current configuration of media and power has created a gaping democratic deficit, an effective movement to remake media would need to intervene in the media field in ways that reshape its power relations to reduce and ultimately eliminate the deficit. To explore the prospects for such change we need to consider how the collective interventions known as social movements have interacted with media, and how contemporary campaigns to democratize public communication actually intervene in the media field.

In this discussion, the concept of a 'public sphere' holds a central place. As we suggested in our Introduction, meaningful democracy requires dialogue, communication, and the ongoing formation of public spheres within which citizens can participate. 'The public sphere', writes Ian Angus, 'is a key component of democracy and also a way of determining the degree of democracy that a society has' (2001: 33). A 'democracy' in which the majority is not able to discuss pressing questions among themselves prior to political decisions becomes, in practice, an oligarchy (Angus 2001: 22). In contemporary societies, the public sphere is (partly) constituted and mediated by mass communication (Schulz 1997: 58), and the prospects for democracy hinge on the patterns of communication and power that media institutions enable. To the extent that media promote discussion free of domination, equality of participation, and rationality in the sense of an appeal to general principles rather than sheer self-interest – characteristics that Habermas (1987) has identified with 'communicative democracy' – they help constitute and sustain a public sphere. Media's democratic roles, then, 'include providing each significant group with a forum to articulate and develop its interests, facilitating the search for societywide political consensus by being universally accessible and inclusive, and reconstituting private citizens as a public body in the form of public opinion' (Zhao and Hackett 2005: 11). As complex social and political arrangements, democracy and media are inextricably bound up with each other through the normative ideal of the public sphere.

In this chapter we focus on social movements as crucial agencies for the promotion of public spheres, and for the democratization of public communication. Media, as we have seen, are not simply conduits or even a single site of power: they comprise a *field*, subject to its own self-transformation as social interests as diverse as corporate owners, journalists, advertisers and media reform activists jostle over possible futures. In the Anglo-American capitalist democracies, and, indeed, throughout the world, this field is a key arena in the struggle for hegemony.

By *hegemony* we mean the practices, cultural codes and social relations through which popular consent to an unequal social order is secured, and the 'system' thus stabilized. In liberal democracies, a successful bourgeois hegemony entails an ensemble of alliances involving (fractions of) the capitalist class as well as other groups and institutions in the cultural and political fields – a 'hegemonic bloc' that presents its interests as universal while selectively dispensing material and symbolic concessions ('bread and circuses') to pre-empt the unification of opposition from below. Within this 'dual perspective' (Gramsci 1971: 169), power is viewed as both concentrated in the state and distributed throughout the organizations of civil society such as the school, the family and of course the media – all of which diffuse hegemonic worldviews into daily life (Carroll and Ratner 1994: 5–6). To the extent that these views become widely adopted as 'common sense', hegemony fulfils a role that naked coercion could never perform: it mystifies power relations and public issues; it encourages a sense of fatalism and passivity toward political action; it justifies every type of system-serving sacrifice and deprivation (Boggs 1976: 40).

Much of what issues from mainstream media corporations serves to reinforce dominant values and worldviews, and in this way media are indeed important agencies of hegemony. Yet media, as we emphasized in Chapter 2, are also a contested terrain: they also figure in the *counterhegemonic* projects of critical social movements. These movements include a great variety of causes, interests and identities arrayed within a multi-organizational field (Klandermans 1992). Despite their diversity, these oppositional forces have the potential to find common ground – to form a counterhegemonic bloc around an alternative social vision (Sanbonmatsu 2004). Such a vision would have to be framed inclusively – not in terms of one or another group's immediate interests but 'through a conception of the world attentive to democratic principles and the dignity of humankind' (Holub 1992:6). To create an alternative hegemony, subaltern groups must engage with the state and capital, but also with civil society and everyday life in a cultural politics to build popular support for a radically democratic order. What interests us here is the recent expansion of movement politics directed at media's democratic deficit. Such activism exemplifies the potentially counterhegemonic role of critical social movements as both 'the crucible for the emergent publics that have altered the face of contemporary politics', and 'the most important source for the renewal of democracy in the future' (Angus 2001: 83).

Movements, media and democracy in the making of modernity

How can we understand these movements? Perhaps the most straightforward definition considers as a social movement 'any sentiment or activity shared by two or more people oriented toward changes in social relations or in the social system' (Ash Garner and Zald 1987: 293). This definition has the virtue of inclusiveness, enabling us to recognize movements that do not always assume a highly visible, 'political' form but may be micro-political and 'cultural' in emphasis, yet it fails to situate movements in history.

As Charles Tilly (1978) has emphasized, contemporary social movements are products of transformations that gave rise to modern national – and now increasingly global – politics. Nineteenth-century movements developed as part and parcel of capitalist modernization. The concentration of capital, the spread of markets, and the consolidation of nation states all spurred development of social movements with new and distinct repertoires of contention – the strike being the most important of the weapons. Print media played a critical role in this process, as they were typically embedded in the practices of social movements organized visibly around the axis of class struggle: the labour movement and the labour press went hand in hand. In short, both movements and media emerged in interaction with the forces producing capitalist modernization. With the consolidation of national states and markets, 'the overall logic of collective action shifted from immediate forms of revenge or resistance directed at local targets to sustained, cumulative pressure campaigns on national centers of decision making' (Buechler 2000: 9). Collective action became national, modular, and autonomous as commercial print media and new forms of association stimulated communication and diffusion of movement strategies (Tarrow 1998). The characteristic form of liberal democracy – the pattern of state-centred claims-making on the part of organized social groups – was an outcome of the movement mobilization and mediatization that accompanied capitalist modernization.

If we follow Chantal Mouffe's (1988) lead we can also see strong historical linkages between democratization and the formation of social movements. She notes the proliferation of *democratic struggles* since the French Revolution, and particularly since the 1960s. The rise of movements as continuing, organized, anti-systemic social forces led to the extension over time of the field of social movements, and of the potential for enhanced democracy, to all aspects of cultural and social life, eventuating in what Meyer and Tarrow (1998) have called 'the social movement society'.

The deep historical links between movements, media and democracy are also evident in the *increasing reflexivity* that has been a hallmark of modernity. Social movements are themselves carriers of this reflexivity, which includes the imagining of alternative ways of life as well as the collective learning processes that occur as activists experiment with strategies for social change. As movements have extended their reach into social and cultural fields they have challenged arbitrary authority and exclusionary practices, such as institutionalized racism and sexism, and have questioned taken-for-granted ways of life, as in environmentalism's challenge to consumer capitalism and the peace movement's challenge to militarism. Such challenges subject various aspects of the social movement society to scrutiny, discussion and debate. In this sense, movements are 'carriers of new learning capacities, proto-public spheres which offer potential solutions to systemic crises in that they presage more fluid and democratic types of organization' (Ray 1993: 73).

A signal aspect of heightened reflexivity is the construction of collective identity (Melucci 1989, 1996). In the pre-modern world, identity was embedded, stable and reified. In (late) modernity, identity becomes the product of conscious action and self-reflection, an ongoing 'project' (Giddens 1991). Activism is motivated and informed by collective identities like 'environmentalist' or 'feminist' that are 'contingent, historical and reflexive creations of those involved in challenging social order' (Buechler 2000:8). If, as Melucci (1996: 68–86) holds, both the social order being challenged and the collective identities mounting the challenges are social constructions, then media as a field of cultural power become a pivot of movement politics.

What Melucci and other social movement theorists provide is an analysis of *new social movements* (NSMs) as distinctive forms of activism arising in the late twentieth century. In good measure, these movements grew out of the political ferment of the 1960s and the first half of 1970s – a wave of intense social activism and political-cultural transformation. Immanuel Wallerstein (1989) has emphasized the world-historical ramifications of the protest wave that crested between 1968 and 1972 in what he calls the revolution of 1968. Significantly, the new movements 'introduced a new emphasis on culture as a terrain of politics and a stress on the cultural impact of movement activism' (Eschle 2001: 51), setting the stage for democratic media activism as an emergent political current. These movements developed in tandem, influencing each other's opportunities and sensibilities. It was their combination that made possible a shift in the definition of the political, to include the personal, the everyday, the cultural, and the environmental (Boggs 1995: 350).

This cultural and intellectual legacy has meant both a widening of the democratic impulse in movement activism to include the cultural field and a further accentuation of reflexivity in movement practice, developments especially salient in contemporary media activism. Out of such praxis, the post-1968 movements forged new *ways* of knowing, new *needs* for knowing, and new *interests* in knowing the social. Whether through feminist consciousness-raising, Greenpeace-style media events or post-colonial critiques of Western hegemony, the cognitive praxis of new social movements has been formed around an interest in developing knowledge that would empower the disempowered, challenge arbitrary authority, and promote democratic practice, from the local to the global (Eyerman and Jamison 1991). *These concerns draw contemporary movements more directly into the media field,* whether as strategic agents interacting with news media, as critical consumers of media discourse, as producers of media, or as advocates for media reform.

From 'movements and media' to democratic media activism

Given the close historical relations between movements, media and democracy, it is paradoxical that until recently the extensive sociological literature on social movements has had little to say on the relationship between movements and media, and even less on the emergence of media activism.[1] Of course, there is abundant evidence to support the claim we made in Chapter 2 that media affect every stage of a social movement's trajectory, from initial formation to success or demise. But the literature has treated the media field as given – as part of the political environment to be dealt with instrumentally by each movement. In this style of 'movements and media' analysis, the former depend on the latter to 'get the message out' (Stone 1993). Movements use 'an establishment institution to fulfil nonestablishment goals: communicating with movement followers, reaching out to potential recruits, neutralizing would-be opponents, and confusing or otherwise immobilizing committed opponents' (Molotch 1979: 71). They make strategic use of the media for various counterhegemonic purposes that include critique of existing social and material conditions, disruption of dominant discourses, codes and identities, and articulation of alternatives, whether in the form of new codes, identities and ways of life or progressive state policies. In her classic manual, *Prime Time Activism*, Charlotte Ryan (1991: 4) observed that movement activists have two goals in approaching mainstream media: (1) 'to turn the news into contested terrain' and (2) 'to use media as a vehicle for mobilizing support'. From this media strategies perspective a key problem is 'getting access' to mainstream media, and Ryan discusses in depth how the daily organizational routines of the news business work against challengers, a point registered strongly in Gitlin's (1980) classic analysis of the role the news media played in the rise and demise of the New Left.

One of the most sensitive formulations in the movements-and-media tradition has been that of Gamson and Wolfsfeld (1993), who distilled many strategic considerations into a model of movements and media as 'interacting systems'. They claimed that the movements–media relation is one of *asymmetrical dependency*: the position of media at the centre of a mass communications network gives media a spectrum of options for 'making the news', while movements have few options beyond the mass media for getting their messages to wide publics. 'The fact that movements need the media far more than the media need them translates itself into greater power for the media in the transaction' (Gamson and Wolfsfeld 1993: 117). Within this asymmetrical relationship, movements need the media for three main purposes: to *mobilize* – to reach their constituencies, to *validate* their existence as politically important collective actors, and to *enlarge the scope of conflict*, drawing third parties into the conflict to shift the balance of forces in a favourable direction. According to Gamson and Wolfsfeld movements are particularly concerned that media discourses grant them (1) *standing* – i.e., a quantity of coverage that places the movement clearly in the public gaze, (2) *preferred framing* of the issues at hand – i.e., a construction of the news that features the terms, definitions and codes of the movement, and (3) *sympathy* – i.e., coverage which is likely to win support from relevant publics.

In fact, movements strive not only to gain sympathetic standing in the media spotlight but to reduce the asymmetric dependency in the media–movement relation (e.g. by producing their own media for movement constituents or by making themselves spectacularly newsworthy: Carroll and Ratner 1999). Research in the movements-and-media tradition has certainly revealed important dynamics relevant to our understanding of democratic media activism.[2] In viewing the movements–media relation as *strategic* these studies advance beyond Gitlin's (1980) analysis of news media as a hegemonic institution that systematically suppresses critical voices. If news is itself a political resource and a modality of power, then 'in media-saturated societies, voice in the news is a key part of making one's "account count" in the public sphere' (Barker-Plummer 1995: 308). But news is also an order of discourse that constrains what can be said, a resource 'whose strategic use requires that sources articulate their experiences within its terms' (1995: 321).

Ultimately, the movements-and-media tradition takes for granted the existing structures and practices of the established media. A project of media democratization simply does not figure in this paradigm. The problematic is purely one of movements devising appropriate strategies to deal with the asymmetrical dependencies that are structured into the system. Thus, for instance, Bernadette Barker-Plummer, comparing liberal and radical feminism, is led to ask about 'the forms of knowledge that can be communicated widely in a media-saturated society' (1995: 320) – with the implication that only highly mainstreamed [liberal] voices will be able to carry widely into the public sphere. The tacit assumption in movements-and-media analyses is that the extant form of mass media is the natural form: in the dialogical relation between media and movements there is space for *negotiation* but there is no prospect of a *radical redesign*. A strategic dilemma sets 'mainstreaming' – aligning with media power and incurring the costs of possible cooptation – against 'disengagement' – refusing media power, with marginalization as the likely outcome. While this has been a real dilemma faced by social movements (Adamson *et al.* 1988), it should not be reified into a permanent state of affairs – either by social movement analysts or by activists (like Gitlin 1980: 290–1). The dilemma between incorporation and marginalization is not an obdurate reality; it is an expression of the democratic deficit, of the narrow bounds of permissible discourse within corporate media, of the lack of viable alternative means of reaching large publics – ultimately, of a shrunken public sphere. The question raised by emergent movements to democratize media is whether and how the *contestation of media power* might constitute a viable counterhegemonic alternative to this Hobson's choice.

The promise of internet activism

In the past decade, with the stunning proliferation of digital communications technologies (including the internet, email, mobile phones and hand-held camcorders) and their insertion into everyday life, the costs of certain kinds of communication have been drastically lowered while their reach and effectiveness have surged. In particular, the internet has emerged as a communications network, and a new political terrain, accessible to an expanding majority in the North Atlantic zone (though not in the so-called South: Curran 2003: 237–8). Even as the concentration of capital within the corporate media spawns transnational media giants – even as the democratic deficit in that field widens — the openings for new forms of media activism seem to multiply.

'Internet activism' has taken two predominant forms. As a *mobilizing resource*, the internet has figured in a series of transnational campaigns that have broadened the field of action beyond the level of individual nation-states by linking local to global concerns. The first dramatic instance of this 'globalization from below' was the Zapatistas' declaration of war against neoliberalism, launched in the Mexican state of Chiapas on 1 January 1994 – the date that the North American Free Trade

Agreement went into effect. This 'first informational guerilla movement' (Castells 1997: 79) has amounted to much more than a series of internet communiques (available at the Zapatistas' website: www.ezln.org/documentos/index.html). At its heart, it is a local, indigenous struggle for land and for cultural and political recognition. Yet in using the internet to transmit its message directly (without mass mediation), and to recruit support internationally, the Zapatistas effected a tactical innovation that has had 'global reverberations' for critical social movements (Atton 2003b: 6). Activist groups opposing the power of large transnational corporations, such as the McSpotlight Website (1996), soon employed similar internet-based tactics, which involve not only web publishing but international networking with other groups to broaden the protest agenda (Atton 2003b: 7). In spearheading the anti-Nike campaign, and the anti-sweatshop movement, Global Exchange made extensive use of the Net in a simultaneous protest outside Nike retailers in twelve countries in October, 1997 which pressured the corporation to alter some of its more objectionable policies in less developed countries (Carty 2002).

Probably the best-known instances of transnational internet activism have been aimed at the major quasi-state institutions of corporate globalization such as the World Trade Organization (WTO). In 1997 the Council of Canadians and allied NGOs used the internet to expose the draft of the Multinational Agreement on Investment (MAI), which was being secretly negotiated in Paris under the auspices of the Organization for Economic Cooperation and Development. Attempts by the OECD to coopt the NGOs into an informal consultation process failed when 560 organizations in 67 countries signed on, via the internet, to a Joint NGO Statement on the MAI, demanding a set of democratizing changes in the substance of the agreement and the procedure for its adoption. This visible and well-organized pressure from below was one factor among several in the unravelling of MAI (Egan 2001). Two years later, in November 1999, the mass media spotlight was on Seattle, where delegations from member countries met to forge a revamped MAI under the auspices of the WTO. The direct actions of thousands of protestors – again facilitated by extensive internet communications – were effective in contributing to the demise of the Ministerial agenda, and in inspiring a series of similar global protests at subsequent elite policy meetings, which have given substance to the fledgling idea of an anti-corporate globalization movement (Smith 2001).

Indeed, a theme running like a red thread through these instances of internet activism has been resistance to corporate power and to the neoliberal agenda of privatizing public goods, deregulating capital and commodifying the world – in short, a critique of global capitalism. The new forms of transborder activism facilitated by the communications revolution have brought to the fore a collection of *transnational advocacy networks* (Keck and Sikkink 1998) centred on groups such as Global Exchange and the World Social Forum. The websites at the centre of these networks comprise a dense configuration of reciprocated hyperlinks that facilitate collective action while informing a shared injustice frame around the critique of capitalist globalization (Van Aelst and Walgrave 2002).

In using the internet as a mobilizing resource, movement groups have often engaged in a form of activism that reaches beyond mobilization of a given constituency for action. They have addressed other audiences, bypassing mass media gatekeepers to communicate directly with the broader public. This comprises a second form of internet activism: *the cultivation of alternative public spheres.*

This second form can also be traced back to the Zapatistas' mid 1990s initiatives, which promoted a direct democratic dialogue that in 1996 brought over 2,000 international delegates to Chiapas for a forum on resisting neoliberalism:

> The Zapatistas inspired a flourishing, widespread, and varied network that afforded them the opportunity to communicate directly with civil society. As a result, civil society was motivated to respond directly to the requests of the EZLN for citizen participation in their project.
>
> (Ford and Gil 2001: 219)

But perhaps the most compelling example of internet activism as a cultivation of alternative public spheres was conceived in Seattle, within a moment of intense political struggle against corporate globalization, where IndyMedia was launched in 1999.

Seattle confirmed new possibilities for bypassing the corporate media. Organized by internet activists and alternative journalists in the lead-up to the WTO Ministerial meeting, the Independent Media Center (IMC) functioned as a 'voluntary communications center', enabling scores of videographers, photographers, print and web journalists to download their reports onto servers in the IMC's temporary site (Downing 2003: 251), 'streaming audio and video footage of the demonstrations, as well as written reports, across the world' (Atton 2003b: 7). From one centre in late 1999, the IMC network has grown to include 144 centres on six continents. Meanwhile, activist sites that in the 1990s used the internet primarily as a mobilizing resource have also become news sites. By 2001, for instance, the anti-sweatshop coalition BehindTheLabel was busy converting its website into 'an Internet news channel to cover the global sweatshop industry and serve as an "online community of people arguing for social justice in the global economy"' (Carty 2002: 137). Sets of politically aligned websites have coalesced into veritable internet communities that offer extensive intellectual and political resources to activists and websurfers alike, as in the 'anarchist web' studied by Owens and Palmer (2003).

There is no doubt that web-based independent journalism offers a powerful alternative to mainstream media news discourse. The interactivity of the Net, the decentralized structure of many (hyperlinked) websites, the democratic form of organization and the norms of open publishing that prevail at IMC transform the communicative relation from monologue to dialogue, empowering those who for mass media are the audience and inviting them to 'be the media' (IndyMedia's slogan). As Couldry puts it, 'every Indymedia consumer is encouraged to be a producer as well, and vice versa' (2003: 45). Moreover, these emergent norms hold beyond the communities of IMC. For instance, London-based openDemocracy has developed from a fledgling website launched in the spring of 2001 into a global magazine featuring news, commentary and discussion on a great range of political and cultural issues. As Curran notes, the key facilitating factor in lifting

openDemocracy from its initially British-based constituency into a 'higher orbit ...
was the internet, which enabled people living in different parts of the world to log
on to a London-generated website'. OpenDemocracy has taken advantage of the
low reproduction and distribution costs of internet technology and of the ability of
online publishers to bypass market gatekeepers and has evolved into a 'hybrid
cultural form' that encourages reader participation with moderated conferences,
linked to its debates (Curran 2003: 235–7).

Internet activism has certainly contributed to the incipient formation of a transnational public sphere (Guidry *et al.* 2000), a global civil society (Curran 2003),
while enabling movements to mobilize and coordinate protest more effectively
on a global basis.[3] (Consider that the largest demonstration in world history, on
15 February 2003 in protest at the impending Anglo-American invasion of Iraq,
was facilitated by a global network of peace-activist websites.) Of course, radical
media and democratic movements have always entailed each other. John Downing
has shown that social movements, local and global, are the 'life blood' of radical
media, and radical media are the movements' 'oxygen' (2001: 390). There has
indeed been a dialectical relationship of intense interdependence between the two,
whether we consider the role of print media in the Reformation, of the labour press
in the nineteenth-century socialist movement, of photomontage in the anti-fascist
politics of the 1930s, or of radical radio in the Algerian liberation struggle of the
1950s (Downing *et al.* 2001: 144, 149, 169, 183). Yet internet activism introduces a
qualitative change in scale as communication networks cross borders, opening up
new opportunities for transnational activism and publics (Keck and Sikkink 1998;
Bohman 2004), while it enables movements to bypass mass media and to implement more dialogical forms of communication. These developments signal major
changes in movement–media relations and offer a possible alternative to the
dilemma between incorporation and marginalization we considered earlier.

Understandably, some leading media analysts have been impressed by the 'new
media power' that the internet seems to give to global activism (Bennett 2003: 17).
In the confluence of rising global protest networks and digital communications
technologies that underwrite more cosmopolitan activism across space, time and
even ideology, Lance Bennett discerns an 'identity shift' toward fluidity and lifestyle politics, as ideologies are replaced by 'issue networks'. In the emerging
networked global formation, coordinated political action need not be based on
common goals and perspectives. Instead, 'the public political vocabulary of this
movement is laden with *memes* – easily imitated and transmitted images that cross
social networks because they resonate with common experiences' (Bennett 2003:
31) – as in culture-jam images equating Nike athletic shoes with sweatshop labour.
Bennett provocatively describes this development as a 'liberation from ideology
[which] creates the potential for crossing many social, cultural, and geographical
boundaries because there is less need for the education, indoctrination, or physical
force that often accompanies the spread of ideologies' (2003: 32).

Bennett seems to be suggesting that 'new media power' promises a more direct
route to media democratization than conventional strategies that rely on
consciousness-raising, the nurturance of alternative public spheres and the long

march through reform of dominant media and related institutions. A similar point of view can be found in Deluca and Peeple's concept of the 'public screen', which they advocate as an alternative to the public sphere, better suited to 'a televisual world characterized by image and spectacle' (2003: 129). If, as these authors hold, the most important public discussions now take place via 'screens' – including computers – conveying spectacular 'image events', then the public screen can be seen as 'an alternative venue for participatory politics and public opinion formation that offers a striking contrast to the public sphere' (Deluca and Peeple 2003: 145).

Postmodern celebrations of the liberating impact of spectacle, image and meme take us a great distance from Zapatista-style dialogic praxis predicated upon the norms of mutuality and sincerity in communication. At least one media theorist has warned that 'liberation from ideology' – the postmodern renunciation of the search for an alternative political consensus – precisely suits the interests of dominant groups. To the extent that activism is based in fluid identities and fascination with images and memes, the field of movement politics fractures into so many independent subcultures, congenitally incapable of finding, through mutual discussion, a moral and intellectual basis for unity. In a world order in which postmodern pluralism celebrates the diversity of consumer choice within the global shopping mall, such fragmentation does not challenge hegemony; it deepens it. The 'liberation from ideology' is entirely compatible with a social-control strategy of 'divide and conquer' (Tetzlaff 1991).

Moreover, while the publics emerging in cyberspace establish some of the conditions for a transnational public sphere, as James Bohman points out, they are not themselves democratic. If they are to promote the interaction *among publics* that is required for deliberative democracy, emergent publics must function within an institutional context. Bohman concludes that

> both network forms of communication and the publics formed in them must be embedded in a larger institutional and political context, if they are to be transformed into public spheres in which citizens can make claims and expect a response.
>
> (2004:146)

Despite the obvious import of internet activism, there are reasons to be sceptical about 'new media power', if the term is meant to imply a superseding of other practices and strategies in the struggle to democratize media. Studies of new media and new movements have shown that although movements have made innovative use of new communications media there is 'little evidence that the internet is becoming a substitute for traditional forms of protest' (Van Aelst and Walgrave 2002: 487). As remarkable as the success of IndyMedia has been, Chris Atton's findings from a study of the Autonomous Centre of Edinburgh may represent a more common outcome of attempts to create internet-based alternative public spheres:

> Since its formation in 1997 as a space whose autonomy from state determination was seen as an indicator of its future strength, the Centre has shown few

signs of expanding either its core organizing collective or its audience. It remains a specialist space, of significance in the main to that small number directly responsible for its maintenance.

(Atton 2003a: 66)

The reason why new communications technologies – whether internet, video or radio – have never in themselves led to democratization of the media is clear enough: 'new technology has not fundamentally changed the underlying economic factors that enable large media organizations to maintain their market dominance' (Curran 2003: 227).

Mobilization on multiple fronts: a dual perspective on democratic media activism

Indeed, it is political-economic factors – including 'the neo-liberal model of largely unregulated capitalism, open markets, and private ownership' – that underlie media's democratic deficit (Ó Siochrú 2005a: 210). That deficit, as we noted in the Introduction, is multifaceted and endemic to the North Atlantic heartland. Internet activism and savvy media strategies to reduce asymmetric dependencies can be no more than elements in a broader politics of media democratization. Below, we provide an initial sketch of media democratization as a nascent, or potential, movement. If democratic media activism (DMA) is actually emerging as a movement in its own right, the frameworks of social movement theory can aid our interpretation of its trajectory. According to Resource Mobilization Theory, movements emerge and have effect on the basis of:

- socially-constructed *grievances,*
- mobilized *resources* that enable collective actions to be mounted (including time, expertise, money and infrastructure as well as the organizations and structures to mobilize and deploy those resources), and
- structural *opportunities* to mobilize resources and to act.

As Klandermans puts it, '*social movements come into being because people who are aggrieved and have the resources to mobilize seize the political opportunities they perceive*' (2001: 276). As they develop, movements create forms of social organization suited to their political projects; indeed any given movement consists of a collection of 'social movement organizations' (SMOs) that differ among themselves in size, structure and strategy (compare, along these lines, a global SMO like Greenpeace with the many local citizen initiatives that also form part of the environmental movement).

Applying this framework, we can surmise that media's democratic deficit provides a *shared grievance* for a variety of groups committed to democratizing public communication. But if grievances constitute a ground for movement formation, they are themselves socially constructed as 'collective action frames' that define certain conditions as grievous, identify sources for those conditions and propose remedies (Klandermans 2001). The list of aspects of the democratic deficit with which we

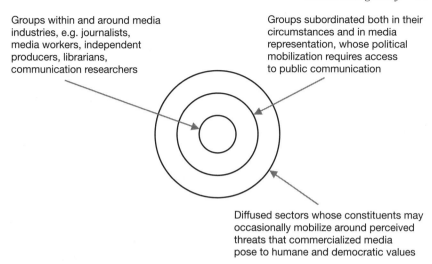

Groups within and around media industries, e.g. journalists, media workers, independent producers, librarians, communication researchers

Groups subordinated both in their circumstances and in media representation, whose political mobilization requires access to public communication

Diffused sectors whose constituents may occasionally mobilize around perceived threats that commercialized media pose to humane and democratic values

Figure 3.1 The social sources for media democratization: a preliminary specification

introduced this book exemplifies the *diagnostic* aspect of such a frame; the goal of democratizing communication represents the *strategic* aspect (cf. Snow and Benford 1992; Ó Siochrú 2005b: 304).

In Chapters 4, 7 and 8 we analyse the action frames, resources, and opportunities for democratic media activism. Here, we offer a few opening observations. Clearly, recent years have witnessed a proliferation of resources for such a movement. Simply considering internet activism, the pace of development of sophisticated websites and networks, underlain by advanced technical expertise and technology and entailing the participation of many thousand amateur journalists and critical readers, is impressive. But the resources potentially at the disposal of a media democracy movement are actually much more diverse. The most important ones are human resources: groups of people whose social interests and life circumstances might lead them to take up media democratization as a cause, in short, the *constituency* for the movement. These social sources for a media democracy movement are, like the democratic deficit, wide ranging. Figure 3.1 shows how they may speculatively be conceptualized in terms of three concentric circles, which partly structure the field of media activism (Hackett and Carroll 2004).

At the centre are groups within and around the media industries, groups whose working life or professional specialization may stimulate awareness of the alienation, exploitation, and/or constraints on creativity and public information rights generated by a commercialized corporate media system. Such groups as media workers, journalists, independent producers, librarians and communication researchers have often been well represented in media democracy initiatives. The second circle comprises subordinate social groups, whose lack of social, cultural, economic or political capital is paralleled in the mass-mediated machinery of representation, and whose interests sometimes bring them into conflict with the social order –

particularly when they are organized in the form of social movements that need access to public communication in order to pursue their political project. The outermost circle comprises more diffuse sectors for whom communication policy and practices are not a central concern, but who may occasionally mobilize around perceived threats that commercialized media may pose to humane, non-commodifiable, democratic values. Parents concerned with media impact on the socialization of the young, communities struggling for local access media or (as in Baltimore) billboard-free public space, citizens concerned with the disconnection between democratic and media agendas, and progressive religious groups advocating ethical standards and human values in communication, all come under this rubric.

Finally, democratic media activism is shaped by the various *opportunities* for collective action that the media field presents. As we have emphasized, the field is only weakly autonomous from capital and the state (power through the media), but capable of intruding upon the functioning of other fields (power of media). This conceptualization helps us to identify several possible strategic approaches that respond to opportunities inhering in the field and its environing conditions.

One broad strategy is to *reform or revamp the media field internally*. Cultural producers and media workers, including journalists, would presumably be the prime agents of such change, whether as trade unionists seeking more collective self-determination in the workplace, or as 'professionals' trying to reform practices and ethos.

A second strategic option is to *create new and parallel fields*, autonomous spaces in civil society, the lifeworld, to bypass the established corporate media and indeed to syphon away some of their control over society's symbolic power. We refer here mainly to so-called 'alternative' media.

A third approach comprises *changing the media field's environing conditions*, particularly the 'field of power'. That shift can happen in several ways. Media reformers attempt to change state communication policies, the institutionalized rules within which the machinery of representation operates. Media educators promote more critical 'consumer' awareness of media. And social movements, pursuing other primary objectives, may succeed in replacing governments or changing their policies. All of these avenues can shift the gravitational pulls exerted on media.

Just as the media field is differentiated and porous, presenting various opportunities for activist intervention, we can expect DMA itself to be differentiated – and anything but a homogeneous collective actor. In fact, the multifold constituencies, sites of intervention and strategies that comprise DMA create a very complex multi-organizational field, subdivided into many groups that are variously aligned with each other and with other critical movements (cf. Klandermans 1992). Certain strategies (e.g. the first one mentioned above) are directed at the main forms of institutional power over communication — the corporate media and the state; others (e.g. the second strategy) are directed at civil society, and within civil society, at specific publics and communities. In the first case, activist efforts are broadly directed at existing *hegemonic institutions*; in the second, at building or nurturing *counterhegemonic media capacities and sensibilities*. Or, placed within the phraseology of Jürgen Habermas's Theory of Communicative Action, the first kind of strategy targets the *system* while the second strives to create change within the *lifeworld*.

Habermas's theory is worth considering at some length here for its insights on the linkages between movements, media and democracy. Habermas understands late modernity as a configuration of *system* and *lifeworld* – of macro-structures organized by markets and bureaucracies (system) and of meaningful everyday life within 'the relations and communications between members of a societal community' (lifeworld: Hewitt 1993: 62). Both these sides of modernity have been subject to processes of *rationalization*, but as the system of advanced capitalism has colonized the lifeworld, the instrumental rationality of corporate and bureaucratic practices has predominated over the communicative rationality, immanent in the lifeworld, that grounds meaningful sociality itself. Even so, critical reason based in a partially rationalized lifeworld has continued to constitute modernity's counterculture – 'a permanent opposition to the dominant forms of instrumentality', one that has surfaced in such emancipatory social movements as socialism and feminism (Ray 1993: 81), and which is integral to the politics of media democratization.

In his original formulation, Habermas argued that new movements express a shift from the old politics of social and economic security to the new politics of participation, quality of life, individual self-realization and human rights (Habermas 1987: 392).[4] Such concerns can be of a defensive nature, as movements attempt to shield endangered ways of life from further systemic colonization, and here we can note that certain kinds of media activism fit this description — a good example being the struggle for indigenous minority language television services, which has become a first priority for certain traditional movements (Hourigan 2001: 93). However, Habermas's formulation is especially instructive in thinking about movements committed to the 'decolonization of the lifeworld' (Ray 1993: 62).

Clearly, a great deal of media activism carries this very impetus. The idea of democratizing communication — of creating inclusive dialogues in place of the monological channels of corporate mass media, of advocating a universal 'right to communicate' which implies a responsibility to listen as well as access to the means of public communication (Husband 1996) — elegantly expresses the aspiration for a decolonized lifeworld, and a revitalized public sphere. Indeed, the recovery of a vibrant public sphere and the decolonization of the lifeworld are necessarily aligned projects, since in Habermas's formulation the public sphere is nothing other than the *public* face of the lifeworld. Distinct from both the system and the *private* realm of everyday life, the public sphere is 'a site for the production and circulation of discourses', by and for publics, 'that can in principle be critical of the state' (Fraser 1997: 70).

However, in contemporary societies wracked by systemic contradictions, the public sphere is not a unified field. It has more the character of a complex of 'interstitial *networks* of individuals and groups acting as citizens' (Emirbayer and Sheller 1999: 156). Modernity's endemic power inequities have led subordinated groups to create *subaltern counterpublics* – 'parallel discursive arenas where members of subordinated groups invent and circulate counterdiscourses, which in turn permit them to formulate oppositional interpretations of their identities, interests, and needs' (Fraser 1997: 81). Such counterpublics are the lifeblood of social movements and counterhegemonic politics. They function not only as arenas for constructing alternative collective identities but 'as bases and training grounds for agitational activities directed toward wider publics. It is precisely in the dialectic of these two functions that their emancipatory potential resides' (Fraser 1997: 82).

This dialectic conjoins what Jean Cohen and Andrew Arato call the 'defensive' and 'offensive' modes of movement activism, the former directed *inward* to civil society and the lifeworld; the latter directed *outward* to state and economic institutions. The 'defensive' aspect of activism is by no means conservative. It involves preserving *and developing* the communicative infrastructure of the lifeworld, through redefining identities, reinterpreting norms, developing egalitarian, democratic associational forms, and securing '*institutional* changes within civil society that correspond to the new meanings, identities, and norms that are created' (Cohen and Arato 1992: 531). The 'offensive' aspect targets political and economic society – 'the realms of "mediation" between civil society and the subsystems of the administrative state and the economy' (Cohen and Arato 1992: 531–2), and struggles not only for resources and political recognition but for influence and institutional reform.

Within this Gramscian 'dual perspective', political society and civil society comprise key terrains for counterhegemonic politics, and movements face the challenge of devising strategies appropriate to both of them. Democratic media activism faces this same double challenge. To revitalize a diverse public sphere requires the advance of democratizing communicative practices both within civil society/lifeworld *and* vis-à-vis the political-economic apparatuses of the system. Evidently, a counterhegemony effective enough to remake media would require substantial movement on both fronts.

Let us systematize some of these ideas into a *typology* of democratic media activism.

Typology of democratic media activism

There is no single, correct categorizaton scheme. Several useful ones have been offered by academics and activists.[5] Our own typology is informed by the following dimensions concerning each form of activism:

- Is it *primarily oriented* towards changing the system, or the 'lifeworld' of civil society?
- As distinct from its target for change, does it *emerge primarily* from within the system, or from the lifeworld?
- At what point in the public communication system does it intervene? Does it engage primarily in the media field per se – producing and distributing news, programmes, reports, and texts, and/or creating new channels of communication (as in the first three levels of Table 2.1)? Or does it attempt to change the media's environing conditions – whether the relevant extra-media institutions in the system, like government regulation of broadcasting, or the

broader cultural context in the lifeworld, including media literacy amongst the population?

Table 3.1 offers a schema employing these categories, with examples in each cell. As with any such schema, ambiguities are unavoidable. It is sometimes difficult to distinguish neatly between the field of media production and its environing conditions. Some projects straddle that border, like media education intended in part to strengthen the political constituency for media reform (a mission for ACME, the Action Coalition for Media Education), or the San Francisco Media Alliance's assistance to marginalized youth in acquiring media skills, producing their own newssheets or websites, and finding a public political voice.

More problematically, where does one draw the boundary between 'lifeworld' and 'system'? This distinction is defined partly by *institutional location* – the 'terrain of the immediate, familiar, everyday, and close to home', as distinct from governments and corporations, including corporate media – 'the large institutions and systems that tower over us, like granite mountains of the social landscape' (Boyte 1992: 340). But it is also defined by the two realms' respective *governing logics* – the discursive reasoning of everyday life, shaped by an implicit search for consensus on shared norms, versus the instrumental rationality employed in the pursuit of profit and power. Importantly, the two criteria – institutional location, and governing logic – are not coterminous. On the one hand, the lifeworld is under constant threat of 'colonization' by the instrumental rationality of domination; on the other hand, Habermas also holds out hope for a reverse process, whereby the 'practically oriented demands of the lifeworld' can be asserted within the institutions of the system itself (Habermas 1992: 444).

So then, where in this map of media activism would we place a public interest NGO, using foundation funding to pursue advocacy within the institutionalized political system on behalf of lifeworld interests, such as media access for the handicapped, or restrictions on advertising to children? What about a university seminar on communications policy, aiming for a rational discussion of democratic norms, yet conducted within a state-funded institution that excludes non-tuition payers and is mandated with credentializing young workers for a capitalist labour market? Arguably, such border zones, at the 'seams' between system and lifeworld, are especially fruitful sites of social movement formation and challenges to system logic.

Despite such categorization challenges, we find that Table 3.1 does usefully map the field of democratic media activism, focusing on projects and groups whose primary mandate is to effect lasting institutional change (as distinct from short-term shifts in media frames), on the basis of progressive values, and in relation to the agenda-setting media of public communication, the 'machinery of representation' (Hall 1986), as distinct from point-to-point, personal or private communication, whether computer-mediated or face-to-face. That focus, it should be noted, leaves aside some contiguous domains which are also part of the broader field of media activism. Most notably, these adjacent areas include the following:

Table 3.1 Democratization of the media: a typology of democratic media activism (DMA)

	DMA centred on lifeworld change	*DMA centred on system change*
DMA centred on the media field per se: the production and distribution of texts, the provision of access to the means of public communication (media workers, routines and organizations)	(a) Emanating from lifeworld • alternative/independent media, distribution networks, access centres • support services and advocacy for alternative media • open source and new technology projects • community broadcasters • witnessing and documentation • media for training, educating and organizing	(a) Emanating from lifeworld • media monitoring as influence on corporate press • PR, strategic communication for/ by social movements • networks of progressive experts for mainstream media
	(b) Emanating from system • state support for arts, community media, minority publications, social animation, cultural sovereignty vis-à-vis hegemonic global media	(b) Emanating from system • internal initiatives to reform news discourse, e.g. public journalism • professional associations and networks for journalists, esp. minorities • state-mandated public service broadcasting, e.g. BBC • media workers' unions, challenging corporate control over media workplace, representations
DMA centred on environing conditions: audience reception, cultural environment, state communications policies (extra-media influences, ideology)	(a) Emanating from lifeworld • culture jamming • media monitoring for advocacy campaigns, public awareness • informal media education, information clearing-houses, public awareness campaigns • critical media research and scholarship • (social justice movements building counterpublics through communication praxis)	(a) Emanating from lifeworld • public interest advocacy groups on communications policy; legislative and regulatory lobbying; legal/ court interventions • (consumers' rights and other public interest groups' occasional interventions on communication policy) • media reform coalitions • advocacy groups and support networks for journalists' rights and media independence (vis-à-vis state) • (social justice movements seeking progressive change in state policy)
	(b) Emanating from system • formal media education in public schools • corporate-sponsored media education? • public school system, libraries	(b) Emanating from system • Parliamentary/Congressional communities, government enquiries on media policy • progressive political parties and formations (e.g. federal NDP Media caucus) • progressive or dissident regulators

- Right-wing content monitoring and policy advocacy intended to shift media structures and frames towards social conservative and/or market liberal perspectives. Examples include Accuracy in Media, the Media Research Center, and the Center for Media and Public Affairs in Washington DC, the Fraser Institute's 'National Media Archive' in Canada, and MediaWatch UK.
- The 'largely unorganized challenges to information monopolies' on the internet (Kidd 2005a), particularly the file-sharing, music-downloading, computer-hacking, software-pirating generation of internet users who are contesting corporate enclosures of cyberspace through their individual actions. While largely inchoate, their combined strength is evident in corporate responses, from the effort to crush Napster to the reinforcement of copyright regimes.
- Activism which addresses communication policy and practices not directly related to the machinery of representation, notably access to and the architecture of the internet and other telecommunications services (Mueller *et al.* 2004). This field is very broad indeed, and increasingly informs more conventional media activism.

Two other types, neither directly focusing on the politics of media, are included in our chart in parentheses, to indicate their indirect or occasional character:

- Public interest advocacy groups which have a broad range of policy concerns, and occasionally make progressive interventions on communications policy – e.g. the American Civil Liberties Union and Consumers' Federation of America (Mueller *et al.* 2004).
- Groups and movements which incidentally or temporarily use media in pursuit of other primary objectives (democratization *through* media). This type of emancipatory communication practices includes not just conventional media relations, but the 'integration of media tools, skills and tactics' in social movement struggles to forge new identities, constituencies and subaltern public spheres (Kidd 2005a). Our typology, however, does include projects intended to build the capacity of progressive causes to intervene in dominant media.

A necessarily brief sketch of the main forms of activism in each quadrant of Table 3.1 provides a clearer overview of their scope and strategic inter-relationships.[6]

Alternative media

The first quadrant – activism centred on changing the lifeworld through producing and distributing media – includes a number of forms. Media makers and trainers act as supporters for advocacy campaigns and social movements, like Undercurrents in the UK: launched in 1993, it provided 'media support to grassroots direct action campaign groups', using camcorders to document, archive and circulate environmental and other protests (see www.undercurrents.org, accessed December 2004). Social animators, perhaps most famously the National Film Board's 'Challenge for Change' programme in Canada during the 1960s, used media to raise public awareness about the realities of poverty, to give a public voice to those without one, and to 'help disadvantaged communities organize themselves and take control of their own destinies' (Henaut 1991: 48). On the whole though, what predominates in this type of media activism is what has variously been labelled radical/oppositional, citizens', participatory, autonomous/independent, community, popular/grassroots, or most commonly, alternative media (Rodriguez 2003: 190). Each of these terms carries different connotations, which however important they be in other contexts, need not detain us here. Alternative media are hugely diverse in orientation, organization and technological form; they range from online zines, political websites and magazines, small independent book publishers, low-power FM neighbourhood radio, access channels on cable TV, organizational newsletters, to weekly urban newspapers, and much else. At the risk of distorting their complex realities, and provoking knowing chuckles from activists who have lived them, we can distil several 'ideal typical' characteristics which distinguish alternative media from dominant corporate media (see e.g. Atton 2002; Downing *et al.* 2001; Hackett and Zhao 1998: 206–13; Couldry and Curran 2003b: 7).

First, in funding, organization and control, they are likely to be relatively autonomous from corporate capital and the state – to be run as cooperatives or small businesses rather than as part of corporate chains or conglomerates; to be funded through supporters' donations, memberships, trust funds or foundations rather than advertising; and to strive for internally democratic and collaborative styles of production and decision-making, rather than bureaucratic hierarchies found in corporate media, however much these may be cushioned by 'employee empowerment' managerial strategies.

Second, in political orientation and content, the 'ideal' alternative medium is progressive, explicitly opposed to particular axes of domination (corporate capitalism, heterosexism, racism, state authoritarianism), openly assumes a stance of advocacy rather than pseudo-'objectivity', experiments with new aesthetic styles, and accesses voices and issues marginalized in hegemonic media.

Finally, alternative media often seek to transform the one-to-many and top-to-bottom paradigm of hegemonic media, and instead to promote horizontal dialogue between subaltern group(s). Audiences are regarded not as target markets whose attention is sold as a commodity to advertisers, but as participants in a community or movement.

In short, at their most 'alternative', alternative media counteract the democratic deficit by circulating counterinformation which helps build counterhegemonic definitions of reality and subaltern counterpublics. And they develop participatory modes which nurture people's 'developmental power', and prefigure more radically democratic ways of communicating. Arguably, they are at their most effective when they have an organic relationship with vital social movements (Downing *et al.* 2001).

As a form of media democratization, alternative media face significant challenges and limitations: their ambiguous relationship with movements (conduit or watchdog?); the trade-off between providing access to community voices and producing content of sufficient 'quality' to appeal to broader audiences; the risk of slipping into a Leninist model of hierarchical organization and party line-ism; or more commonly, the challenges of collective self-management, such as maintaining connection with broader democratic currents in society, and avoiding the 'tyranny of structurelessness' (Downing *et al.* 2001: 70–1). Perhaps the most important limitations, though, are these:

- Alternative media that reject the logic of commodifying audiences typically find it difficult to maintain a revenue stream, and thus to become organizationally and economically sustainable.
- The temptation of commercialism thus emerges as a means of survival. The retreat of North American urban weeklies from the countercultural barricades to the more profitable embrace of the entertainment industry bespeaks the implications – although as Benson (2003) shows, under the right circumstances, it is possible to combine advertising dependence with political content, critiques of capitalism, and supportive framing of social movements. The risk of absorption comes from another direction as well, as major media corporations adopt edgy styles and launch their own 'alternative' media (like urban weeklies) when the independents become uncomfortably successful.
- Alternative media typically remain ghettoized, preachers to the choir. They face structural bottlenecks to distribution (including the much-touted internet, which has drastically reduced distribution costs but not the need for promotional resources to attract attention in an environment still dominated by media, software and telecommunications giants). And there may be psychological comfort in sticking with a familiar niche in the obscure corners of the public communication system. As one member of a now-defunct Vancouver alternative newspaper collective told us in the 1990s, he was content to let the corporate press 'do its own thing' so long as his circle had its own print vehicle.

And yet – alternative media have substantial strengths as a democratization strategy. They do not require the long nurturing of a political constituency and/or expertise in elite discourse needed to gain a hearing in official policy circles. The skills they do require, and their characteristic autonomist, do-it-yourself ethos, are more in tune with a technologically-savvy younger generation of activists. Even if alternative media producers are mainly concerned with 'defensive' lifeworld struggles – with community-building or cultural politics rather than contesting state policy or corporate media – their relatively autonomous centres of skills, power, and meaning comprise an implicit challenge. Combined with their accessing of new voices and counterpublics, their creation of a parallel and (debatably) prefigurative media field is absolutely central to media democratization.

Changing the lifeworld as media environment

The lower-left quadrant of Table 3.1 comprises efforts to shift consciousness, identities, skills and the distribution of political, economic and social resources in the lifeworld, in ways that would transform the context of the media field per se. In

Shoemaker and Reese's levels of influence on media content (depicted in Table 2.1), these would comprise extra-media institutions, and 'ideology', the articulation of cultural narratives with the overarching power structure of the social order.

Conceptually, this quadrant itself can be broken down into several sectors. First, some emergent forms aim to transform how audiences understand the media and their frames. Critical media educators, both inside and outside the formal school system, encourage students to recognize and analyse the link between the textual (mis)representations and the political economy of media. A prime example is University of Massachusetts professor Sut Jhally's Media Education Foundation, which distributes DVDs and videos on the objectification of women in music videos, right-wing pressure on the media, and much else. Content analysis and other forms of monitoring media messages can be a useful adjunct to media education, and can indeed help mobilize campaigns for better representation. An example is the Global Media Monitoring Project spearheaded in 1995 by MediaWatch in Canada, and in 2000 by the World Association for Christian Communication (WACC). This periodic one-day snapshot showed how much the world's press, radio and television news under-represents women and the issues of particular concern to them (Gallagher 2001: 26–8).

A less 'academic' approach to de-naturalizing media texts – to rendering the familiar strange – is that of culture jamming, or as some prefer, 'direct action media critique'. Internationally popularized though not pioneered by Vancouver-based magazine *AdBusters*, culture jammers fuse political, media and artistic activity to try and reverse or subvert the meaning of spectacular images and events. A billboard slogan for a cigarette brand is 'edited' under cover of darkness to read 'Are we dead yet?' An SUV driver finds an official-looking ticket on his windshield citing him for ozone depletion and climate change. Bleary-eyed morning commuters do a double-take passing the newsbox: the daily paper is wrapped in a graphically familiar but semiotically jarring front page, marked by politically satirical headlines ('British Columbia government merges with forest company'). Using and parodying familiar codes, attempting to deliver consciousness-raising 'mind bombs', culture jammers seek to disrupt the flow of consumerist spectacle (Lasn 1999). It is now widely recognized as a tactic rather than a fully-fledged strategy, one that works best in conjunction with other tactics (such as lobbying or boycotts) in social change campaigns.

Media education and culture jamming clearly have limits: they can be too easily divorced from social movements, media education in particular is a very long-term process, and both are vulnerable to corporate cooptation, whether by countersatirical marketing gimmicks (like the Australian billboards for brand-name sneakers boasting of being '100% pure sweatshop'), or through corporate funding of 'media literacy' associations and materials. Speculatively, they are more likely to be effective when embedded in supportive communities and practices, and connected to strategies for institutional change. Media education and culture jamming can be loosely considered as interventions intended to transform audience consciousness, and thereby, in the long run, to transform – or replace – the hegemonic corporate/consumerist regime of signification.

By contrast, another set of lifeworld-based practices may well be more important, even though they are more diffused and less media-centric. We refer to the use of communication networks, technologies and practices by social movements, which are articulators or bearers of democratization processes in civil society. The very networks and information technologies at the centre of neoliberal globalization have also been appropriated by its opponents, and earlier in this chapter we discussed some examples of this communicative judo – the Zapatistas, the defeat of the MAI, the Seattle IndyMedia Center at the WTO. Sreberny (2005: 246–51) extends this analysis to a less dramatic but at least equally profound example – women's transnational advocacy for gender justice. She discusses four dimensions of this struggle: *rights* (civil, political and communicational), *representation* (in its double sense: both political influence, and media portrayals), *recognition* (developing spaces 'where women can talk among themselves, find a voice, articulate concerns and demands, and receive recognition from each other'), and *redistribution* (of economic and communicative resources). In the struggle to articulate and disseminate these 'four Rs of democratization', media and information technologies – from print, the post, and telephone, to community radio, fax and internet – have been central as 'the tools and infrastructures of connectivity, as spaces for debate, as channels of voice' (2005: 251). Women's media activities are thus significant not only as spaces for the further articulation of political issues, but as 'significant organizational and cultural activities in their own right' (2005: 250).

At their best, social movements are both a source and a model of democratic communication. Indeed, Robert A. White (1995) goes so far as virtually to equate the two phenomena. What are his reasons? Given its own mandate and needs, he argues, a progressive movement needs to practice democratic communication internally. It needs to build horizontal communication networks in order to attract members and earn their loyalty, to challenge hegemonic definitions of reality, to enhance its cultural capital and emergent identities, and to project its symbols into the cultural arena. Moreover, for White, democratic communication entails not only institutional reform, but also normative and cultural change – validating skills and knowledge which are repressed by technocratic rationality ('system logic', in Habermasian terms), and spreading participatory communications throughout the system and lifeworld, to the workplace and family, for instance. New social movements, for White, are the birthplace *par excellence* of such cultural practices.

White's view of movements is perhaps unduly romantic, expressing a sense of redemptive action and pure space, uncontaminated by the sins of domination. Still, democratization *through* the media provides vital impetus for democratization *of* the media, in several ways.

First, in using hegemonic media in campaigns to heighten public awareness on a given issue, say the environment, activism can help diversify the range of voices and perspectives in the media. That itself is a form of media democratization.

Second, activists and advocacy groups sometimes gravitate towards struggles over media policy and representations, for both negative and positive reasons. Negatively, hegemonic media often loom as impediments to non-media-centric struggles; positively, the communication skills and networks produced through those struggles can be mobilized as resources explicitly to contest media power. Women's transnational advocacy networks display this combination of motive and means, as many women's groups participated in civil society interventions in the venues and debates surrounding global media governance. One example is the CRIS campaign, which emerged prior to the UN's World Summit on the Information Society in 2003 (Sreberny 2005).

Third, media education, culture jamming and the communicative activities of social movements can sometimes transform the environing conditions within which media operate. If movements succeed in shifting public consciousness, hegemonic media may be forced to respond – abandoning previous stereotypes, or allowing more space for new voices. Whether by forging new communities and identities in the lifeworld, by directly challenging media representations, or by campaigning to change state policies, social movements are often the key to cultural and political change, thus shifting the gravitational field, the environing conditions, of media. The gay rights movement exemplifies all three approaches. In the lifeworld of the North Atlantic societies, apart from sectors still dominated by religious fundamentalism, it has succeeded in transforming the definition of Queer from deviance to a source of pride, something to be celebrated in massive annual parades in major cities. Queer activists have sought to improve the mass-mediated images of gays, whether through the insider tactics of the Gay and Lesbian Alliance against Defamation (GLAAD), or the confrontational theatrics of Act-up. And they have sought equal rights under the law, with Canada's legal recognition of same-sex marriage in 2005 comprising a landmark victory. Not surprisingly, the representation of gays – at least, white, middle-class, males – on American network television has improved over the decades. A similar story could be told with respect to ethnic minorities; during the 1970s, the US TV networks created consultative mechanisms and improved, at least marginally, the representation of minorities in prime time (Montgomery 1989).

Most important, by de-naturalizing dominant media for significant elements of their mass audiences, lifeworld-oriented activism can foreground media as objects for critique and for political action. The 'problem of the media' thus becomes a *political* issue, one subject to democratic debate and policymaking (McChesney 2004).

Reforming the public communication system

The right-hand column of Table 3.1 signals those forms of media activism which are at the heart of this book – mobilization to reform, in liberal or radically democratic ways, the public communication 'system', including the state policy framework which helps shape the structure, performance and content of media. The upper quadrant highlights efforts to democratize mainstream media, and in particular journalism as a key genre in the media field.

Journalists and media workers inside the 'machinery of representation' have sometimes undertaken organized efforts to democratize both their workplace and media discourse. Historically and geographically, unions in the North Atlantic countries have differed in their degree of interest in questions of ownership structure or editorial control, beyond bread-and-butter workplace issues. But even journalists' unions' efforts to secure more job security and editorial autonomy vis-à-vis corporate employers are incipiently democratizing – and sometimes, they may win space for more favourable (or less hostile) representation of subaltern groups. (For instance, the National Union of Journalists' Code of Conduct in the UK enjoins members not to distribute material which promotes hatred or discrimination against various groups, and to afford those criticized in the news a right of reply. Were the Code effectively enforceable in the workplace, the British tabloids' vilification of asylum seekers or other marginalized people would be far more difficult.) Media unions also sometimes lobby on communication policy more broadly; a notable example is the extended project by the Communications, Energy and Paperworkers Union (CEP) to develop a detailed policy document, *For a Democratic Canadian Media*, in 2004.

Another basis for reforming journalism from within springs more from a 'professional' than a trade unionist sensibility. Two recent examples suffice:

- During the 1990s, a 'public journalism' movement arose within US media. It aimed to rescue American democracy and journalism from their perceived state of malaise by involving journalists in actively promoting public discourse, rather than simply 'covering' elite sources (Hackett and Zhao 1998: 200–6). This movement floundered in part because it ignored structural and power-related constraints on the media, and thus, the more fundamental roots to the crisis of media and democracy.
- NGOs like Reporting the World have emerged to promote 'peace journalism', which is conceived simultaneously as a mode of analysis and evaluation of potentially dangerous patterns of conflict reporting, a source of practical alternatives, and a challenge to everyday news discourse which typically comprises 'war journalism' (Lynch and McGoldrick 2005a, 2005b). While its success remains to be seen, the emergence of this reformist movement is hopeful.

From outside media organizations, progressives and academics have created ongoing monitoring projects to provide empirical benchmarks of media content, which in turn can be used in campaigns to inform and pressure editors (as well as mobilize the 'victims' of media coverage). Examples include Project Censored in California, which identifies the most newsworthy stories ignored each year by the mainstream press (usually jaw-dropping tales of corporate and government perfidy); Media Lens in the UK; NewsWatch Canada; and Fairness and Accuracy in Reporting (FAIR, in New York), which content-analyses selected issue coverage in the most prestigious American news media.

A related strategy entails finding the 'openings' in news discourse for progressive messages or counterinformation. Public interest advocacy groups and movements sometimes try to reduce the asymmetry of their relationship with media, by making themselves newsworthy. The idea is to identify the actions and issues which are news, formulate strategic key messages (appealing to such 'news values' as drama, novelty and conflict), and communicate those messages. Some media activists, like the Strategic Progressive Information Network (SPIN) in San Francisco, specialize in training community groups to conduct such news-oriented campaigns; others (like Public Media Center in San Francisco) design campaigns which revolve around paid advertising. These strategies have advantages. It is far easier to attract interest groups to a media-oriented campaign directly relevant to their primary goals, than to 'democratic media' as an abstract issue. And they can sometimes achieve short-term successes (raising issues, establishing a group's legitimacy) in diversifying media frames, as well as building media skills amongst subaltern groups. There are also limits and risks to such campaigns (Ryan 1991). They are typically reactive. They sometimes run afoul of the obduracy of established media frames and stereotypes, and even if successful in re-framing an issue, they leave long-term media structures intact so that the problem simply re-emerges on other issues. Such media-centred campaigns can lead to coverage of protest actions rather than progressive issues, and can suck resources and distort priorities. This very difficulty of redressing the asymmetry of media–movement relations through conventional public relations provides one of the incentives to change the policy framework of public communication.

The last (bottom right) quadrant in the map of media activism, then, calls attention to public interest interventions to address the regulatory practices (notably state communications policy) that constitute an environment for media production. Here, as elsewhere, progressive social movements are relevant, even when they do not directly address media reform. Contrary to some of the more extreme claims of New Social Movement theory, contemporary movements are interested not only in re-configuring the daily culture of the lifeworld. Their 'four Rs of democratization' – rights, recognition, representation, redistribution of resources – imply demands on the system: the state, corporations, and supra-state institutions of governance, such as the WTO. As we noted above, as successful movements acquire more political and economic resources for subaltern groups, as they put their issues on the political agenda and gain recognition from official policymakers, those movements can shift the gravitational pulls exerted on media; they change the political world to which journalism orients. To take a simple example, if more women assume positions of political leadership, the news will generally portray more women, simply as a by-product of its orientation to elite sources. To put the point in more structuralist language, altered power relations in the political field will usually have pertinent effects in the media/journalism field, whose autonomy (we argued above) is relatively weak.

This book focuses particularly, however, on attempts to build broad coalitions for democratic media reform – state-enacted policies and regulations to reduce the media system's democratic deficit. One of the longest-standing such efforts in the North Atlantic, and perhaps the Western world, is the Campaign for Press and Broadcasting Freedom (CPBF) in the UK. Its story is told in Chapter 6. It has inspired similar groups in North America, including a Canadian CPBF, and Free Press in the US.

Media democratization: a nascent movement?

What does our account of the forms of democratic media activism suggest about it as a nascent movement? In lieu of a definitive conclusion, we offer a hexagon of observations.

First, there appears to be a well-advanced division of labour between groups. Our typology suggests an organizational ecology with distinct niches. At the same time, significantly, there are many groups which consciously combine strategies like ACME, noted above.

Second, the most significant cleavage is between (a) autonomist strategies, aiming to create parallel communication spaces and practices outside the system; and (b) reform-oriented strategies, aiming to improve the existing regime. These are associated with contrasts of style, generation and ideology.

Third, despite this cleavage, there are encouraging indications of efforts to build bridges, or find the synergies, between different strategies. Alternative media sometimes publicize critical media monitoring; the *Bay Guardian*, for instance, publishes the annual Project Censored underreported story list. Academic content analysis (George Gerbner's Cultural Indicators Project) inspired an early attempt at a media reform coalition (the Cultural Environment Movement) in the 1990s. Media reformers ring the bells for public service television and access media; alternative media producers become involved in policy issues, such as postal rates or cable TV franchise agreements in the US, when their livelihoods are at stake. Progressive lawyers file court challenges on behalf of low-power FM microradio activists. Such collaboration seems to work better between groups with complementary but distinct mandates, rather than within a single group trying to incorporate them all.

Fourth, social movements are direct or indirect contributors in every type of democratic media activism, confirming the connection between democratization through and of the media.

Fifth, at the same time, democratizing initiatives can emerge from within sectors of the system itself, particularly the state. Contrary to dogmatic anarchism, radical democratic gains, if they are to be institutionalized, need to be registered by and through the state; dissident individuals (like Commissioners Copps and Adelstein at the FCC) or semi-independent agencies (like Canada's National Film Board) can help catalyse change.

Finally, given the political, cultural and economic resources of the hegemonic media, as well as the range of democratizing tasks (implied in Table 2.1) and strategies (sketched in Table 3.1), it seems likely that a successful and lasting democratization of media would need to advance on all fronts we have identified – lifeworld and system, media field and environing conditions. In so doing, the movement would foster expansive, media-literate counterpublics among subaltern groups; it would transform the societal public sphere; in short, it would challenge hegemony.

A challenge of this sort requires what Gramsci (1971) called a 'war of position' – a *sustained* struggle to win space for democratic practice on various interconnected fronts in civil society and lifeworld, in the workplace and in the state. Such a struggle cannot be discontinuous and episodic. Notwithstanding the ebb and flow of protest waves, it must occur as a cumulative series of coordinated campaigns directed at 'changing the rules', rather than simply forging identities and building networks. And in advancing a new communication paradigm, such a struggle would need to be morally and philosophically grounded in an alternative worldview to the reigning neoliberal discourse about democracy. Whether there is sufficient ideological cohesion for such a counterhegemonic initiative is the subject of Chapter 4.

4 Visions and divisions
Normative commitments of media democratization

August 10, 2004. On Ottawa's Parliament Hill, thousands are protesting against the Canadian Radio-television and Telecommunications Commission. The CRTC has just denied licence renewal to CHOI-FM, a commercially successful Quebec City radio station, on the grounds of 'abusive comment ... personal attacks and harassment' – such as a 'schlock jock's' on-air suggestion that mental patients be killed. His views, and the day's mood, were described as a nihilistic, Darwinian 'look after yourself anti-politics' (Aubin 2005). The station's defenders sport black T-shirts proclaiming 'Liberté', and a placard reading 'Death penalty for being different ... If that's democracy, I want no part of it!'.

Rewind to 7–9 November 2003. In Madison, Wisconsin, the newly-formed non-profit organization Free Press is holding its first National Conference on Media Reform. Inflamed by US corporate media's perceived complicity with Bush's Iraq war policy, by rabid right-wingers' domination of talk shows and networks, and by the FCC's waterboy subservience to media corporations, 1,700 people from across the US are loudly applauding broadcaster Amy Goodman, Free Press co-founders John Nichols and Bob McChesney, and other progressive media all-stars (Hackett and Carroll 2004). They are riding the wave of an ultimately successful grassroots campaign to reverse the FCC's proposed liberalization of media ownership rules. That unprecedented uprising – spanning the political spectrum – involved about three million Americans (McChesney 2004), most of whom would consider themselves supporters of free speech. Precisely because of that commitment, they favour more, not less, government regulation of media ownership concentration.

What do these contrasting events suggest about media activism? First, media issues do have the capacity, at least episodically, to stir people to take political action and to link media policies with stakes broader than personal preferences – liberty, democracy, press freedom, global peace. But, of course, those principles can differ. In this book, we are interested primarily in *progressive* forms of media activism – those that prefigure new forms of democratic participation, and/or promote the more equitable sharing of economic, political and cultural resources. Equally, however, economic and social conservatives, seeking to extend the hegemony of capital, to deepen privilege and/or further marginalize subaltern groups, have also employed monitoring, boycotts and other forms of 'flak' (Herman and Chomsky 1988) against what they perceive as 'left-liberal' media, especially in the

US. Notwithstanding influential political and theoretical currents attempting to blur the distinction,[1] history shows a meaningful contrast between reactionary and emancipatory movements – between, for example, nationalisms which seek the colonization or 'ethnic cleansing' of other peoples, and those (like the Kurds in Iraq) pursuing self-determination against an historically repressive state. Similarly, in the field of media activism, Downing *et al.* (2001: 94) see an irreducible difference between radical media of the Left, and those of the Right, whose 'deepest principle' is hierarchy, evident especially in the Right's uniform rejection of feminism as the pursuit of gender equality.

At the same time, progressive media activism is not monolithic. In Chapter 3, we glimpsed the range of its strategies and socio-institutional locations. Here, we briefly consider its ideological cohesion and diversity. In terms of vision, values and goals, do media activist groups have enough in common to form the nucleus of a coherent movement, a common project of transformation? Conversely, are there potentially crippling fault lines between them? Overall, what kind of project would it be, politically?

Equally important, does it matter? As noted in Chapter 3, some theorists see the displacement of political programmes by memes and lifestyles, and of movements by issue networks. We argued against that view. Our interviews suggest that it trivializes the aims of activists themselves: they do plan campaigns, build coalitions and pursue political goals. A collective, transformative project must comprise more than a network of disparate groups with shared grievances, and more than a series of unconnected protests and expressive outbursts. The search for an alternative political consensus is integral to any movement which is genuinely emancipatory and *counterhegemonic* – as distinct from one that is *anti-hegemonic*, ultimately rejecting the project of building a new and sustainable society, in the name of endless opposition, micro-politics, and differentiation (Sanbonmatsu 2004: 44, 129–31).

An adequate treatment of the normative/political dimensions of media activism would take at least an entire book. Here, we can only sample tantalizing slices of the pie. First, we outline contending political narratives on media and democracy, as a reference point to situate ideological currents within media democratization. Next, we sketch several contending ways that activists themselves frame media democratization, in the context of historical divisions within the Left. We then analyse a manifesto that represents a broad-based, collaborative attempt broadly to outline the principles of a democratic media system – the People's Communication Charter. In light of the Charter's commitments, we conclude by considering whether a coherent vision or paradigm informs that project.

Media and democracy: three perspectives[2]

In Chapter 1, we sketched North Atlantic media's democratic deficit. But, we now confess, there is no universally shared definition of that deficit. As we saw in Chapter 2, how the media interact with political life is a highly debated question. Moreover, even if we could agree on what the media's 'effects' actually are, how we evaluate them depends greatly on what 'grading' criteria we use. There are contending perspectives on what democracy entails, what the roles of media (in particular journalism, as its most politically relevant and contested form) ought to be, and how well media are performing those roles. Competing conceptions of democracy are not simply matters for policy wonks. They are both reflections of, and 'weapons' in, fundamental political divisions related to conflicting interests, and ultimately at stake are alternative futures.

In this section, we sketch three broad contemporary perspectives on media and democracy, as one useful way of placing DMA politically.

Market liberal and conservative critiques

In the 1980s, in the US at least, there was a modest uptake in 'conservative' advocacy and activism directed towards media and communication policy, partly in response to the surge of media-oriented liberal public interest groups a decade earlier (Mueller *et al.* 2004: 30, 51–2). But like 'liberalism', the term 'conservatism' is vague. It implies opposition to rapid change, scepticism towards human malleability and political utopias, a wish precisely to conserve valued traditions. In the name of traditional or 'family values', social conservatives, the most vocal opponents of abortion and same-sex marriage rights, protest the media's perceived violations of morality or social order – too much sex, violence, sensationalism, invasion of privacy.

Yet support for tradition over change hardly typifies conservatism's currently dominant incarnations. For nearly three decades, self-described conservatives in the North Atlantic countries have driven socially disruptive processes of economic liberalization and global corporatization, while the Left has found itself on the defensive, attempting to *conserve* social welfare programmes, public service broadcasting, and much else on the right-wing hit list.

Since the 1980s, the British Conservatives, the Canadian Conservative Party (newly rebranded after a decade of fragmentation), and especially the American Republican Party, have cleverly brought together apparently contradictory strands into a single hegemonic project. If self-styled Conservatives have been out office since 1997 in the UK, and from 1993 to 2006 in Canada, it is partly because parties of other names have adopted much of their agenda. Surveying the Republicans' 'propaganda mill' of right-wing radio, policy institute reports, and much else, American essayist Lewis Lapham (2004: 41) asks what principles, if any, could possibly reconcile conservatives' declared support for both small government and an imperial army, for self-reliance and government subsidies to business, for conservative compassion and the unfettered free market. Lapham can find only two common beliefs: that 'money was good for rich people and bad for poor people', and that truth is transcendent, the distinction between Good and Evil unambiguous. We suggest, following Downing's point above, that conservatism's core principle is *hierarchy* – whether the entrenched but waning cultural power of whites and heterosexual males, or (especially) the wealth of corporations and the power of capital over subordinate social groups and alternative modes of social organization.[3]

Since the 1980s, the most consequential form of 'conservatism' might be better described as market liberalism (or neoliberalism). This ideology holds that 'the world's resources are basically private property, that public affairs should be regulated by private parties on free markets, and that the state should retreat from most – if not all – domains that affect people's daily lives' (Hamelink 1995: 33) – with the exception of the state coercion (laws, police, military) needed to uphold property rights and market relations themselves. Democracy is seen not as an end in itself, but as normally the best institutional arrangement to maintain political stability and a political culture of individual rights and choice, particularly economic rights of ownership, contract and exchange. Here, market liberalism overlaps with libertarianism, a thoroughgoing version of liberalism which rejects social and legal constraints on individual autonomy, particularly vis-à-vis the state.

Though it often adopts a populist stance, the 'free market' vision actually fits well with a 'competitive elitist' version of democracy, classically articulated by Joseph Schumpeter (1942; cited in Baker 2002; Held 1987: 164–85). His model meshes with market liberalism's emphasis on private consumption rather than public virtue. Given the complexity of modern political issues, the vulnerability of the masses to irrational appeals, and the risk of overloading the political system with competing demands, Schumpeter argued, ongoing public participation is neither necessary nor even desirable. Policymaking elites need considerable autonomy from the mass public; and periodic elections, entrenched individual political rights, and a free press are enough to hold them accountable. In this view, democracy is a procedure for selecting leaders, with citizen participation confined mainly to voting every few years – essentially, the role of consumers in a political marketplace.

Journalism in this model would have several roles, including the 'watchdog' function discussed in Chapter 2 – exposing the abuse of power by government, which is considered by market liberals the main threat to individual freedom. The press 'need not provide for nor promote people's intelligent political involvement or reflection', since 'meaningful understanding of social forces and structural problems is beyond the populace's capacity' (Baker 2002, 133); nor need it raise fundamental questions about state policy or the social order. But journalism, particularly the 'quality' press, can play a useful role in reporting intra-elite debates and in circulating 'objective' information useful to elites themselves – a mandate articulated as early as the 1920s by the legendary American political columnist Walter Lippmann (1963).

If market liberals see a democratic deficit in contemporary journalism, they usually focus on one of two perceived problems. One is the influence of the state, whether through informal manipulation of journalists by politicians, through formal laws and regulations, or through subsidies to public service broadcasters, which allegedly distort the market's ability to satisfy consumer demand.[4] The second bogeyman for the conservatives, especially in the US, is the alleged anti-authority or 'left-liberal' bias of journalists themselves – a more politicized version of the 'mad dog' metaphor discussed in Chapter 2. Both of these assumptions have been actively promoted by market liberals, especially in the US, as part of their current hegemony over public policy discourse. Yet progressive critics have compellingly refuted them both. Journalists are neither raving lefties, nor do they control the news (McChesney 2004). And as we noted in Chapter 2, commercial media do not simply 'give people what they want'. Many structural factors refract or undermine the expression of consumer preferences. Consumers are not sovereign, and public broadcasting helps to offset corporate media's systemic democratic deficits (Baker 2002).

Moreover, as a normative ideal, consumer sovereignty assumes that media should serve people as consumers rather than as citizens. The two concepts differ radically. 'Citizen' implies active participation in civic affairs; 'consumer' implies the more private and passive role of material consumption. In democracies, citizens are in principle equal; in market economies, consumers are unequal, their access to commodities dependent upon their purchasing power.

In reality, people express their values in many ways, not just through consumer purchases. Citizen-oriented journalism, like public health, universal schooling, and some other socially necessary goods, cannot easily be supplied solely through market mechanisms (Baker 2002). But that limitation is relevant only if the goal is participatory rather than elitist democracy.

'Public sphere' liberalism

The elitist model of democracy has been widely criticized. It underestimates citizens' capacity for informed civic engagement, and overestimates the competence and accountability of political elites, absent ongoing public participation. The Iraq policy fiascos of the Bush and Blair administrations have underlined the point.

Similarly, the related market liberal approach to democracy overlooks the excessive influence of concentrated wealth over policymaking processes. It dismisses the threat, posed by the growing gap between rich and poor, to political equality and even meaningful individual freedom. And it ignores the erosion, by a culture of acquisitive individualism, of the sense of community underpinning democratic governance.

Such considerations have strengthened an alternative vision that accepts the elitist democrats' support for individual rights and an independent 'watchdog' press, but places a much higher value on popular participation through established political channels. Participation can be valued as a means to produce more just and legitimate policies, and to develop the democratic capacities of citizens. This vision of a liberal democracy functioning in accordance with its own legitimizing principles of representative government, citizen equality and civic empowerment informs much social movement activism in the North Atlantic societies. As it applies to the politics of communication, it typically calls upon the media to facilitate or provide a democratic public sphere – 'that realm of social life where the exchange of information and views on questions of common concern can take place so that public opinion can be formed' (Dahlgren 1995: 7).

How should media structure be democratized to meet this public sphere criterion? For Baker (2002: 129–53), it implies that participatory democracy needs two offsetting types of media. In a 'republican' version, we need media organizations that can facilitate the search for society-wide political consensus by being universally accessible, inclusive (civil, objective, balanced and comprehensive), and thoughtfully discursive, not simply factual. Such has been the mandate of public broadcasting at its best. But in a 'liberal pluralist' view, we need a segmented system which provides each significant cultural and political group with a forum to articulate and develop its interests. We can link such segmented media with Nancy Fraser's (1997) call for subaltern counterpublics, detached from, but able to intervene in, the broader societal public sphere. Interest-specific and alternative media fit this bill.

Political scientist Pippa Norris (2000: 25–35) proposes a more specific checklist of 'public sphere' tasks for journalism. First, if news media are to provide a civic forum that helps sustain pluralistic political competition, do they provide extensive coverage of politics, including a platform for a wide plurality of political actors? Do media provide 'horizontal' communication between political actors, as well as 'vertical' communication between government and governed? Are there multiple sources of regular political news from different outlets, underpinning effective government communication, multiple venues for public debate, and reduced costs to citizens for becoming politically informed? Is there equal or proportionate coverage of different parties? Finally, as an agent in mobilizing public participation, does journalism stimulate general interest, public learning and civic engagement vis-à-vis the political process?

Around these questions, debate rages. In one corner, a 'media malaise' thesis, a refined version of the 'mad dog' metaphor unleashed in Chapter 2, blames infotainment, audience fragmentation, scandalmongering journalism, and other putative media malpractices, for many of the public sphere's perceived woes – voter cynicism, low participation, the 'disconnect' between politicians and citizens, the 'dumbing down' of public debate (Blumler and Gurevitch 1995; Fallows 1996; Norris 2000: 4–12). In the other corner, a more optimistic reading critiques these 'narratives of decline' (McNair 2000: 197) as conceptually misdirected or empirically unsupported. For instance, Norris (2000: 318) finds that 'exposure' to news media, and trust/participation in the political system, are a mutually reinforcing 'virtuous circle'.

Critical public sphere liberals, those who hold the 'malaise' position that media are not contributing properly to democratic dialogue, provide intellectual and political ammunition for media reform. This position straddles the seams between hegemony and counterhegemony. It challenges the hegemony of market relations over public communication, seeking to infuse the dialogical ethics of the lifeworld into the media and political systems. At the same time, its voice is not one of marginalized outsiders but of disappointed insiders. It supplies the terms of respectable debate among legislatures, academia, middle-class NGOs, journalism schools, and sometimes media practitioners themselves – one thinks of the writings of the American editor James Fallows, or the reformist 'public journalism' movement, involving experiments by newspapers to facilitate community discussion of public issues, rather than simply to report on official sources (Baker 2002: 158–63).

The case for media reform is often articulated through the language of public sphere liberalism and its adherents. Their concerns are legitimate, and have some purchase within the media and political system. Yet much of the grassroots energy for challenges to hegemonic media derives from outside, from the more marginalized reaches of the lifeworld – from bitter political struggles, like those of British trade unions fighting Thatcherism in the 1980s, or from subaltern strata, like non-white communities jackbooted daily by racism and poverty. From these social spaces, more radical visions can emerge.

Radical democracy and the media

Public sphere liberalism usefully critiques aspects of the democratic deficit, especially relating to journalism practices, but it is less likely fundamentally to question the commercial basis of media, and still less the social and political order. Radical democrats offer a more robust set of benchmarks for evaluating media performance. If market liberals emphasize 'negative' individual freedom from constraint by government, and public sphere liberals highlight public deliberation about policy, radical democrats add a third dimension – a thoroughgoing view of democracy as not just a set of procedural rules, but a societal environment which nourishes developmental power – a 'positive' freedom, everyone's equal right to 'the full development and use' of their capabilities (Macpherson 1977: 114; Downing *et al.* 2001: 43–4).

Such a standpoint transcends public sphere liberalism in several respects. First, radical democrats seek not just to reinvigorate the existing system of representative democracy but to expand direct and equitable participation in decision-making in the neighbourhood, workplace, and family/gender relations – the lifeworld.

Second, they prioritize equality as a core principle of democracy, one which has come under increasing assault by neoliberal governments in the US, UK and Canada since the 1980s. Citizens should have not only formally equal legal and political rights but also approximate equality in access to the resources needed to participate meaningfully in public life.

Third, radical democrats have a more critical orientation towards the social order and its embedded inequalities. They are more likely to regard power relations in zero-sum terms, as antagonistic: the power of economically, politically or culturally privileged groups derives at least partly from excluding, exploiting or oppressing others.

Thus, radical democrats understand power holistically. A democratic public sphere cannot be insulated from power hierarchies embedded in state, economy, gender and race; so long as they exist, they will tend to undermine equality of voice in the public sphere. If public sphere liberals aim to improve quality and equality of participation in public communication through reforming media practices and laws, radical democrats may be aiming for nothing less than the transformation of (in bell hook's notable phrase) white supremacist capitalist patriarchy (cited in Riordan 2002: 13, n. 3). Or, as a Toronto activist has put it, the media system is undemocratic because our society is undemocratic. The state of our media is an extension of an oppressive nationalist-corporate state. It's not a problem to be fixed within the system, but a lesson in how the system works.

(Baines 2004: 91)

As for expectations of media, most radical democrats would nevertheless accept parts of the market-liberal and especially the public sphere models, including the watchdog and public forum functions. But they would add criteria, favouring social equality and participation, such as these:

- Enabling horizontal communication between subordinate groups, including social movements as agents of democratic renewal (Angus, 2001). By giving public voice to civil society, media can facilitate needed social change, power diffusion, and popular mobilization against social injustices.
- Providing access for, and diffusion of, events, issues and voices which are socially important but outside, or even opposed to, the agendas of elites.
- Counteracting power inequalities found in other spheres of the social order. As McChesney (1999: 288) has put it, 'unless communication and information are biased toward equality, they tend to enhance social inequality'.
- Contributing actively to public awareness in favour of environmental sustainability and other extra-market values integral to a just and humane society.

Given these criteria, radical democrats find much to criticize. Whereas some public sphere liberals worry about public mistrust of government, radical democrats like Herman and Chomsky (1988) worry that 'lapdog' media are altogether *too* successful in 'manufacturing consent' for unjust state and corporate policies. In many ways, discussed in Chapters 1 and 3, news media structures are in tension with values of democratic equality, equitable political representation and informed participatory citizenship. Indeed, our sketch of the democratic deficit in Chapter 1 is animated by the radical democratic critique.

Fault lines in the Left

Yet radical democracy is hardly a unitary standpoint. It is marked by the broader divisions of the Western Left over the past century. The competing traditions included, on the one hand, the now rightly discredited Communist faith in the capacity of a vanguard party and state to force-march a new classless social order into being and, on the other hand, the anarchist rejection of the state and all its doings as an instrument of oppression. In between these extremes of twentieth-century Leftism, we find (particularly in Europe and Britain) democratic socialism, committed to achieving social reform through electoral and parliamentary means, for implementation through legislation and administrative bureaucracy; and the student-based New Left of the 1960s, particularly vocal in the US and France, but with echoes around the world, with its goal of participatory democracy, a society where people would collectively shape the decisions affecting their lives, in the workplace and community. The Western Left incorporated conflicting views not only of the state, but of modernity itself – from classical Marxism's wish to liberate the forces of production from the fetters of capitalism, to the New Left's romantic rejection of consumerism, industrialism, bureaucracy and efficiency-worship – perhaps typified by the slogans of French student rebels of May 1968: 'Be realistic, demand the impossible!'; 'Under the paving stones, the beach.'

Notwithstanding their intent to sweep away the bases of human oppression, these longstanding radical traditions also had their blind spots. Two other late-twentieth-century currents made that clear. First, various strands of feminism (liberal, radical/essentialist, psychoanalytic, socialist) critiqued the masculinist biases that the Left shared with the broader social order, including the neglect of gender as an axis of inequality, and a public/private dichotomy predicated upon a taken-for-granted gendered division of labour.

Second, postcolonial theory, so-called identity politics, and racial justice struggles strove to articulate the perspectives and knowledges of the non-white, non-Western majority of humanity – and to challenge, on behalf of the marginalized, the West's dominant political and cultural discourses and (sometimes) structures. In the name of 'equality and well-being for all human beings on this earth' (Young 2003: 7), these politics problematized the Eurocentrism of the Western Left, its acceptance of citizenship in national states as the basis for political rights, and its relative indifference to the subordination of indigenous and colonized peoples, as the dark flipside of Western nation-building. From this perspective, Western democracy may appear as a set of rules to preserve stability within an affluent gated community, and to keep the world's impoverished rabble outside.

Add to this already frothy brew the pseudo-radicalism of postmodernism, rejecting the totalizing meta-narratives of modernity, including Enlightenment concepts like reason and progress. Postmodernism ultimately denies the possibility of progressive, counterhegemonic politics in favour of the micropolitics of anti-hegemony, noted above – even though, arguably, postmodernism's critiques smuggle in through the back door the very universalizing criteria which it had so noisily evicted out the front.

But neither rant nor potted history is intended here. The point is that the complexity, dilemmas and multiple standpoints of progressive challenges to hegemony in general also have implications for the specific field of media activism. Here, we have space to highlight just a few of those challenges.

Reformism or radicalism?

How fundamental and far-reaching is the object or target of change? Is the project about fixing a temporarily broken media system, or, as Malkia Cyril of the Oakland Youth Media Council put it at the 2005 Free Press conference, is the goal 'to dismantle and rebuild' it? For public sphere liberals, the goal is to reform public communication so that it better serves the existing processes of liberal democratic governance; for others, media activism is just a piece of a much broader struggle against social, racial and economic injustice, and for the redistribution of wealth and power.

Related to that normative question (what is media democratization for) is a more 'empirical' one: Does media democratization depend upon changes in the media field's environing conditions? The answer depends upon how autonomous media are from other social institutions. Most would probably agree with Jakubowicz (1993) that communicative democracy must be accompanied by other democratic rights and structures, and could not last long in an otherwise authoritarian or hypercommercialized society. But for some activists, media democratization entails an egalitarian redistribution of material resources and cultural competence, whereas for others, a democratic public sphere can be insulated from the effects of social inequality – for example, through ceilings on political campaign spending.

A related question concerns orientations towards the state. In Chapter 3, we noted the state's dual role: its policies (subsidies, regulation, direct provision of media services) can help remedy the democratic deficit; yet it also contributes to the deficit (manipulation, surveillance, harassment of dissent and so on). We also noted the distinction between lifeworld- and system-oriented forms of DMA. The distinction is both strategic and ideological. Social democratic media reformers (like the CPBF) emphasize the state's potential for enforcing reforms against corporate power and commercialism. Libertarians and anarchists are more likely to see the state as inherently repressive, and to advocate building autonomous communication spaces. Indeed, Downing (2003) sees an ideological affinity between the Independent Media Centers, and the political tradition of socialist anarchism. An American microradio activist told us that 'mass mobilization and the people taking to the streets' rather than electoral politics was the path to 'change in this country'. Similarly, microradio pioneer Stephen Dunifer described reform as 'a waste of our effort; we're much better off creating our own models'.

Populism versus moral leadership

Media democratization theory manifests conflicting impulses. On the one hand, cultural populism denigrates corporate and state elite control of media, in the name of the values and rights of ordinary people – a position which may be difficult to disentangle from the market liberal celebration of consumer choice. On the other hand, the critical concept of hegemony implies that popular consciousness is distorted by power relations and is not genuinely autonomous, that if sexism and racism (for example) have deep roots in everyday culture, then a straightforward populism – a demand that politicians and media reflect mass preferences – is not an unambiguously progressive politics. Yet this counterhegemony position also has its risks, those of a cultural politics of elitism or vanguardism. Questions of vision as well as strategy are in play: to what extent should democratic media actively and consciously cultivate democratic subjectivity?

Freedom versus moral order

Characterizing Western political thought as a whole since the Enlightenment, this is perhaps the greatest theoretical conundrum for media democratization. For communications philosopher Clifford Christians (1995: 78), communicative democrats share the Enlightenment 'cult of human personality in all its freedom', in which human beings 'were declared a law unto themselves, set loose from every faith that claimed their allegiance'. This ideal is one of the normative underpinnings of free expression against state or corporate constraints. At the same time, communicative democrats hope and expect that the exercise of such freedom will enhance other social values, such as peace, democracy and universal human dignity and integrity. As debates over censorship of pornography and racist propaganda show, one problem arises when freedom of expression and broadened media access are used to attack rather than support human rights and dignity. But Christians identifies another problem, more subtle and profound than balancing free speech with protection from violence and hatred. It concerns the need for commitment to community, and to other-oriented moral values. Like many of the writers associated with the WACC, Christians argues that a culture of self-gratification and narcissism 'has rendered public life virtually impossible and simultaneously hollows out our personal sphere as well'; ultimately, it is incompatible with 'genuine democratization of empowered citizens' (Christians 1995: 81–2).

What does media democracy look like – in the long term?

Some theorists (e.g. Christians 1995; White 1995) argue quite cogently that media democratization is very much a matter of transforming ethos and practices in the culture, the lifeworld. But if it is also a matter of changing rules and structures in the system, then a very policy-relevant challenge arises: to devise policies and models that effectively address the democratic deficit, and are also economically, politically and organizationally sustainable in a complex society with an advanced division of labour. Activists and academics may be attracted to access and alternative media based largely on volunteer labour, but Polish theorist Karol Jakubowicz (1993) cautions soberly that this is an outdated '1960s' paradigm of communication democratization based on a number of fallacies, including the assumption that broad swathes of people actually want ongoing participation in media production. Similarly, Mueller *et al.* (2004: 59, 64, 80) argue that media democrats have not yet adequately countered the 'economic realism' enshrouding their neoliberal opponents' arguments. To be sure, activists can respond that simply placing media reform on the political agenda is a higher priority than detailed blueprints. But just as plausibly, economically credible alternative models could help media reform earn a political hearing.[5]

Contending frames

Philosophical and policy conundrums like those sketched above have concrete implications for movement alliances and frames. If media democratization is conceptualized as inside-the-system reform separable from the broader social order, then liberal professional elites are the most likely leaders, and alliances with cultural conservatives on some issues (such as media violence and hyper-commercialism) become more plausible. On the other hand, if media democratization and progressive social change are inseparable, they are most likely to be spearheaded by a revitalized political Left.

As resource mobilization theory suggests, successful movements create their own 'action frames' as integral to support-building strategies. Typically, such frames will evoke shared values and goals, name a problem and potential solution, identify opponents whose power needs to be challenged, and propose a strategy or collective action repertoire (Snow and Benford 1988). Borrowing from Keck and Sikkink (1998), Ó Siochrú explains that

> constructing 'cognitive frames' is an essential strategic activity for advocacy. It enables other actors to comprehend the issue raised from within their own context, and they can then encourage and guide collaborative actions. 'Frame resonance' refers to the extent and manner in which a network's interpretative work can influence broader public understanding, involving both internal coherence and alignment with the broader political culture. The formulation of various frames, including competing frames, is characteristic of the early stages of a campaign or movement, but over time they can become embedded in the campaign's common 'reservoir of symbols' from which future and deeper frames can be built.   (2005b: 297)

For media activism, finding a frame that is both shared and that resonates with potential supporters has proven to be a major and still unresolved challenge.

Our interviews with activists suggest at least five potential frames in play:

- A *free press, freedom of expression* frame. In the US, it makes reference to the Constitution's First Amendment, and the public responsibilities of the media implicit therein. It thus invokes mainstream liberal values, but seeks to extend the concept of media autonomy from government, to autonomy from unaccountable corporate power. The struggle against censorship (both governmental and corporate) is a common theme within this frame.
- A media and democracy, *media democratization*, or democratic communication frame. This frame differs from the free press frame, in more directly incorporating egalitarian and participatory notions of democracy as informed, collective self-government. It directly addresses the media's democratic deficit while offering a radically democratic vision of public communication. This concept is probably dominant within American media activism, and it provides the shorthand language that we use most frequently in this book.

- A *right to communicate* frame, which implies a connection with struggles for other human rights, as well as a legalistic focus: the recognition and entrenchment of 'rights' in international law, particularly Article 19 of the UN Declaration of Human Rights, concerning freedom to seek, receive and import information and ideas. Like the free press frame, this implies an expansion of the liberal right of free expression, which classically means freedom from government censorship or punishment. But in this case, the extension is to the right of access to the means of public communication, the right to place ideas effectively into the public domain. Interestingly, among our informants this frame was invoked almost exclusively by activists working at the international level, on issues of global media governance, rather than those working in national contexts. One reason for this may be that the right to communicate has arisen from UNESCO and NWICO, and from the framework of international law, rather than from within national policy domains. Another reason may be that in the US and UK, a human rights frame is more difficult to disarticulate from the liberal notion of freedom of the press.

- A *mental or cultural environmental frame.* This frame implies a struggle against a toxic culture, exemplified by formulaic violence, fearmongering and consumerism in the media, and driven by hypercommercialism, the pursuit of profits above all public service considerations. It de-emphasizes the process of democratic participation, in favour of the desired outcome: a more humane culture. It implies a parallel with the relatively successful environmentalist movement.

- An emerging *media justice* frame, articulated in particular by American community and media activists of colour. This frame re-positions the project as one of social justice in a world organized around globalized capitalism, racism and patriarchy, and directly connotes the need for alliances, even integration, with other progressive social movements (Hackett and Carroll 2004: 18). While relatively new, this frame's foregrounding of equality for the marginalized, and the redistribution of wealth and power, resonate with broader Left traditions, like socialism and postcolonialism.

A multiplicity of frames is not necessarily a barrier to movement mobilization; there is even an advantage in that different frames can appeal to different constituencies. But lack of a common frame becomes an obstacle if it inhibits alliances or the sense of shared interests or identification with a common project. The problem is compounded if different frames, as they are deployed by activist groups, not only compete with but undercut each other. Some of the activists we interviewed indicated that such is sometimes the case.

Thus, for a variety of reasons, the concept of 'democratic' communication strikes many as problematic. Aliza Dichter, now with the Center for International Media Action (www.mediaactioncenter.org, accessed 18 October 2005) notes that in some transition societies of the global East and South, the term 'democracy' is a loaded one: 'It can be a Trojan horse for capitalist imperialism, to be pretty blunt.' John Anner, of the Independent Press Association, suggested that the concept of 'democratic media' is too broad and amorphous: 'It's so easily definable by whoever is in the room that we could decide right now that we have a democratic media and then we could all go home. We need something a little more specific' to fight for. Peter Franck, a progressive communications lawyer, likewise notices an ambiguity: does 'democratic media' imply internally democratic decision-making within media institutions, or, as he prefers, does it indicate the role of media within democracy as a political system – a media 'that isn't governed by commercial principles but really structured to have a broad variety of social views'.

Kim Deterline, at We Interrupt This Message, acknowledges that framing the project as 'a democracy issue' will appeal to 'some people who have the resources to think that's the primary issue, as opposed to people who have really frontline issues to deal with, who might think that democracy is important but having food on the table for my kids, and the people in my neighbourhood not being shot, is more important to me'. Holly Minch at the Independent Media Institute's SPIN project agrees with the priority of such issues, but argues that a 'media democracy analysis' does play a role; while helping them with local campaigns, the SPIN project also teaches grassroots community groups very concretely about media structure and how that affects media representations of the community. Praxis founder Makani Themba-Nixon, who works with ethnic minorities and prefers the 'media justice' frame, argues that 'democracy' precludes a sense of redistributive justice. As she and other American activists of colour assert, for non-white minorities in the US, 'democracy' may be irretrievable from connotations of conquest, slavery and tyranny of the white majority.

At the same time, the media democracy frame is probably the predominant one. It certainly has its defenders. Andrea Buffa, at Media Alliance, argued that in the US, media democracy connects with a widely held mainstream political value. Her colleague Ben Clarke suggests that more than environmentalism (for instance), a media movement requires a participatory democratic politics, in order to relate to the real concerns of supportive constituencies: 'If you organize a democratic media environment without a message, you certainly will never mobilize a constituency.' And alternatives to the media democracy frame also have their critics. A feminist political economist with the Union for Democratic Communication argued that the concept of 'cultural environment' too readily erases the question of power inequalities, and of the policy-shaped nature of the cultural industries. A media justice activist at the ACME Summit opposes mainstream environmentalism as a model: it is 'like a whites' rights movement. Look at who defines what nature is … Why are most people who are setting the environmental agenda white, and why are most people who suffer most of the negative impacts of an unhealthy environment people of colour? … There's something systemic here … I don't want to see it happen in the media democracy movement.'

As for the communication rights frame, San Francisco scholar/activist Dorothy Kidd argues that it can educate disempowered people to their potential power, but it is important that people not 'get limited by the existing framework of rights' – one should move into (broader) notions of democratization. 'People don't see their information rights in the same way as they see their civil rights', says Ben Clarke. He implies that on media issues, people respond to concrete and local concerns,

Substantive moral reform		cultural environment	media justice
		media democratization	
Democratic procedure	free press	right to communicate	
	Free individuals		**Collective solidarities**

Figure 4.1 Five action frames for remaking media

such as the cancellation of a valued radio programme, rather than to abstract principles. At the international level, the notion of a Right to Communicate has proven
quite contentious (Ó Siochrú 2005b). Right-wingers see it as a reincarnation of
NWICO, a rationalization for government regulation of the 'free flow' (in corporate-dominated markets) of information. But progressives too challenge it, on
grounds of both strategy (it is too legalistic, it could divert energy from concrete
local campaigns, it could counterproductively unleash a rollback of internationally recognized rights), and principle (it could facilitate bureaucratic interference with journalists' autonomy). For such reasons, its supporters in the
Campaign for Communication Rights in the Information Society (CRIS) have
tactically retreated from the concept of a singular Right to Communicate to more
general 'communication rights'.

Amid this dissensus as to what the movement might be about, it is nevertheless
possible to see these frames as inhabiting a shared conceptual space. As counterhegemonic visions for remaking media, they differ along two dimensions: first,
whether the goal is mainly to secure *procedures* for democratic communication, or to
implement *substantive moral reforms* that alleviate pathologies stemming from the
current order; and second, whether the process is the *freeing of individuals* from
unnecessary constraints, or the construction of *new collective solidarities*.

Figure 4.1 offers a heuristic mapping of the five frames in this two-dimensional
space. Both the free speech and the right to communicate frames emphasize
procedural changes (winning of autonomy and rights) as key, but the latter moves
in a collectivist direction by envisaging a future in which subaltern groups are
empowered to participate fully in public discussion, implying an alleviation of
subalternality. In contrast, the media justice and cultural environment frames both
advocate extensive substantive change in the direction of a new moral order, with
the former more than the latter, emphasizing the need for new collective solidarities. The media democratization frame, which comes closest to the vision of radical
democracy discussed above, strikes a certain balance between the poles of both
dimensions, and for this reason might be a candidate for pulling various strands of

the movement together – so long as 'democracy' can be redeemed to carry a strong egalitarian and participatory theme.

The People's Communication Charter

Diversity and debates can be taken as signs of vitality rather than causes for dismay. Differing political commitments have not precluded activists from collaborating on campaigns for specific objectives, such as supporting public broadcasting in the UK, or opposing ownership liberalization in the US. And media democrats have been able to agree on an impressive number of manifestos and statements of principle. One of the most influential has been the People's Communication Charter, which we explore in this section for further insights into communicative democracy's political vision.

Written in a universalizing language of human rights, the Charter's text evolved during the 1990s, through an intense process of debate and study by NGOs and activists around the world. Organizational sponsors included the Centre for Communication and Human Rights in Amsterdam, the Third World Network (Malaysia), the AMARC-World Association of Community Radio Broadcasters (Peru/Canada), and the Cultural Environment Movement (CEM) with its dozens of affiliated organizations. The Charter's initiators aimed explicitly to propose a set of criteria by which to organize and evaluate communications, drawing upon recognized international agreements and standards, particularly the Universal Declaration of Human Rights (UDHR) and other UN-mandated international agreements (Duncan 1999: 175–6). Noting the genesis of the Charter at a meeting of social activists in Malaysia in 1991, one of its key drafters, Dutch communications scholar Cees Hamelink, explained that it was also intended to educate and mobilize people (personal interview, 2001). The initiators hoped that, combined with campaigns around more concrete political objectives, the Charter would help transfer the mass influence of peace and human rights movements in the 1980s to the seemingly abstract issues of communication and culture in the 1990s.

The Charter's 18 articles (see summary in Table 4.1) can be grouped into a smaller number of themes and principles.[6] The Charter's opening clauses endorse classical liberal (and libertarian) commitments – people's entitlement to respect and rights (Article 1), and freedom of expression (2). The Charter also calls for strengthening, in the communications field, other rights already recognized in liberal theory – for example, legal protection for journalists (6), privacy (13) and fair trial (15). Indeed, Hamelink (1995) grounds the ethical case for democratic communication precisely in its greater contribution to human rights and dignity, compared to state- and corporate-controlled forms of public communication.

But the Charter (in common with other declarations produced by the Campaign for Press and Broadcast Freedom, the Media and Democracy Congress, and the CEM) transcends the classical liberal conception of free speech and free press in several important ways.

First, it avoids conflating free speech with commercialism, and critiques the

Table 4.1 People's Communication Charter (excerpts)

Article	Text
1 Respect	People are entitled to be treated with respect, in accordance with the basic human rights and standards of dignity, integrity, identity and non-discrimination.
2 Freedom	People have the right to freedom of expression without interference by public or private interests, and to … communication channels independent of governmental or commercial control.
3 Access	In order to exercise their rights, people should have fair and equitable access to local and global resources and facilities for conventional and advanced channels of communication …
4 Independence	The realization of people's right to participate in, contribute to, and benefit from the development of self-reliant communication structures requires … international assistance …
5 Literacy	People have the right to acquire the skills necessary to participate fully in public communication. This requires literacy in reading, writing, and storytelling; in critical media awareness … computer skills; and education about the role of communication in society.
6 Protection of journalists	Journalists must be accorded full protection of the law, including international humanitarian law, especially in areas of armed conflict …
7 Right of reply and redress	People have the right of reply and to demand penalties for damage [from] … inaccurate or misleading and damaging information …
8 Cultural identity	People have the right to protect their cultural identity. This includes respect for people's pursuit of cultural development and the right to free expression in languages they understand. People's right to the protection of their cultural space and heritage should not violate other human rights or provisions of this Charter.
9 Diversity of languages	People have the right to a diversity of languages. This includes the right to express themselves and have access to information in their own language, the right to use their own languages in educational institutions funded by the state, and the right to have adequate provisions created for the use of minority languages where needed.
10 Participation in policymaking	People have the right to participate in public decision-making about the provision of information; the development and utilization of knowledge; the preservation, protection and development of culture; the choice and application of communication technologies; and the structure and policies of media industries.
11 Children's rights	Children have the right to mass media products that are designed to meet their needs and interests, and foster their healthy physical, mental and emotional development. They should be protected from harmful media products and from commercial and … other exploitation …

continued overleaf

Table 4.1 People's Communication Charter (*continued*)

Article	Text
12 Cyberspace	People have a right to universal access to and equitable use of cyberspace ... [Their] rights to free and open communities in cyberspace, their freedom of electronic expression, and ... their privacy against electronic surveillance ... should be protected.
13 Privacy	Media should respect people's private, family and home life, physical and moral integrity, honour and reputation ... However ... the protection of privacy [should] not unduly interfere with the freedom of expression or the administration of justice.
14 Harm	Media should resist incitement to hate, prejudice, violence and war ...
15 Justice	People have the right to demand that media respect standards of due process in the coverage of trials ...
16 Consumption	People have the right to demand useful and factual consumer information, and to be protected from misleading and distorted advertising, promotion disguised as news and entertainment ... and from the promotion of wasteful, unnecessary, harmful or ecologically damaging goods and activities.
17 Accountability	Media should establish mechanisms ... that account to the general public for their adherence to ... this Charter.
18 Implementation	... national and international mechanisms will be organized ... to monitor and assess the performance of media in light of these Standards ...

Source: www.wacc.org.uk/wacc/our_work/thinking/communication_rights/the_people_s_communication_charter, accessed 8 October 2005. For consistency with other versions of the Charter, Articles 8 and 9 have been reversed.

latter. The Charter implies that not only government but also private centres of power can censor, monopolize, or distort public communication. Article 2 refers to independence from 'governmental or *commercial control*' (emphasis added). Other clauses (11, 16) refer to protecting people, particularly children, from the excesses of media commercialism.

A second departure from libertarianism is the Charter's emphasis on *responsibility* and *accountability* in the media's exercise of power. Mechanisms of media accountability to their publics include 'self-regulatory bodies' (17), and people's 'right of reply' to media misinformation (7). The Charter sidesteps debates about the regulation of pornography or hate speech; without advocating censorship, it simply calls on media to avoid 'incitement to hate, prejudice, violence or war' and 'stereotypic images that distort the realities and complexities of people's lives' (14).

But while the Charter advocates responsibility on the part of professionals in the established media it also demands direct popular *access* and *participation* in communication – a third extension beyond 'free speech'. To be rendered meaningful, freedom of expression requires that 'All people are entitled to access to the resources they need to communicate freely within and between their societies', in the words of the Charter's preamble. This clause parallels, in the communication field, the socialist position that political and legal equality must be supplemented by access to social and economic resources. The Charter can be seen as an articulation of the *right to communicate* frame, discussed above. Articles on access (3), literacy (5), and the right of reply (7) elaborate specific aspects of people's ability actively to participate in public communication. They entail not only people's right to produce their own alternative or citizens' media but also public participation in broader communication policymaking (10). In short, the Charter implies both autonomous media within the lifeworld, and challenges to the dominant logic of the system.

In a fourth departure beyond classical liberalism, the Charter intimates a conception of *equality* broader than citizens' formally similar legal/political rights (voting, fair trial). While a vital principle, such formal equality can be rendered a mockery by the differential impact of seemingly 'universal' laws, and by the ability of the wealthy to hire high-powered lawyers, to bankroll election campaigns, to lobby politicians, to blackmail governments with the threat of investment withdrawal. Such economic and political imbalances are hardly compatible with democracy conceived as 'equality of entitlement to the conditions of self-empowerment' (Hamelink 1995: 31). Similarly, as we have seen, formal equality in the right of free speech coexists with concentration of the means of symbolic production in few hands, and with the systemic marginalization of political/cultural practices that cannot be profitably commodified. *Effectively* equal free speech rights imply a just (re)distribution of the resources needed to participate in public communication. Illustratively, the Charter (12) advocates 'equitable use' and 'universal access' to cyberspace.

Fifth, the Charter also endorses *diversity* and *pluralism* – including diversity of languages (9), and 'a range of cultural products designed for a wide variety of tastes and interests' (3). At first sight, that commitment to diversity seems to be shared by market liberals, who talk of consumer choice and a 'marketplace of ideas'. But their commitment is to individual choice expressed through consumer purchases and contractual relations in 'the market place', not to diversity as such. In their view, freedom of expression vis-à-vis direct government censorship can be guaranteed by constitutional protections, but diversity cannot. The market ensures some level of diversity, but if it fails to represent every significant view, market liberals would argue, there is little that governments can or should do about it; any form of state intervention would be more likely to harm than promote free expression (Hackett *et al.* 2000: 70). The Charter, by contrast, rejects such free market fundamentalism, mandating governments to take active responsibility for protecting linguistic and cultural diversity. Certainly, the Charter recognizes that state practices can repress diversity; indeed, one of the Charter coalition's major public interventions was a non-official Tribunal in the Hague, on five cases of state suppression of the right to communicate in minority languages (Media Development 1999). On the other hand, progressive media democrats can also point to press subsidies, public service broadcasting, minority language education, and other state policies, particularly in western Europe and Scandinavia, that have successfully promoted media and cultural pluralism without state censorship.

Sixth, while many of the Charter's provisions imply popular and state mobilization for progressive social change, they are in some measure offset by commitments to *community* and *solidarity*, to the preservation of the most humane and nurturing elements of the current social order. In Chapter 1, we identified the threat to community as part of the media's democratic deficit. The value of community is manifested in several Charter clauses: the protection of children from harmful media products and commercial exploitation (11, 16), the media's avoidance of hate-incitement and 'other violations of human dignity and integrity' (14), and the protection of cultural identity (8).

The Charter thus does address Clifford Christians' concern, discussed above, that freedom and emancipation can degenerate into narcissism. Notwithstanding the postmodernists' dubious claim of a retreat from universal moral values, the Holy Trinity of Enlightenment political thought – liberty, equality, fraternity (or community, in less gendered terms) – continues to inform Western normative media theory too. Thus, expectations of the media include not only freedom and fairness but also contributions to public order, solidarity and social identity (McQuail 1992: 237–73). Those concepts can of course be used rhetorically to justify authoritarian repression; but they have positive and arguably necessary aspects – the formation and maintenance of personal identity and group cohesion, the transmission of values from one generation to the next, the protection of a way of life from global homogenization. Partly in the name of such values, democratic governments have placed certain restrictions on market forces and individual behaviour – from laws against the possession of child pornography, to content quotas in Canadian and European broadcasting to ensure 'shelf space' for domestic productions.

Finally, note that the Charter speaks in the explicitly anti-postmodernist language of universalism. Hamelink (1995: 28) argues for the defence of human rights as the 'universally valid principle' to guide media democratization. There is a faint genuflection to moral relativism in the Charter's cultural identity clause (8), but it is immediately qualified by the proviso that such protection 'should not violate other human rights'. At least in principle, media democracy activists seem to be willing not merely to critique and challenge hegemonic media but to reconstitute public communication (and potentially much else) on the basis of values that they broadly share, that they consider to be universally applicable, and that (notwithstanding differences of strategy and vantage point) collectively distinguish them from their opponents. That is a powerful reason to consider progressive media democratization a potentially coherent social movement.

Locating democratic media activism

Social solidarity and community, egalitarian social change, individual freedom from state or corporate power – to varying degrees, these are core values of progressive media activism. They may coexist uneasily, yet surely no more so than those of the currently hegemonic Right, which has nevertheless been able to bring social conservatives and market liberals, libertarians and theocrats, into the same political tent.

Where does democratic media activism 'fit' in relation to the market liberal, public sphere, and radical democratic perspectives on media and democracy discussed above?

In using the language of human rights, as well as other broadly legitimized concepts such as fairness, balance and diversity, communicative democrats situate themselves within the ideologically hegemonic tradition of liberalism, avoiding the instant marginalization that would greet anarchism, Marxism or other revolutionary discourses. With the collapse of Communism and the hegemony of market liberalism during the last two decades, the Western Left largely abandoned socialism and Marxism as counterhegemonic challenges to capitalism, and (unevenly) took up the defence of actually existing democracy against the encroachments of capital. Many of the themes expressed in media reform conference panels and manifestos, and in our interviews, resonate with public sphere liberalism – accountable government, access to information, citizen-relevant programming, an informed and engaged citizenry, the public service ethos in broadcasting and other media, and the critique of fragmentation and infotainment.

At the same time, democratic media activism often entails pushing liberal democracy to live up to its stated claims, and sometimes points beyond them – not just at the level of ideas but in terms of the logic of struggle. The defence of popular self-government, in the media and other fields, now implies a challenge to capital – and it is that challenge which makes democratic activism radical. Radical democrats might sign on to many liberal themes, including those of the public sphere, but their actions as well as their manifestos problematize the liberal assumptions about power, rationality and the potential for consensus which underlie it. Radical media democrats highlight direct and widespread citizen participation in producing media, the support (but not subordination) of media to progressive social movements as agents of social justice and democratic renewal, and especially, social, cultural and economic equality outside the media field as corequisites of democratized communication.

The relationship of democratic media activism to conservatism (including market liberalism) is a little more complicated. For the most part, the neoliberal and socially conservative Right is the 'other' against which progressives mobilize. Market liberalism in particular is the chief ideological weapon for attacking public broadcasting, for leaving corporate media giants unrestrained by public interest regulation, for most of the very democratic deficiencies which have catalysed media activism.

And yet – the conservative camp is not a monolithic, reactionary mass. On a number of communications issues, democratic media reformers and different stripes of conservatives could well find overlapping interests if not a common cause. Social conservatives often oppose excessive media commercialism and the consequent intellectual and moral vacuity of so much media fare – 'the raw sewage, the ultraviolence, the graphic sex, the raunchy language that is flooding their living rooms day and night', in the words of conservative media activist Brent Bozell (cited in McChesney 2004: 280). Libertarians, defending civil liberties and individual freedom vis-à-vis the state, would generally oppose official censorship. Many conservatives as well as progressives lament the loss of local ownership and programming, as conglomerates like ClearChannel homogenize the airwaves. Even market liberals generally favour competition in media industries, however reluctant they may be to endorse state action against monopolies. Many of these factors motivated thousands of American conservatives to join the populist campaign against the FCC's media ownership rule changes in 2003 (McChesney 2004: 280–1).

At the same time, there is an irreducible distinction between media politics of the left and right. As two of the Free Press co-founders note, 'conservative critics, in the end, are handcuffed by their allegiance to the maintenance of corporate and commercial rule, so they are incapable of providing real explanations for, and real solutions to, the problems they describe' (Nichols and McChesney 2000: 109–10). At conferences and in interviews, we heard broad support for policy principles that would be anathema to most market liberals and many social conservatives – increased subsidies and autonomy for public broadcasting and for independent and community media, more taxation and public interest regulation of large media corporations, 'common carrier' and 'open architecture' principles in developing new communications technology (notably broadband and the convergence of broadcasting, cable and internet), opposition not only to government authoritarianism and censorship but also to corporate enclosures of knowledge.

It is possible to see media democratization not only as a coherent movement but also as prefiguring a new paradigm of public communication. It comprises efforts to change media messages, practices, institutions and contexts, including state communication policies, in a direction which enhances (rather than contains) participation and equality (rather than hierarchy and exclusion), and helps to build a social order which nurtures the autonomy of individuals and their 'developmental power' (Macpherson 1977). For Jakubowicz (1993: 41), a core principle of democratic public communication is the ability of each segment of society 'to introduce ideas, symbols, information, and elements of culture into social circulation' so as to reach all other segments of society. Social theorist Robert White (1995) defines it similarly, as the institutional organization of public communication so as to enable all individuals to actively participate in constructing public cultural truth.

These principles entail the intertwined projects of both democratization *of* and *through* the media – expanding the range of voices accessed through the media, building an egalitarian public sphere, promoting the values and practices of sustainable democracy, and offsetting or even counteracting political and economic inequalities found in other fields (Hackett 2000: 65). Social movements, especially the struggles of subaltern communities, are arguably the backbone of media democratization. Having sketched it ideologically, in the next two chapters we attempt to situate it historically, and consider the evolution of two of the most important media democracy advocacy groups in the US and UK.

5 The long revolution and the Media Alliance

How does media activism in the North Atlantic compare, in terms of ideological orientation and social support, with previous struggles? Under what historical conditions is such activism likely to arise, and to succeed? How does it relate to the trajectory of social movements? Does it make sense to think of different historical 'waves' of communicative democracy as part of a single tide, or are they irreducibly unique?

We cannot do full justice to these issues here, but we can selectively draw lessons from overviews of long-term historical trends, especially several waves of media activism in the past four decades. We then outline the trajectory of two of the longest-standing organizations promoting more democratic media in the US and UK, in this chapter and the next, respectively.

The long, unfinished revolution

British communications historian Raymond Williams described the contradictory cultural consequences of industrialization, including the growth of a reading public, as a 'long revolution' (Macey 2000: 399; Williams 1961). The democratization of politics and culture has also been described as an 'unfinished revolution' (Tehranian and Tehranian 1995: 38–9). It is both.

The Tehranians regard democratization as a series of bottom-up responses to mainly top-down processes of modernization, defined as 'an accumulative process of accelerating change achieved by successive applications of scientific and technological knowledge' (p. 46). Sweeping over ten thousand years since the agrarian revolution, the authors define a series of accelerating waves of change or 'tsunamis', each associated with interacting territorial spatialization, economic and political systems, technologies, ideologies and communications institutions and elites. Always uneven and never linear, these phases of democratization include the spread of ideas of freedom, equality and community on the wings of universalist and egalitarian religions; the spread of individuation and secularization following the Renaissance; the liberal-democratic revolutions in England, the US and France by the end of the 1700s; the resistance of a revolutionary working class within and against the capitalist imperial heartlands of the nineteenth century; the post-1945 Third World independence movements; and in the contemporary post-

Cold War period, resurgent particularist ethnic, religious, and tribal loyalties challenging 'the authority of the existing state systems' (p. 62).

At each stage of modernization and democratization, technologies, elites and institutions of communication played a 'pivotal' role (p. 48), in reinforcing or challenging established power, and in expanding and transforming its spatial dimensions, from city-states to industrial empires to planet. The Greek Agora, the Gutenberg Bible, the printed pamphlets of revolutionary liberals like Thomas Paine, the subsidized distribution of newspapers by the post office during the early American republic (McChesney 2004: 33–4), the electrification (telegraph, telephone) and mass circulation of information which facilitated mass movements in Europe and Asia challenging the imperial systems – all these show that the process of democratization *through* the media has a long historical pedigree, one that is hardly exclusive to Western liberal democracy.

What about democratization *of* the media? We should not overrate the autonomy and power of the communications field, but the transition from one communications technology (and its associated elites) to another may well yield a broadening of the society's collective conversation – breaking older elites' former 'monopoly of knowledge' (Innis 1951: 3–32). Such transitions create potential openings for other social and political forces to re-structure the communications field. The internet's destabilizing impact on previously established technologies and regulatory regimes may be such a critical juncture (Mueller *et al.* 2004). Other forms of crisis in the existing media or political system may also generate widespread questioning of established policies (McChesney 2004: 24). Public engagement with media issues is likely to be higher at such potentially democratizing moments.

Yet history also teaches us patience. Neither Berlin walls nor global media behemoths are toppled every day. Critical junctures are not always present, but seemingly marginal activism can contribute to subterranean cultural shifts, even if the results are not visible for generations. Thus, socialist newspapers in the nineteenth century paved the way for labour rights and social security programmes in the twentieth (Downing *et al.* 2001: 148–9). Moreover, the pace of historical change – the sequence of tsunamis – is accelerating exponentially. For some, this gives hope that not only communicative democracy but also counterhegemonic challenges to corporate rule may be achievable sooner than expected, even in an era of seemingly irresistible global pan-capitalism. Moreover, if the political opportunity for media democratization climaxes at critical junctures of disruption, then this helps explain the current absence of mass involvement in media activism. The historians' accounts are cause for optimism, not defeatism. They suggest repeatedly the courage and persistence of human demands to receive and share ideas, and to participate in collective dialogue – from the sixteenth-century European printers and vendors of 'heretical' books who faced 'severe or terminal' punishment by the authorities (Downing *et al.* 2001: 145), to the twentieth-century *samizdat* publishers in the Soviet Union.

Perhaps history's most important lesson about oppositional and transformative communication is its connection, structurally, with social movements and, historically, with upsurges in broader 'cycles of protest' (Tarrow 1989) and even political revolutions throughout the modern era. Consider alternative media as vehicles for subaltern public spheres and potentially broader challenges to hegemony. Such media are most effective politically when they fuel, and are fuelled by, the energies of social movements. From hundreds of possible examples, we can highlight the roles played by alternative media in challenging the crustacean dictatorships of the former Soviet bloc. In Poland, for example, underground publications helped create an alliance between dissident intellectuals and industrial workers in the late 1970s, contributing to the growth of Solidarnosc, the largest mass opposition movement in eastern Europe prior to the 1989 collapse of Soviet-style communism (Downing *et al.* 2001: 368–83).

Journalist/activist and theorist Michael Traber (1993) links demands for participatory communication and the expansion of communication rights with political revolution, when typically people's stories, actions and protests are especially prominent in popular communication (and often repressed in dominant or official media). Traber identifies three such waves of change in the era of modernity. The eighteenth-century middle-class revolutions in France and America established the democratic rights of the individual vis-à-vis despotic government. The early-twentieth-century socialist upheavals in Mexico and Russia posited a second generation of human rights in which the state has in principle a positive role in promoting citizens' well-being. Though these revolutions in practice produced prolonged one-party rule, especially brutal in Russia, such innovations as the 'right to information' clause in the Mexican constitution of 1917 arguably symbolized new conceptions: of the state as a resource, not simply a constraint, vis-à-vis communication rights; of the need to overcome economic as well as governmental constraints on free expression; and of collective communication rights, whereby popular social groups, not just individuals, are ensured access to public communication. Traber's third wave of human rights derives from the postwar Third World anti-colonial struggles, which proclaimed the political self-determination of peoples, equality among races and cultures, equal status of nations at the international level, and ultimately 'a duty to place common human interests before national and individual interest' (Traber 1993: 25).

All three aspects of communication rights – individual expression, access to the means of communication, and responsibility in relation to global social justice – have left a legacy in contemporary media activism, as we suggested in Chapter 4.

While these historical accounts imply the interdependence of communication democratization, and broader political struggles, the substantive meanings and priorities of 'democratization' vary with historical and cultural contexts. For example, the introduction of market relations in feudal Europe or the former Soviet Union could certainly help break up the erstwhile economic monopolies of landowning elites or state-entrenched bureaucracies, empower consumers in new ways, and provide a material basis for expanded political participation. But in the contemporary capitalist global order, the further intensification of market relations to new areas of social life can further entrench inequalities, and undermine diversity and indigenous cultures.

Conversely, the 'content' of repression is also context-dependent. Certain cultural forms considered regressive by contemporary standards of gender equality, were once engines of subversion. In a sweeping history of radical media as embodiments of subaltern public spheres, Downing *et al.* (2001: 146) instance the use of printed pornography in pre-revolutionary France as a weapon to ridicule the high and mighty. Similarly, history challenges the stereotype of politicized religion as homophobic, national chauvinist, patriarchal, fundamentalist, divisive, exclusionary and repressive. While such reactionary forms may currently predominate, mass-mediated religion has sometimes been the medium of progressive protest, and a force for the expansion of political and communication rights – from Martin Luther's use of the printing press to challenge the Catholic Church hierarchy in the 1520s, to Martin Luther King's riveting televised 'I have a dream' speech in the 1960s.

Contemporary media activism[1]

Clearly, communicative democratization assumes a variety of forms and histories, so diverse and wedded to broader political projects that considered globally, it may not constitute a coherent 'field' in the sense that Bourdieu applies to journalism and media. Still, whether or not they comprise a field, it is useful briefly to scan the globe for major waves of media democratization during the past four decades, as summarized in Table 5.1, in order to help situate recent democratic media activism in the North Atlantic.

The Sixties

The social unrest now known iconically as 'the Sixties' spawned waves of democratization through and of the media, in the heartland of global capitalism – western Europe and North America. Challenges to the narrow discourse of dominant media grew organically from the youth 'counterculture' and the new social movements of the period. Socialist and nationalist revolutions in the Third World influenced the North Atlantic's political climate, giving the Left a sense of having history on its side. Segregation and the Vietnam war provoked mass protest in the 1960s; less drastically, the Watergate scandal in 1973 opened a window for political reform.

The energies of social movements impacted the media field in at least two directions. First, alternative media, especially the 'underground press', mushroomed, expressing the political and cultural alienation of middle-class youth. Second, a system-oriented media reform movement emerged from and alongside other movements of the civil rights era: 'Minorities, women, children's advocates, seniors, organized labor, education advocates, and gays and lesbians, in coalition and separately, identified mass media policy as a site of struggle for equity and access' (Aufderheide 1999: 18–19).

Within the civil rights movement, the United Church of Christ's struggle against racist-held broadcasting licences set a key precedent in gaining legal standing for public interest groups vis-à-vis the FCC in 1966. In Washington, public interest

Table 5.1 Waves of media democratization, 1965–2005

Wave	*Social/political impetus*	*Target/opponent*	*Contribution to media democratization*
'The Sixties' (mid 1960s– early 1970s)	New Left, counter-culture, national liberation, new social movements	The 'Establishment', war, racism, social conformity	Enhanced reflexivity – spurring critiques of media content; proliferation of independent media
Movement for a New World Information & Communication Order – NWICO (1970s)	Third World post-colonial struggles conducted at levels of states and movements; development of alternative and grassroots communication forms	North–South disparities in media and imbalances in content and flow; imperialist threats to information sovereignty; commodification of information	Despite defeat institutionally, the staking of claims for cultural sovereignty in postcolonial contexts and for participatory communication in the lifeworld
Neoliberal reaction: right-wing media activism (since 1980s)	Consolidation of the New Right: growth of neoliberal think tanks and right-wing media monitoring	'Left-liberal' media bias and the state's provision and regulation of media	Significant policy victories, widening the democratic deficit via deregulation and liberalization of public communication
Post-Communist media reform (since 1990)	Transition from Soviet-style to liberal regimes via democratization from below, elite-engineered reforms and outside pressure	Statist authoritarianism and the absence of rights-based legal frameworks for public communication	Currently unclear: possible recovery of civil societies and public spheres
Democratic Media Activism comes of age (since 1990s)	Digitization and convergence of media technologies, spurring both neoliberal globalization and globalization from below; escalating media concentration and commercializa-tion; emergence of transnational progressive networks and policy advocacy vis-à-vis digital media	Media's democratic deficit in its various manifestations; the neoliberal regime of global media governance	Proliferation of independent media, internet activism, media education and culture jamming; emergence of a media reform movement, internationally and especially in the US

groups advocated during the 1970s 'on behalf of consumer price and quality issues, expansion of the range of expression in media, encouragement of [consumer] access to media, and ... of the development of new uses of technology' (Aufderheide 1999: 19).

The achievements of this wave of media democratization were modest. The liberal media reformers 'marginally extended the gains of civil rights and related social movements', and institutionalized some of their cultural and social norms (Mueller *et al.* 2004: 47, 64). US television networks conceded modest changes in programming, but they also turned advocacy group pressure into a self-protective form of feedback (Montgomery 1989: 217). Media reformers' success in moving beyond content issues to transform the economic and regulatory framework of media was 'much more limited' (Mueller *et al.* 2004: 47). The conservative hegemony of the Reagan years and the waning of the Sixties' movements left Washington-based reformers without much leverage within the system.

As for the more radical and grassroots forms of media activism, they often exhibited a McLuhanesque overconfidence in the emancipatory potential of 'hand held media' (Halleck 2002), and in the capacity of activists to manipulate the dominant media. Media attention to black civil rights, the anarchistic Yippies, and the Greenpeace environmentalists (Dale 1996) initially seemed to validate such optimism. Only in retrospect were the destructive dynamics of the anti-war student-based US New Left's dependence on corporate media evident (Gitlin 1980).

By contrast with the US, the new social movements overlapped with a surge of working class militancy, catalysed by economic problems and often inspired by socialist ideals, in Quebec, the UK and western Europe. In Italy, the re-energized Left spawned a daily newspaper and radio stations; in Portugal, radical media helped spark an anti-fascist revolution in 1974–5 (Downing *et al.* 2001). Labour radicalism and the youthful 'new' movements occasionally converged, as in the May 1968 upheaval in France, and in the Quebec independence movement; but often their respective 'materialist' and 'post-materialist' values, though overstated by new social movement theorists, yielded divergent political sensibilities. As we see in Chapter 6, union and socialist militancy generated a distinct form of media activism in the UK, focused squarely on radical democratic structural media reform.

The New World Information and Communication Order

Playing out in the 1970s and 1980s, NWICO was integral to the third revolution described by Traber: Third World postcolonial struggles for independence and development. Indeed, the demand of Third World governments via the UN for a New World Economic Order, characterized by more favourable terms of international trade, helped spawn NWICO in the mid 1970s. Its culminating document was the MacBride Report (International Commission for the Study of Communication Problems 1980), which Carlos Valle (1995: 205–10) argues sought a response to five global problems: the excessive commodification of information; the huge gap between North and South in the distribution and control of communications media and technology; imbalances in the flow of information and media content between North and South; threats to various countries' information sovereignty through such foreign interference as transnational corporate control over data; and the development of grassroots or alternative communication forms, as tools for popular education, expression, and mobilization. Thus, NWICO expressed two potentially contradictory aspects of democratization: cultural and communicative sovereignty for postcolonial countries (a 'system' or state-centred concept, but arguably also a prerequisite for meaningful democracy within a nation), and participatory communication in the lifeworld, to empower citizens within states, a thrust more akin to radical democracy (Zhao and Hackett 2005: 13).

NWICO's impetus was similarly bifurcated. The official NWICO debate was conducted at the level of state and interstate institutions, where it was decisively defeated by the intransigent hostility of the US (Reagan) and UK (Thatcher) governments, and their corporate media allies. But NWICO was arguably also 'a people's movement' involving a wide range of grassroots actors and communicative forms, from Latin American workers' radio to Indian popular theatre, in addition to government policymakers (White 1988).

Right-wing reaction

By the 1980s, smarting from various cultural and political insults – progressive reformers, rebellious youth, victorious Vietnamese – the American Right had marshalled a counterattack. Its ideological diversity was noted in Chapter 4. Bringing together cultural/religious, economic (market liberal) and nationalist (America First) conservatives into a hegemonic project, it articulated a hostility to perceived 'left liberal bias' in the media, and waged campaigns against 'indecent' rock lyrics, sex and violence in prime-time television, and alleged anti-business bias in the news. The Right has employed media monitoring organizations, more confrontational tactics like boycotting advertisers (Mueller *et al.* 2004: 55), and heavy investment in setting up its own propaganda infrastructure, particularly policy institutes and broadcasting outlets. The conservatives' most significant victories have come in the policy field, where market liberal intellectuals and institutes, allied with industry interests, have provided the vision and models for deregulation and liberalization in telecommunications, broadcasting and cable (Mueller *et al.* 2004: 56–62).

From the public sphere liberal and radical democratic perspectives, the Right typically seeks to intensify the democratic deficit, and left-leaning media watchdogs like FAIR vie for influence with their right-wing counterparts. Yet, as we noted in Chapter 4, Right and Left may also sometimes find common foes in the media field, from commercial schlock to entrenched monopolies.

Post-Communist media reform

The collapse of the Soviet system after 1989 sparked another wave of media democratization – media reform, in conjunction with political and legal liberalization, in societies in transition from authoritarian to more nominally democratic forms (Price *et al.* 2002). This wave has combined democratization from below (popular movements like Poland's Solidarnosc, as well as journalists and other cultural producers yearning for freedom of expression), from above (liberal elements within the previous regime, most famously Mikhail Gorbachev), and from outside (Western NGOs, experts and media organizations). Whether such reform has been effective and whether it is a springboard toward a vibrant civil society, rather than incorporation into a globalized, de-politicized consumer culture, are debatable questions. It may be less about democratization, in the radical democratic sense of popular sovereignty and participation, and more about liberalization, the regularization of media laws and individual (and corporate) rights of expression vis-à-vis state repression. And even that project is hardly secured, as Vladimir Putin's Russia backslides towards earlier practices, and China finds ways to combine modest media liberalization and commercialization with one-party rule – market authoritarianism (Zhao 2005). But generalizations are difficult and nuances abound. Even in Western efforts to promote reform in the transition societies, there is competition between American-style commercial (market liberal) and European-style public sphere models of broadcasting (Zhao and Hackett 2005: 16).

DMA in the internet era

This book, however, is mainly concerned with aspects of the fifth wave of media activism which has been gathering steam since the 1990s. Described briefly in Chapter 1, it derives partly from the first wave noted above – labour and the new social movements of the 'Sixties'. But it has been stimulated by the new conditions of the past decade.

First, the digitalization and convergence of media technology which fuelled the accelerating process of globalization has also generated new opportunities for democratization *through* the media (such as transnational communication channels for social movements like the Zapatistas, noted in Chapter 3), and new incentives for democratization *of* the media, as computers and the internet bring new policy issues to the fore. In the US, advocacy groups concerned with the governance of digital media began forming and surfacing at the national level in the 1980s, engaging in policy battles around encryption (privacy protection vs. government surveillance), censorship and content regulation on the internet, and intellectual property rights – such as trademarks and internet domain names, the online sharing of copyrighted entertainment content, and software patents and the 'open source' principle (Mueller *et al.* 2004: 74). Such activism arguably reflects 'a new epistemic community' of technologues, infused with a libertarian ethic which sometimes contradicts the regulatory impulses of earlier liberal media reformers (Mueller *et al.* 2004: 64). But, more importantly, it has helped diversify the agenda of public interest advocacy on communications policy in the US. Advocacy organized around problematizing media messages, the overwhelmingly dominant focus in the 1970s and 1980s, has been increasingly supplemented by advocacy for individual communication rights (privacy, fair use and so on), and attempts to influence the political economy of media (market regulation, media concentration, subsidies) (Mueller *et al.* 2004: 11, 28).

Second, something of the spirit of MacBride is returning. Historically, the First and Third Worlds are mutually constitutive, most dramatically in the repressed historical reality of slavery's role in Western development. Yet with some exceptions (Halleck 2002: 73), NWICO's calls in the 1980s for a global communications regime change found few public advocates in the North, and an asymmetrical cultural divide between movements in the North and South was still quite evident when the CEM was publicly launched as a national coalition in the US in 1996 (Tomaselli 1999). In the meantime, an emergent neoliberal regime of global media governance has become increasingly entrenched. Supranational institutions and agreements, like the WTO and NAFTA, have assumed a greater role relative to national governments in setting policy frameworks; and notions of public service and public access are giving way to market logic and the interests of transnational corporations (Zhao and Hackett 2005: 8). But there are signs in recent years of challenges to that regime, from transnational advocacy networks and NGOs with roots in civil society and local media activism – for example, the World Association of Community Radio Broadcasters (AMARC), the Association for Progressive Communications (APC), the now-defunct Videazimut, the World Association for Christian Communication (WACC) and the Campaign for Communication Rights in the Information Society (CRIS), which seeks civil society participation in international standard-setting and policymaking bodies (Ó Siochrú 2005b: 292).

Third, such transnational networks have been paralleled at the national level since the 1990s by efforts to build broad progressive coalitions like Free Press, focused specifically on media reform. While the issue agenda for communications advocacy has arguably expanded considerably since the Sixties wave, many of the activists we interviewed confirmed that the question of the content and control over society's means of symbolic production – the means of public communication – are still at the heart of what motivates people to engage with the media field as a political problem. And while global media governance has acquired greater importance, local communities and national governments still constitute the prime locus for media activism in the US and UK.

The expanding agenda, transnational links, and the forging of media reform coalitions, suggest that media democratization has broadened and matured as a sustained collective project. In the rest of this chapter, we consider the trajectory of one key American component in that project.

Media Alliance[2]

In its 7 January 2002 cover story on media reform, the respected progressive periodical *The Nation* recognized Media Alliance in San Francisco (now Oakland) as one of several 'crucial organizations' for building media democracy in the US (McChesney and Nichols 2002b). The seed from which this non-profit media advocacy group sprouted was the post-Watergate generation of journalists, against the backdrop of a high tide of liberal reformism in American politics. The tumult of the Vietnam war era had receded following the withdrawal of US troops, but the movements which it had engendered were impacting the State machinery. Lawmakers and courts were moving forward on environmental protection, reproductive rights, women's equality and other issues. Buoyed by the liberal zeitgeist but frustrated by the conservative disposition of mainstream media, about 50 journalists began meeting in 1975–6 to socialize and discuss media and political issues (Wolschon 1996). Larry Bensky describes his fellow founding members as journalists, especially freelancers but also many employed in both corporate and alternative media, people dissatisfied with corporate media coverage of events in the Bay Area (like the Vietnam war and the anti-war movement), and hoping to change that. After months of debate, the Alliance adopted a mandate to 'support, in all ways necessary, media workers faced with attacks on their human, constitutional, and professional rights and obligations' (Wolschon 1996).

By contrast with its more recent history, the original Media Alliance began as an organization of 'insiders', albeit marginalized ones – people involved in news production, but hardly at its apex. Moreover, while critical of the performance of the corporate media, it was then the Alliance's main field of action – something potentially reformable, and from within. A not unusual view at the time; after all, hadn't Bob Woodward and Carl Bernstein, the *Washington Post*'s celebrated investigative journalists, brought down the corrupt presidency of Richard Nixon?

As a geographical and cultural context, the vibrancy and creativity of the San Francisco Bay area has been fertile ground for movements and media activism. The Bay Area's assets include its rich cultural diversity, with large populations of Asian, Latin American and African as well as European descent, and its large and politically active gay community. (Gays have unquestionably contributed to the city's diversity and social liberalism, but relatively little directly to media activism. Tracy Rosenberg, a former MA staffer, suggests that gays' economic and political success in the city grants them access to dominant media not available to other minorities; and moreover, their main battles are in the legal and political rather than media fields, over such issues as property rights, same-sex marriage, and employment discrimination.)

Notwithstanding the conservatism of city authorities in some respects (vis-à-vis the homeless, for example: Edmondson 2000), the city is known for its relatively strong popular traditions of labour militancy, progressive politics, and cultural innovation. Venues like City Lights Bookstore still manifest the heritage of both the 1950s Beatnik poets, and the youthful counterculture's 'summer of love' a decade later. 'That whole people's cultural movement is still really strong here', contends Dorothy Kidd of the University of San Francisco, and in addition, the city is near the Hollywood 'dream machines', with an infrastructure for film and video production. Moreover, she points out, nearby Silicon Valley has brought expertise and capital to build the computer, software and multi-media industries. (Among its many effects, the dot.com boom during the 1990s fuelled enrolment in the Media Alliance's computing skills courses, which in turn helped cross-subsidize its advocacy work.) These rich media production capacities and oppositional popular traditions – the first and second 'circles' in the potential constituency for media democratization, described in Figure 3.1 – have combined to increase awareness of, and activism against, the commercial media's 'blockade' of the distribution of diverse and progressive media. The density of media-savvy advocacy groups by the 1990s in the Bay Area has provided a fertile organizational ecology for networking. And the reputed mediocrity of the San Francisco daily papers (the *Chronicle* and *Examiner* have nothing like the stature of the New York or Los Angeles *Times*), contrasted with the global image of the city, provide a paradox to mobilize around.

What is impressive and distinctive about Media Alliance itself? It is not so much institutionalized and permanent successes in the media field, which few progressive advocacy groups can claim in the past generation of neoliberal hegemony. Rather, what distinguishes the Media Alliance are two characteristics.

First, its sheer longevity, its organizational growth and survival. By contrast with industry and professional associations, which by definition have an economic base for their advocacy work, public interest groups organized around political ideas have a precarious existence. Moreover, compared to their industry counterparts in the media field, public interest advocacy groups have been more prone to dying off rather than adapting their mandates or merging with other groups in response to a shifting political environment (Mueller *et al.* 2004: 28, 52). Bucking this dismal tradition, Media Alliance has now survived three decades. A key to its initial growth and long-term survival has been its provision of exclusive or discounted services and benefits to its members, thus minimizing the 'free rider' problem facing many public interest groups. These benefits include access to health and dental insurance (a significant draw in the US, where a profit-oriented medical system leaves millions of citizens uninsured), a credit union, a job-listing service, and discounts on journalism and computer skills classes and computer rentals. And the chance to join the MA softball and volleyball teams!

With such incentives, membership reached about 4,000 at one point in the 1990s; member fees, along with course tuition, enabled MA to generate 75 to 85 per cent of its half-million dollar average annual budget internally, with the rest deriving from external project grants and donations. (In the late 1990s, membership was restructured to distinguish between a basic category, and those paying more for access to MA's benefits and services.) In effect, that benefit-driven internal revenue stream has reduced MA's vulnerability to the vagaries of foundation funding, and has cross-subsidized MA's political work, enough to hire a staff of ten (four of them part-time) as of 2001, headed by an executive director accountable to a Board – a standard pattern for US non-profit advocacy groups, with the commendable (and, as became clear in 1996, fateful) exception that the Board is elected by the membership.

MA's second notable achievement is its linkage of different constituencies and tasks in concrete steps towards media democratization. Over the years, it has provided a social as well as a political outlet for journalists; it has enjoyed the support both of freelance journalists and those employed by media corporations; it has combined training for the media with critique of the media; in later years, it has coalesced different ethnic communities in common cause; and it has worked in different venues and with a range of tactics, from nonviolent civil disobedience to interventions at policy hearings. It does not fit easily inside the strategic quadrants that we identified in Table 3.2. At the same time, as we shall see, there are still limits to how far such boundary-crossing can go.

The MA's roots in the muckraking, you-can-beat-city-hall optimism of 1970s journalism are evident in the pages of *MediaFile*, the newsletter which MA has produced with only occasional interruptions since 1978. Its headlines in the first fifteen years read much like a progressive journalism review: political and ethical issues facing journalism (censorship, source confidentiality); critical analyses of corporate media coverage of city and state politics, of minority rights, of movements and their issues (nuclear disarmament and Central America in the 1980s, the 1991 Gulf War); occasional surveys of local, minority, independent, alternative, movement, gay, and ethnic media, ranging from the laudatory to the sympathetically critical; some attention to regulatory and legislative issues affecting news media (freedom of information versus national security, deregulation of radio and cable, even Unesco's NWICO debate); profiles of the winners of the annual Media Alliance Meritorious Achievement (MAMA) awards; financial, legal and technological developments affecting Bay Area journalists and their rights, particularly freelancers, along with occasional professional advice.

Building in the 1980s

The Alliance's campaigns during the 1980s were, for the most part, activities that progressive-minded journalists could endorse without compromising their occupational self-image as independent truth-seekers. During its very first year, MA voted overwhelmingly to support Newspaper Guild and Typographical Union workers, striking at the weekly *San Francisco Bay Guardian* for guarantees against job losses due to the use of freelance material. *Guardian* editor and publisher Bruce Brugmann defeated the strike, but the solidarity effort defined MA as a political entity, united MA members, and attracted many of the strikers to its ranks (Wolschon 1996). (Interestingly, Brugmann and MA became allies vis-à-vis the corporate dailies in later years.) In 1994, MA staff, board and members again walked picket lines, this time in active support of striking workers at the two San Francisco dailies. As if to balance the ledger between freelancers and employees, MA successfully negotiated a contract with Pacific News Service in 1978, setting fees and freelance rights for PNS contributors – reputedly the first such agreement between a freelance group and a news organization.

In 1979, MA united in a long, hard legal battle on behalf of two of its own. As a result of their 1976 investigative articles on a 1972 Chinatown murder, freelancer Lowell Bergman and *Examiner* reporter Raul Ramirez were sued for $30 million by a former district attorney and two police detectives. The *Examiner* refused to provide the pair with legal counsel. MA members responded with a defence committee which raised $60,000 in legal fees until the pair's exoneration in California Supreme Court in 1986. Commented Ramirez of the ordeal, 'Individuals are powerless; you have no idea how energizing, inspiring and encouraging it was to have a group of people standing behind you' (Wolschon 1996).

By contrast with such solidarity, a 1981 controversy over the journalistic ethics of *MediaFile* itself foreshadowed how bitter internal disputes could become. In a debate over a story on prisoners' rights, a letter to *MediaFile* by the story's two authors betrayed confidential, and potentially life-threatening, information that had been supplied to them by a source. The source, Eve Pell, happened to be then-president of the MA board. *MediaFile* readers responded with a stream of letters, some questioning the editor's judgement in publishing the exchange, culminating in his resignation and an apology from MA staff. MA's executive director later commented that the controversy was 'a shock', a case of 'devour[ing] your young' (Wolschon 1996).

Nevertheless, during the 1980s, a burgeoning Media Alliance moved quarters to historic Fort Mason overlooking the Bay, created internal committees, launched its JobFile system and computer classes, and published a directory of local news media, a valuable tool for community and advocacy groups. It initiated the annual MAMA awards, intended to recognize both social responsibility and outstanding achievement in Bay Area journalism. While they drained MA's resources until their abandonment after 1994, they could be seen as a means of attracting mainstream journalists' interest, and influencing media performance. Throughout its history, the Alliance has also hosted panels and forums relevant to journalism, from skills (for example, 'Writing and editing for online publications') to the politics of media ('Smoking out the truth: The CIA, drugs, and media coverage'). Presciently, the MA helped mount a Media and Democracy conference in 1992, with keynote speaker Ralph Nader, and analyses of campaign coverage (Wolschon 1996).

During the 1980s, MA's agenda was influenced by the political ascendancy of the 'great communicator', Ronald Reagan, and much of the US media's servility to his reactionary politics ('on bended knee' was how journalist/author Mark Hertsgaard (1989) described the press's relationship with the administration). One of MA's major projects during the 1980s was the Propaganda Analysis Review Project, intended as a media education tool exploring the connection between politics and the manipulation of symbols and ideas. It produced several issues of a magazine, which eventually foundered from funding and mission difficulties; some of its originators feared that an exclusive focus on right-wing propaganda made the magazine itself a propagandist tool of the Left. A second project was the Central America Committee, whose purview later expanded to Latin America and the Caribbean. It undertook critical analyses of mainstream coverage of the region, including US intervention, produced a resource guide for journalists, and attempted with some success to expand the Bay Area media's breadth of opinion and reportage on the region.

So, on the one hand, MA has served the professional and career needs of its members and tried to influence mainstream journalism. On the other hand, it has sought to promote progressive political goals, in the face of North American journalism's waning but still hegemonic 'regime of objectivity' (Hackett and Zhao 1998). Striking a balance was a constant challenge during the first two decades. To be sure, many of MA's founding members, like liberals and rationalists generally, would deny any contradiction: journalism at its best – truth-telling (in the public interest) and democratic governance are mutually supportive. Tell the truth to the people, and it shall set them free. That's the view expressed in the *Bay Guardian*'s summary (on 13 March 1996) of MA's mission: to seek 'excellence, ethics, diversity, and accountability in all aspects of the media, in the interest of peace, justice, and social responsibility' with the goal of a 'free and unfettered flow of information and ideas in order to achieve a democratic and just society'. An unpublished statement of purpose commits MA 'to bringing about a more humane and democratic society by protecting freedom of speech and freedom of the press; by fostering genuine diversity of media voices and perspectives; by holding the media accountable for their impact on society, their hiring practices, and the integrity of their products; by working together with other groups and individuals who share our goals; and by providing services, support, and a sense of community for media workers committed to these goals'. Founding member Ken McEldowney put it simply: 'This was not an organization of dispassionate reporters who sat on the sidelines and wrote stories in the form of Journalism 101. We were concerned about the content of news' (Wolschon 1996).

Even so, MA's direct engagement in overtly political campaigns has been limited by its media-oriented mandate, its concern for political independence, and its tax status as a 'charitable organization': Section 501(c)(3) of the tax code precludes attempting to influence legislation as a 'substantial part' of its activities, or participating at all in campaign activity for or against political candidates. Rather, MA typically analyses biases and blind spots in media coverage of political issues and progressive constituencies – Asian-Americans, gays, refugees and immigrants, the environment, Hispanics, community youth issues. In 1991 the MA served as an information clearing house for members on events related to coverage of the Persian Gulf War. The Alliance has also partnered with community groups to conduct joint projects, typically adding the 'media piece', such as skills training and strategic communication advice. Some collaborative projects have included tours to Cuba for American journalists (with Global Exchange, a human rights organization); a summer internship and training programme for reporters of colour (with Independent Press Association); media training on domestic violence (with community press and legal aid associations); co-sponsorship of events with the Society for Professional Journalists, the National Writers Union, the Film Arts Foundation, the National Lesbian and Gay Journalists Association, and many others. By contrast, MA's links with Bay Area organized labour (apart from journalists' unions) have been minimal, other than through the efforts of individual rank-and-file activists like writer David Bacon, who has served on the MA board. Somewhat by contrast with Britain and Canada, the conservatism of American labour leadership, and the lower rate of unionization in the workforce, has arguably impeded American media activism in general; it has certainly contributed to its distinctive form, with a greater orientation towards the countercultural Left and minority group struggles for equality. Occasionally, MA has assisted other groups, and even helped launch them, by accepting tax-deductible funds on their behalf, saving them the tedious process of acquiring 501(c)(3) tax status. (One relatively recent example is the Bay Area Independent Media Center, which was centred on local community organizing rather than a major anti-globalization action.) Such fiscal sponsorship is 'a way to make friends and alliances', explains a former MA staffer.

While turf issues are more likely to arise than with non-media community groups, the MA has also partnered with other media-related advocacy groups, especially where there is a history of mutual support and complementary expertise. San Francisco's rich organizational ecology has offered many such partners. One example is We Interrupt This Message, a national media strategy and training centre, which former MA staffer Kim Deterline helped launch in 1996. Others include the Independent Press Association, Community Press Consortium, Project Censored, the Center for Improvement and Integrity of Journalism, FAIR, the Public Media Center, and alternative media like Pacific News Service and the *Bay Guardian*.

Transition and renewal in the 1990s

By the 1990s, a decade of conservative hegemony had shifted the political environment to the right. By contrast with its apparent momentum in the 1960s and early 1970s, the US Left had fragmented into factions seemingly more intent on self-expression and identity-assertion than on coalition-building and broad societal transformation (Sanbonmatsu 2004). In the media field, corporate priorities and hypercommercialism were becoming more blatant and seemingly more difficult to challenge from within newsrooms, where the public service ethos was withering (Hallin 2000; McChesney 2004: 87). The post-Watergate generation of journalists, MA's original membership base, had aged; acquiring family responsibilities and career success, they no longer needed the professional and social support of MA (including its renowned 'great parties'). Parties aside, some felt that the organization was losing the fire in its belly and its sense of purpose.

Media Alliance was ripe for renewal. Its critical juncture came in 1996 initially disguised as chaos. In the first contested board election in MA history, seven petition-nominated candidates defeated a board-nominated slate after an acrimonious campaign. Led by Van Jones, a young African-American civil rights lawyer, the reformers promised to energize the Alliance by making it more accessible to the poor and minorities, only to run into a sea of troubles once in office: sour relations between MA's still divided board and staff, a high rate of staff burnout and turnover, and 'a perilous financial situation', according to a 1998 letter from Jones to the membership. After nearly two years of 'miserable frustration and floundering', a new executive director, appointed from within the ranks, took the helm. With an activist sensibility and a consensus approach to administration, Andrea Buffa is widely credited with helping to save MA from self-destruction, and to energize and build an activist-oriented staff. According to Jones, Buffa's leadership 'completed the coup' and 'made it possible for the organization to move in a different direction'. In Jones' view, 'an old boys' club' of 1960s/70s media professionals was transformed into one reflecting MA's younger activist members and more relevant to contemporary media realities – including online and alternative media, as well as 'the monopolization of all media by corporations as a dire problem for democracy'. For Jones, the old guard had failed to grasp how corporate media had become 'an absolute barrier to any kind of social change, whether the issue be homelessness, police issues, whatever'.

Veteran and former members we interviewed are divided on MA's new direction. For some, the outcome was a rediscovery of MA's original sense of mission. For founding member and former *MediaFile* editor Larry Bensky, the shift was both generational and political. It enabled MA to tap the energies of the new hip-hop protest movement, for whom diversity is a serious issue.

For others, the organization has marginalized itself, its critiques no longer to be taken seriously. An editor at the *Chronicle*, and one of MA's founding members, says he drifted away from the organization a few years after it was formed because it had become 'more ideologically driven than craft driven', predictably supporting every radical demand, such as the release of controversially-convicted African American death row inmate Mumia Abu Jammal. Some of these members blame Van Jones personally for an unnecessarily confrontational transition. Even Raul Ramirez, the journalist who had benefited from MA's legal defence fund, observed in *MediaFile* (March/April 2001) that his colleagues think of MA as having 'drifted much farther into the political world than they feel comfortable mingling with', and that MA is no longer the 'vehicle for the internal self-examination of mainstream media'. He attributes this distance to the traditional ethos of objectivity: 'Don't get involved in the story, translated into, "You're not a part of the community."' The further that MA's advocacy extended beyond safeguarding the First Amendment and journalists' rights, the more reluctant that working reporters (and still more their superiors) became to associate with MA's campaigns.

The Alliance's projects, campaigns and tactics since 1996 reflect its more activist and outsider strategy. One indicator was MA's 1996 picketing of the *New York Times*' San Francisco bureau, as part of a national 'Melt the Media Snow Job' campaign to protest dominant media's lack of coverage of alleged links between the CIA and the drug trade. This classic outsider tactic earned the ire of some within the media, like the *San Francisco Weekly*, who might otherwise be sympathetic to MA critiques. In a similar vein, MA brought together media activists from around the country to San Francisco to protest at the 2000 convention of the National Association of Broadcasters, the powerful corporate lobby group.

In 1998, MA campaigned to expose perceived biases in media coverage of Proposition 227, a referendum initiative to abolish bilingual education in California, thus restricting Spanish-speakers' access to public education in their own language. (This policy was one of the alleged violations of language rights adjudicated by the People's Communication Charter's unofficial tribunal at The Hague in 1999: Media Development 1999.) The campaign's goal was to ensure that pro-bilingual voices were not shut out in the media. Andrea Buffa recalls regretfully the difficulty MA had in persuading mainstream media, notably National Public Radio, to participate in its public panels, which NPR officials considered 'biased' because they reflected majority expert opinion in favour of bilingual education. (The referendum passed, but its implementation was delayed by court challenges.)

Media Alliance did not altogether abandon its links with mainstream journalists – for example, it helped organize protests when the *Chronicle* removed one of its few progressive columnists from the op-ed pages in the political aftermath of the 9/11 attacks. But MA's new focus had clearly become training community groups and political activists how to tell their story more effectively, whether through creating their own media or framing messages for the corporate media (though as Buffa conceded, better coverage certainly cannot be guaranteed). Critiques of corporate media coverage were still offered, but were seemingly intended less to encourage mainstream journalists to do better, and more to persuade activists to identify, and strategize against, corporate media bias.

It was, however, a landmark battle within the field of *alternative* media that re-energized the Alliance and encouraged its activists to start redefining it as part of a broader media democracy movement. The campaign centred on resistance to the Pacifica Foundation's crackdown on KPFA in Berkeley, one of the five stations in Pacifica's radio network. We cannot elaborate here the station's half-century history as America's first listener-supported independent station, its distinctive programming with the stated intention of supporting peace, social justice, the labour movement and the arts, and its relatively democratic, participatory and often conflict-laden structure (see Downing *et al.* 2001, Chapter 21). Instead, our story begins with a decision by Pacifica's national board, which legally owned the station and was accountable to no other body. In 1995, the board began to develop and implement a plan to transform Pacifica's programming and operations, for reasons not fully and publicly explained: it may have been an effort to win broader audiences for public service radio, and to address the perceived problem of 'the stranglehold of ... stick-in-the-mud local programmers' over Pacifica's output (Downing *et al.* 2001: 348). Opponents, though, saw it as a kind of corporate coup; for veteran MA member and KPFA broadcaster Larry Bensky, at stake was 'the survival of a unique institution dedicated towards speaking truth to power – free speech radio, non-corporate and democratically and locally controlled'.

Whatever its motives, the board's tactical tools included secrecy, central directives, gag orders, firings and lockouts of staff, and a covert contract with a union-busting organization. Not surprisingly, such tactics met with resentment and resistance within the stations – and among listeners, especially in the Bay Area, where the station had deep roots, and where the confrontation became a crisis in 1998–9. Firings, demonstrations, sit-ins, even an on-air confrontation between a talk-show host and private security guards ensued. A sympathetic student of radical media sees the conflict as another example of the Left's 'self-devouring virus', with the board and local programmers

> locked into position by rival messianic drives, fed by a shared conviction that Pacifica was the single beacon of light in a broadcasting wilderness. Each side

saw itself as a savior and its opposite as the most infuriating and illegitimate of obstacles to survival and success.

(Downing *et al.* 2001: 346, 349)

For Media Alliance, however, the issue was clearcut, and it 'jumped into the leadership role in the campaign', as Andrea Buffa put it,

> organizing everyone from nonprofit organizations to journalist groups to local politicians in a demand that the station be reopened. We did everything. We did civil disobedience at the station, we started a campsite in front of the station, it was operating 24 hours a day. We organized activities at the station every day.

MA also helped organize a march of ten to fifteen thousand people, probably one of the largest protest rallies on a media issue in American history.

By contrast with the outcome at other Pacifica stations, in Berkeley the board eventually backed down, the station remained on the air, and the staff stayed on their jobs. One could argue that the campaign was reactive, that at best it recaptured ground previously held and made no new inroads into the corporate media monolith. But for *MediaFile* editor Ben Clarke, the campaign was a victory, even if it further marginalized MA in the eyes of some mainstream journalists. It 'made people more willing to take risks to defend media democracy' as embodied in workers' rights at a free radio station; and it produced 'a distinctly more engaged staff and membership, a greater visibility and reputation in the community'.

The new century: taking on media reform

MA's new sense of purpose was illustrated not only by the Pacifica struggle, but also by other lifeworld-based projects to claim media space for subaltern groups. A particularly important one was the Raising Our Voices programme, initiated in 1999 to challenge media myths by offering training in media skills to the victims of those myths, particularly the poor and the homeless. According to executive director Jeff Perlstein, the programme, which ran for several years, was 'a strong example of the political agency and engagement that follows from people claiming their voice'.

Notwithstanding MA's new resolve to do battle with corporate media, however, the idea of structural media reform was not yet on MA's radar screen, Andrea Buffa told us in 1998. Although *MediaFile* had kept members abreast of some communications policy issues since the late 1970s, MA had little tradition of actual intervention in state policy processes. But by 2001 Buffa and MA staffers were singing a different tune, however tentatively; and by 2003 'organizing local communities around media policy' was part of MA's public mission statement (Center for International Media Action 2003: 35). By the turn of the century, something resembling a self-defined media reform movement was emerging in America. Microradio activists had succeeded in persuading the FCC to legalize hundreds of outlets, and it took the Republicans' electoral sweep in 2000 to quash that near-victory. More and more activists were making the connection between bad communications legislation, bad media, and bad political outcomes on other issues.

Thus, in 2001, campaigning against corporate giant Clear Channel Communication, Media Alliance explicitly framed the issue as one of media democratization. The campaign centred on the firing of David Cook ('Davey D'), a popular and respected African-American radio talk show host at KMEL in Oakland, part of the 1,200-station radio empire amassed by Clear Channel after the 1996 Telecommunications Act's passage. Davey D's microphone had often been open for social justice groups, and many of them, with little prior interest in media politics, joined MA in the campaign, including civil rights lawyers, the Latino Issues Forum, and youth groups organizing against the city government's plans for a super-jail in the Oakland area. While the immediate goal was Cook's reinstatement, Media Alliance linked the campaign to broader issues: Clear Channel's abuse of its prominent position in Bay Area radio broadcasting, the grave implications of media deregulation and consolidation, and the culture of media silence and complicity engendered by 9/11 (Cook was fired a week after he interviewed Barbara Lee, the only member of Congress to vote against giving the Bush administration carte blanche to invade Afghanistan and launch a 'war against terror'). MA worked against post-9/11 chill in other ways too: a sign-on letter campaign in support of press freedom and diversity, and communications training for anti-war campus groups and for South Asian and other minorities being victimized by media hysteria.

Another campaign, around cable franchises, further enabled Media Alliance to combine community and policy concerns in 2002. The proposed merger of two of America's largest cable companies, AT&T and ComCast, meant that the new post-merger firm would be required legally to renegotiate the contracts with each of the 2,000 municipalities where the two pre-merger companies had franchises. Two Washington DC-based public interest organizations, the Consumer Federation of America and the Center for Digital Democracy, saw in the franchise transfer an opportunity to extract concessions from the cable companies. They identified 80 affected cities for intervention, and supplied logistical and informational support for local advocacy groups, thus reducing their costs of mobilization. In San Francisco, Media Alliance organized a broad coalition that included local advocacy groups and school-based community centres in eight neighbourhoods. Campaign goals included discounted cable rates for seniors and low-income residents, open access to the cable infrastructure for independent service providers, and more resources and channels for community access production and programming. As Jeff Perlstein explains, the campaign strategically presented an opportunity to encourage community activists to expand their repertoire, from alternative media production to policy intervention. It was also a chance to educate the broader public, which is aware of cable TV but generally overlooks the implications of increasing cable company control over broadband and high-speed internet. As the MA website explains, citing the American Civil Liberties Union, in a deregulated monopoly environment,

Not only will [cable] be allowed to charge whatever toll they want, they will be able to discriminate against other ISPs ... cable companies could engage in various forms of discrimination against consumers, from reviewing e-mails to extracting marketing data to slowing down transmission speeds to Web sites that compete against cable-affiliated products. 'An ISP controlled by a politically inclined CEO or board could use the network to promote political positions ...,' the ACLU said. 'It could block or slow access to the Web sites of rival candidates, or redirect users to the preferred candidate's site.'

(www.media-alliance.org; accessed March 2005)

What did the Pacifica, Davey D and cable transfer campaigns have in common? *They all challenged threats to the ability of community activists to disseminate their messages publicly.* As Ben Clarke observed, that threat may be the strongest stimulant for media-related activism.

In sum, Media Alliance's project for its first two decades was system change from within the media field – reforming corporate journalism, through defending media workers' rights, critiquing 'bad' journalism and celebrating the 'good', and training aspiring journalists (including those with little interest in MA's politics).

Since 1996, MA has found its main constituencies amongst those marginalized within the media field and the broader field of power, communities seeking racial and economic justice and an effective public voice. MA is rooted within the lifeworld, with a focus on media production and content, but also increasingly on media policy – an environing condition of media production. In 2002, Jeff Perlstein explained the rationale behind this shift:

In order to achieve systematic change, activist organizations must be willing to do policy work, political lobbying, and broader base-building at the grassroots level, and we have to figure out what the entry points are in the local media policy that can ripple up to national media policy.

He notes that some constituencies who have been 'making their own media' or 'accessing the mainstream media' have not been previously engaged in media policy reform. Accordingly, Media Alliance has been consciously attempting to link strategies:

Those two pieces (alternative media and strategic communication) are really crucial, because what that does is build an understanding on a very gut level around what we mean by changing media policy. You're making your own media, and you find out well, all the great alternative media distribution networks still aren't really getting it out there quite enough just yet. There's still this (structural) barrier ... that we're hitting.

Since 2001, the policy focus has been evident in a steady stream of *MediaFile* features (on FCC proposals, media concentration, telecommunications politics, postal rates for independent magazines, and much else). As it has shifted emphasis away from working with mainstream media workers and towards training the marginalized to create their own media, MA is also paying more attention to the substance and processes of government media policies, mobilizing for interventions in regulatory processes (FCC hearings, industry conventions, cable franchise negotiations) from a public interest perspective. It appears that journalism's objectivity regime may have been a greater impediment to policy engagement than younger activists' distrust of the state and electoral politics.

With varying intensity and at different times, MA has worked within all four of the sectors identified in our schema. Its history illustrates the permeability of the boundaries between the different sectors of media democratization we sketched in Chapter 3, as well as the potential for a particular vector of media democratization – from subaltern communities in the lifeworld, via alternative media or media training, to interventions in media structure and policy. It also shows the integral links between media activism's trajectory, and the energies of broader political currents, particularly those of social movements.

In the next chapter, we consider a British media advocacy group launched at about the same time as MA, one that adopted a politically radical and policy-oriented mandate from the start.

6 Campaigning for press and broadcasting freedom in the UK

As a case study in the politics of media reform, the Campaign for Press and Broadcasting Freedom offers an instructive contrast with the Media Alliance, discussed in Chapter 5.[1] The CPBF is British rather than American, mainly national in scope rather than local, oriented primarily towards influencing state policy more than journalistic or lifeworld practices, and has stronger roots in the labour and socialist movements than in 'new' social movements, journalism or Britain's non-white minorities. What the two organizations do have in common are the wide variety of their actions and issues, the richness of their experience, and their sustained capacity to challenge the media's democratic deficit for nearly three decades. While there are other media reformers in the UK, we focus on the CPBF given its longer history, its relationship to other progressive forces, and its radically democratic intention to reform the media system in fundamental ways.

After a quarter century of neoliberal globalization, it may be difficult to imagine the climate which gave birth to the CPF (Campaign for Press Freedom, as it was originally known) in 1979. In Britain, it was a time of polarization and hope, struggle and crisis, now known as 'the winter of discontent' – industrial militancy by trade unions after a period of wage controls and IMF-imposed government austerity, high inflation and unemployment, declining economic output (Minogue, n.d.) and emerging racial tensions and authoritarian manifestations in popular culture, symbolized by a media- and state-fuelled 'moral panic' over 'mugging' (Hall *et al.* 1978). Yet many on the Left hoped that Britain could lead the Western world in a transition from capitalism to socialism – notwithstanding the defeat that year of James Callaghan's social democratic Labour government by Margaret Thatcher's Conservatives, a sharp shift to the right with hegemonic implications that few foresaw at the time.

Proposals to create the CPF did not emerge from a vacuum; they were preceded by growing interest in, and resolutions about, democratic press reform within the Labour Party and the Trades Union Congress (TUC), Britain's main labour confederation. The CPF itself began to take shape at a March 1979 conference of the Institute of Workers' Control (a radical-democratic concept no longer current, but no less important, in today's context of extraordinary power and mobility for capital). Immediate catalysts were the threat of massive job losses among unionized print and clerical workers as major newspaper corporations introduced new computer-based production technology, as well as 'a vicious propaganda war' by British media against organized labour, especially militant public sector unions, just as corporate interests were mobilizing to elect Thatcher (Richardson and Power 1986: 195). Strategically, the idea was to promote solidarity between media workers and other unions, and to influence the policy platforms of both the Labour Party and the TUC.

The CPF was launched at a union meeting that September, with a founding document that sold 10,000 copies within three months. The bimonthly journal *Free Press* was launched soon afterwards, with an initial circulation of 3,000, peaking at 11,000 in the mid 1980s. The CPF filled an intellectual as well as political gap, as there was little research or 'reforming activity' on press issues at that time (Richardson and Power 1986: 197). In 1982, following some internal debate, and after the disheartening defeat of the newspaper print unions after major dailies abandoned their venerable Fleet Street premises for new high-tech facilities in London's Wapping district, the Campaign added broadcasting to its name and mandate.

As it evolved, and by contrast with the typical US public interest advocacy group with a board and legally incorporated status, the Campaign created an elected National Council, with guaranteed representation for regional and particular interest groups, and a committee to oversee daily management. Notwithstanding its mainly national focus, CPBF developed a regional presence during parts of its history, one appropriate to the importance of regional broadcasting in the UK. During much of the 1980s and '90s, the Campaign had regional organizers and semi-autonomous branches based in such centres as Manchester and Huddersfield in the north of England, and its regional events (such as a public meeting in Leeds on the 1991 Gulf War) were sometimes larger than those in London.

By 1986, in its heyday, the Campaign had over 900 individual members and 472 affiliated organizations, including national trade unions representing 7.5 million workers (Richardson and Power 1986: 197, 208), a staff of five full-time workers, and an annual income of £56,000. Some of these figures, of course, are misleading; the CPBF is an open organization that has been sustained by the work of a few extremely dedicated intellectuals, trade unionists and political activists. Mike Power and the late John Jennings helped keep CPF rooted among print union militants; Jennings overcame scepticism within SOGAT, the print union for which he was communications officer, to obtain office space until CPF acquired its own premises. Media academics James Curran and Tom O'Malley provided intellectual gravitas. With a background in both journalism and socialist activism, Granville Williams has poured prodigious energy into fundraising, public talks, and editing the *Free Press* over the years; some of his colleagues credit him for the Campaign's survival. Media professionals were amongst the CPF's key founders, for instance columnist and later TV producer Anna Coote, National Union of Journalists' (NUJ) activist Mike Jempson, and Aidan White, who became General Secretary of the International Federation of Journalists. Various Labour Party luminaries have also been CPBF activists, including at least two (Dennis MacShane, Michael Meacher) who eventually became cabinet ministers, and several journalists who were or later became Labour MPs.

This account of CPBF's origins suggests several points. As resource mobilization theory predicts, a key to movement formation is to reduce the costs of organizing by accessing existing resources. Though the CPBF has never had active mass support, trade unions, Labour Party ridings, and progressive foundations (like Rowntree), provided staff support, office space, organizational memberships and bulk subscriptions to *Free Press*, thus subsidizing those costs. However, it took motivated individuals ('movement entrepreneurs', to use one of sociology's uglier terms) to obtain and aggregate such resources.

From the viewpoint of Bourdieusian field theory, the CPBF was launched not by thoroughly marginalized social strata but by dissidents on the fringes of the media and political fields – groups with a certain amount of cultural, symbolic, political and even economic capital but who had significant 'issues' with dominant media representations and policies. Indeed, one CPBF National Council member in the early years devoted efforts to building community support, since 'it always seemed top heavy with big names from the media, trades union movement and the academy, and lacked a comfort zone that would persuade more lowly folk it could be for them too'. Arguably, oppositional social movements tend to emerge at the seams between system and lifeworld, establishment and the marginalized, inside and outside.

Goals, commitments and strategies

The Campaign's initial statement of purpose (Curran *et al.* 1986: 241–2) bespeaks a pro-union and socialist orientation, one still reflecting the 'old' Left understanding of social class as the primary axis of domination. The statement calls for fewer legal restrictions on freedom of publication and for more effective mechanisms to redress press bias, but it moves beyond these reformist liberal positions in several ways, including its critiques of the 'myths' of impartiality, objectivity and the equation of press freedom with private ownership. Indeed, the very name of the organization signalled an intention to campaign for rather than against something, and to recuperate the concept of press freedom from its conservative libertarian equation with media owners' autonomy from government. For the Campaign, a society's media freedom could be measured by whether 'the power to communicate is available equally to *all* groups and classes', so that media 'fairly represent the fullest possible range of opinion and experiences from the *whole* of society' – and government policy could and should potentially support such freedom (Oakley 1986: 216; emphasis in original). In contrast to market liberalism, the CPBF called for industrial democracy and for debate on alternative forms of ownership in media. Reducing media sexism and homophobia, and promoting equal opportunity in media for women, were goals added in the 1980s; its 1996 Manifesto extended this egalitarian commitment to ethnic origin, gender, disability, class, age and sexual orientation (www.cpbf.demon.co.uk/manifesto.htm, accessed 2002) but, as we shall see, some of these concerns were in effect add-ons to its core mandate.

Perhaps not surprisingly, the CPBF reflected the gender and ethnic composition of labour and political leadership in Britain; most of its founding activists were white male journalists, academics and/or trade unionists – demographics that, despite occasional fluctuations and CPBF's best efforts, are still much evident today. The decline of the women's movement, with many middle-class feminists abandoning activism once they had broken through the 'glass ceilings' of white-collar professions, has also been offered as an explanation for the apparent shortage of female media activists in Britain. However, women members remain active within the media unions, especially the NUJ, and there are now more caucuses and professional organizations providing support for women pursuing media careers. Moreover, women with experience in media, trade unions, labour communications, disability rights and NGOs have been active in the CPBF.

Two decades after CPBF's founding, its website concisely summarized its enduring commitments: a media more accountable to the people it is meant to serve; the break-up of media concentration to promote greater diversity; rights of citizens to redress for unfair coverage; rights of journalists to report freely. These commitments imply changes in journalism practices, media structures and state policies, potentially entailing many of the activism types identified in Table 3.1. Indeed, the Campaign has pursued a range of strategies, including numerous conferences and public forums, publications, media interviews, a boycott of newspapers (in response to Murdoch's attempt to break unions), media monitoring, and support for journalists and members of the public in individual cases of media accountability, and legislative campaigns.

Thus, the CPBF has adopted both insider and outsider strategies – pursuing reform through established political channels, and striving for influence within media institutions in collaboration with media workers, but also radically challenging dominant policies and sometimes adapting confrontational strategies. At the same time, the insider/outsider contrast does not have the same import as in the US, where, with brief exceptions (such as during the 1970s), the Left has been largely frozen out of media and policy institutions, and has organized primarily through its own subaltern political spaces. To adapt a concept from Marxist theorist Nicos Poulantzas (1975: 79–84), strong working-class movements and socialist parties in the UK and elsewhere in western Europe have had 'pertinent' effects on the state, which inscribed (though also arguably domesticated) certain progressive dynamics. By 1979, Labour had been in office for almost half the years since World War II, and had enacted reformist labour and social legislation. Thus, during its (narrowly) victorious campaign in 1974, Labour had promised 'to bring about a fundamental and irreversible shift in the balance of power and wealth in favour of working people and their families', rhetoric almost inconceivable from a major US party (see www.socialistworker.co.uk/1784/sw178413.htm). Radical, minority, community and artistic projects, including the CPBF, received funding from the Greater London Council (GLC), the capital's left-oriented metropolitan government, until Thatcher abolished it in 1987, (Mulgan and Worpole 1986). Moreover, the CPBF has always had journalists amongst its ranks; it worked from the very start with the NUJ, and it developed links (including membership in its regional management committees) with newsworkers in the regions, such as the team whose documentary on the regional TV programme *World in Action* helped release the Birmingham Six, a group wrongly convicted of an IRA bombing. The CPBF's founding expectation, of working within the system (notably the Labour Party and parliamentary/electoral politics) to enact radical democratic reforms that could significantly reshape the public sphere, was not unreasonable in light of postwar British history.

Notwithstanding the variety of its tactics, a review of CPBF's major campaigns shows the energy it has put into advocating communications policy reform, through public campaigns and legislative lobbying. One of its most consistent campaigns has centred on the 'right of reply' – the principle that 'if individuals or groups have been seriously misrepresented in a newspaper or magazine, they should have a chance to put their case to the readers of that publication' (Richardson and Power 1986: 199). The right of reply, to be adjudicated by an independent committee with a statutory mandate, was seen as both a principled step towards press accountability, accuracy and diversity, and a 'tactical point of entry for the Campaign's wider strategies' (Oakley 1986: 219). Though unions victimized by the British press's propaganda assault had good reason to support the right of reply, it probably resonated with concerns across the political spectrum, about tabloid sensationalism, inaccuracy and the trashing of people's reputations. The Campaign was aware of the limitations of this concept – it was reactive, it could actually institutionalize bias if news organizations left it up to 'the misrepresented' to reply, it was not a substitute for structural change to 'break the grip of the monopolies' (Power 1986: 222) or to enable people to actively use the media to set their own agendas and not just respond to those of the powerful (Oakley 1986: 219). But, argued Mike Power (1986: 222), 'the need for such strategic changes will gain credence if the right of reply is won'.

The Right of Reply campaign brilliantly provided a focus for a range of actors – academics, media unions, Labour parliamentarians and members of the public. The CPBF sponsored conferences and publications, inspired industrial action at two tabloids to win space for the mineworkers' union to respond to 'an incessant barrage of abuse' (Richardson and Power 1986: 200), and created a Right of Reply unit in 1984 to help people challenge individual cases of media bias. Most impressively, during the same decade that the Reagan administration was dismantling the Fairness Doctrine in US broadcasting, the CPBF successfully lobbied to have versions of right of reply legislation introduced, by supportive individual Labour MPs, at least five times in the British House of Commons. Despite obtaining support from individual MPs in other parties, including the governing Conservatives, and passing first and second reading on several occasions, each bill was stalled, or defeated at the third and final reading, by the government. Newspaper publishers and editors were particularly vocal in opposing the proposed legislation, at least once hiring a public relations company to lobby against it (*Free Press*, April 1989).

The CPBF extended its concern with press standards and accountability to challenges to Britain's Press Council, and its successor, the Press Complaints Commission (PCC). As proposed by a 1947–9 Royal Commission on the Press, these bodies were intended to promote professionalism and public service in the press. In practice, however, they became little more than adjudicators of public complaints, widely regarded as ineffective due to three basic problems: lack of sanctions, too narrow a mandate, and financial dependence on the very industry they supposedly monitored (Curran 2000: 40–1). The CPBF created an independent Commission of Enquiry in 1980, chaired by Geoffrey Robertson, to consider alternatives to the Press Council, and has not stopped critiquing it since then. It has sometimes taken on the government as well – particularly the 1989 Calcutt Committee on Privacy and Related Matters, which (in an apparent effort to deflect growing concern over press policy and growing support for right of reply and privacy legislation) led to the replacement of the Press Council with the equally toothless and industry-dependent PCC.

From its inception, the CPBF has critiqued, and sometimes campaigned against, other aspects of the democratic deficit. As early as 1981, it collaborated with the Minority Press Group to publish a pamphlet and create a working committee on market- and monopoly-related blockages in the wholesale distribution system for newspapers and magazines. It has consistently decried media concentration and cross-media ownership as threats to diversity. In 1986, the Campaign denounced the treatment by media moguls Rupert Murdoch and Robert Maxwell of their unionized workers during the implementation of new job-cutting printing technology.

The CPBF campaigned not only against industry but also state constraints on democratic journalism, including outright censorship entailed by aspects of the Official Secrets Act and the longstanding broadcasting ban against militant Irish groups, notably Sinn Fein, the IRA's political wing. Indeed, while broadcasters and freedom of expression groups like Article XIX denounced the ban, the CPBF went further, helping to lead an active campaign against it through events and publications, and critically analysing biased reporting about the Northern Ireland conflict. The post-Thatcher Conservative government of John Major quietly lifted the ban in 1994 in the context of peace talks.

Similarly, the CPBF welcomed the launch in 1984 of a new group, the Campaign for Freedom of Information; with overlapping membership on their respective Councils, the two groups lobbied for legislative reform in this area. While in opposition, Labour promised to introduce a FOI law but once in office, introduced a bill that the CPBF regarded as 'feeble, flawed and ... weaker than the existing code' (*Free Press*, July/August 1999). The Campaign had long argued for 'wholesale reform' of libel laws, particularly given their 'gagging effect' on investigative reporting; in 2001, it renewed that call following the settlement of a libel suit brought by Barrick Gold in response to a piece on corporate malpractice by Greg Palast (*Free Press*, September/October 2001). In wartime – the Falklands/Malvinas war against Argentina in 1982, the Gulf War of 1991, the invasion of Iraq in 2003 – the CPBF held forums and expressed opposition to constraints on journalism, whether by intimidation of dissenting newsworkers, state restriction of information, or the 'jingoistic gung-ho attitude' of the tabloids. CPBF coordinator Barry White speculates that given the apparent permanence of the Bush administration's post-9/11 'war on terror', the militarization of reporting may become an enduring challenge.

On the other side of the ledger, the CPBF has consistently called not only for more journalistic freedom, but for more responsibility and better standards, while shunning the authoritarian approach of state sanctions or censorship. Thus, in

1982 the Campaign called upon journalists to respect the NUJ's code of conduct, and two decades later, it was still addressing such issues as, for example, the practice of publishing paid-for editorials. Indeed, media historian Tom O'Malley regards helping to set the terms of debate on journalism standards as one of the CPBF's most signal contributions.

By the mid 1980s the CPBF had shifted its focus from the press to the media more generally, particularly broadcasting, as the CPBF lost activists from among the defeated and newly unemployed print workers, and replaced them with 'recruits from the expanding sectors of media studies and independent television production' (Curran 2000). Its efforts here have centred on the defence of public service broadcasting against the perceived threats of privatization and commercialization of the BBC, deregulation of ITV and other private broadcasters, and liberalization of ownership ceilings. During the long night of Conservative rule, from 1979 to 1997, the CPBF's work was largely reactive to government enquiries, proposals and actual legislation, including the 1986 Peacock Report on BBC financing, Broadcasting Acts in 1990 and 1995–6, the auctioning of ITV franchises in 1991, and the BBC's Charter renewal in 1996. The CPBF's support of public broadcasting was not uncritical, however; after all, during the 1970s, leftist academics had popularized a trenchant critique of the ideological biases the BBC shared with commercial media, and trade unions had good reason for discontent with BBC coverage (e.g. Glasgow University Media Group 1976). In that spirit, CPBF argued for more transparency and accountability at 'the Beeb', for democratization of its governance, such as parliamentary review of appointments to its board, for curtailing its internal market mechanisms and commercial activities, and for more regional input to policy and content. The Campaign also addressed the expansion of cable and satellite television services, again with a view to protecting the priority of public service values.

While the *Free Press* began discussing the importance of the internet as early as 1994, the CPBF has maintained its focus on 'the machinery of representation', and has not addressed point-to-point computer-based media or telecommunications more than incidentally. Other aspects of globalization, however, have affected the CPBF's work since the 1990s. The regional integration of Europe, and the growing relevance of European policy for British media policy, especially since the 1997 election of the Blair government which moved to incorporate the European Convention on Human Rights (ECHR) into British law, has encouraged the CPBF to develop connections with sympathetic members of the European Parliament. The Campaign has also made links with the Council of Europe, an intergovernmental forum of European states, whose media policy is guided by the ECHR. On CPBF's National Council, Gary Herman specialized in European policy issues. More recently, the CPBF has begun to make links with the European Social Forum and the WACC, groups working against neoliberal hegemony over global media governance.

It would be misleading, however, to portray the CPBF strictly as policy wonks. To be sure, some of its academic supporters (Tom O'Malley, James Curran, Mike Jempson, Jonathan Hardy and others) certainly have policy expertise. Curran in particular contributed to numerous policy working groups within the parliamentary Labour Party, and was an adviser to a Royal Commission on the Press. More recently, Hardy and others have continued doggedly to prepare detailed responses to government initiatives. But the CPBF has never been part of high-echelon wonkdom, setting the terms of policy discourse for governments. Even during its wilderness years in opposition, the Labour Party always had other voices whispering in its ear, including journalists and industry interests. Its turn to the right under Blair, and the rise of the policy think tank industry, spewing out position papers as funding opportunities arise, have both displaced the CPBF as policy advisers. CPBF's policy positions consistently reflected well-defined counter-hegemonic political values – and partly for that reason could be dismissed as irrelevant or doctrinaire by those within the established policymaking field. If the CPBF's academics aspired, in Gramscian terms, to be 'organic intellectuals' for a radically democratic government, the tide of hegemony has flowed in the opposite direction.

Moreover, lobbying on national media policy has not been the CPBF's sole vocation. It has also adopted activities and issues more akin to the 'lifeworld' and community orientation of the post-1996 Media Alliance – the mis- and under-representation of minorities and marginalized groups; challenging sexism; supporting alternative and radical media; media training, literacy and monitoring. During the 1980s, with the intent to 'activate and involve all sections in society subject to media distortion', the CPBF incorporated the Campaign Against Racism in the Media, and developed 'special autonomous groups' to work on behalf of women, gays and lesbians (especially in the wake of AIDS hysteria), blacks and the disabled (Richardson and Power 1986: 202). Often working with the NUJ, these CPBF Groups helped develop guidelines for media coverage of their respective constituencies, held public meetings and conferences, published analyses of coverage (including a book on racism in the Murdoch tabloid, the *Sun*). The women's group initiated a debate within the CPBF when its research and advocacy led to a private member's bill in the House of Commons to curb the distribution of pornography. Despite support of MPs from all three main parties, the Bill was defeated in 1990. The Bill caused much controversy on the Left; print unionists saw it as an attack on their livelihood, and others called it an exercise in censorship (*Free Press*, May/June 1990).

In principle, CPBF welcomed the expansion of independent, progressive media. In 1980 it helped develop the *East End News*, a weekly paid-for local London paper run as a 'workers and readers' cooperative. In 1981 it backed the re-launch of the Welsh alternative paper *Rebecca*, and helped fundraise for several others. According to Tom O'Malley, the Campaign had good links with community media throughout the 1980s when funding was stronger, but a divisive internal debate over supporting 'community radio' (local, independently owned, specialized stations) proved to be a 'political disaster'. As summarized in *Free Press* (August 1985), the debate revealed fault lines in progressive British media activism. On one side, community radio supporters argued that conventional broadcasting, including the BBC, was dominated by a 'white, middle-aged, male and conservative Establishment', including the Tory government. They rejected the 'sophisticated Stalinist' assumption that media can be run only by the state or corporate capitalism, and the strategy of waiting for a Labour government to reform the management of the BBC and the independent (private) broadcasters. A report by Justin Lewis identified the unemployed, working people and ethnic minorities as the keenest supporters, and indeed 'black' media activists argued that community radio was a way for Asians, Afro-Caribbeans and other minorities to counteract their marginalization in British media. They weren't waiting for government approval. Foreshadowing the American microradio movement a decade later, 'pirate' stations were sprouting around the country, forcing the Tory government's hand: it announced 20 pilot projects in July 1985.

By contrast, opponents like O'Malley 'argued furiously against endorsing community radio' on the grounds that it could provide the government with an alibi for reducing public service obligations on the major media, thus leaving them uncontested; it could result in marginal enterprises that did not serve their surrounding communities; it could undermine unions by breaking up British broadcasting into small low-cost units run by volunteers and low-paid free-lancers; and it could open the floodgates of commercialization and concentration evident in the US. Given the Tory government's market liberal privatization agenda, and its plan to implement 'community' radio with advertising and without regulation, these were plausible arguments, and they won the day. The CPBF opted instead to campaign 'for greater access and public accountability within the present system'. Contrast that with the US context, where public interest regulation of media is historically much weaker than Britain's, and where media activists almost axiomatically support alternative media as a counterweight to corporate behemoths that many of them regard as unreformable.

That decision did not mean that CPBF altogether turned its back on the strategy of building new radical media. On the contrary, it supported the creation of a national progressive newspaper. In 1982, the TUC began to move seriously towards launching this long-debated project. As a way to gain a public voice and to diversify the press system, a mass-circulation labour paper was a supplement, and arguably an alternative, to legislative reform. And it was not without precedent: from 1922 until the 1960s, the British Left had both published its own dailies and had 'powerful press allies', making Labour 'a stakeholder in the system' (Curran 2000: 38). The death of the TUC-owned *Daily Herald*, noted in Chapter 1, changed that situation (Curran 2002: 102). In 1984, the CPBF organized a national conference on the question of a labour paper. Notwithstanding early misgivings about the TUC's plans (no clear editorial policy, no survey of advertisers, insufficient consultation with media unions), the same 1985 CPBF annual general meeting that had rejected community radio endorsed the labour paper.

The *News on Sunday*, a left-leaning tabloid weekly, was launched in 1987. It collapsed within eight weeks. In an autopsy on the paper in *Free Press* (October 1987), Mike Power concluded that it was conceived as a political rather than journalistic project but that in order to raise six million pounds in start-up costs, the founders had to appeal to 'respectable' bankers and thus downplay its left-wing stance. Internally, the staff lacked real leadership or shared political vision, and experienced a disastrous split between its editor and a senior journalist, John Pilger. Other powerful institutions in the media field – the BBC, the tabloid press, advertisers, the Newspaper Publishers Association distribution committee – were reluctant to give the radical upstart coverage or material support. Conflicting vested interests, an inadequate financial reservoir, and an inability to overcome tensions between politics, journalism and business, killed the paper. One member of the paper's board, until he was removed for criticizing its direction, concurs that the tabloid was under-capitalized and 'too right-wing, too up-market'. The bitter experience of *News on Sunday* has probably precluded this strategy for a generation.

Other more modest media strategies, more similar to the Media Alliance approach, have been less contentious – training workshops, public education, and monitoring. The Campaign has at times sponsored seminars to train union members to deal with media, as well as media literacy and independent media production courses (in collaboration with adult education institutions). While much of its news coverage has derived from the trade press or sympathetic dailies, notably the *Guardian*, the Campaign has occasionally found openings in the broadcast media. In 1983, for instance, the BBC televised a 30-minute CPBF programme hosted by two leading actors, Julie Christie and Billie Whitelaw. 'Why their news is bad news' was intended to 'encourage action against bias and distortion in the media' and sparked a flood of supportive calls and letters to the CPBF's office.

The Campaign's educational and monitoring activities continued into the 1990s and beyond, for example major conferences on the state of British media in 1993 and 1995 (the latter in a European context), and media monitoring exercises on partisan bias, organized by the Campaign and conducted by *Free Press* reader-volunteers during the 1992 and 1997 national election campaigns. The CPBF issued a revised Media Manifesto in 1996, and in 1999 joined with other media democracy organizations for the first official British commemoration of World Press Freedom Day.

But the CPBF's story, unfortunately, is hardly one of uninterrupted progress and expansion. In 1987–8 the Campaign was forced to confront a major resource crisis, partly due to Thatcher's eradication of politically troublesome city government bodies (like the GLC). CPBF had to reduce its staff, which at one point comprised five workers, some of them specializing in gender and race issues in the media. The forced reassessment of priorities inevitably triggered bitter internal debates. At the end of the day, the Campaign decided to retrench to its core mandate – 'in key policy debates around the regulation of broadcasting, we had to be there', as Granville Williams put it. This retrenchment foreshadowed another challenge to come: the ebbing of its traditional sources of support.

Alliances – and abandonment?

While the CPBF has collaborated with other groups across the political spectrum on particular campaigns, it did not originally set out to be the nucleus of a broad coalition for media reform. Rather, for its first decade and beyond, the CPBF operated in a classic British left mode – an alliance between organized labour and political reformers, anchored around the Labour Party. To be sure, some CPBF activists have found their primary political home in Trotskyist or Communist parties, and its objectives have also enjoyed support from further right along the political spectrum. In its first year, the Campaign was endorsed by the youth wing of the centrist Liberal Party; and even within the governing Tories, some MPs sided with it on specific issues, such as Right of Reply and press standards.

Moreover, over the years, the Campaign has made overtures to other movements, such as environmentalism. As early as 1984, the Ecology Party joined the CPBF; in 1998, CPBF organized a public event and *Free Press* articles on media and the environment; it has made connections with Friends of the Earth on genetically modified foods, and with the World Development Movement, a lead civil society organization on cultural policy within the GATS and WTO agendas. Still, CPBF's ability to forge links with new social movements has been limited by the self-reinforcing dilemma of the white male 'old left' demographics, the lack of resources since the 1980s to run broad campaigns that could appeal directly to other movements' priorities, and arguably, the lack of coalition-building vision and energy on the part of movements themselves. The movements have too narrow a focus to include media as part of the big picture, lamented some CPBF members, or, like the women's movement, they have become politically quiescent.

What about other media reform groups? The CPBF's right of reply campaign spawned PressWise (now MediaWise, www.mediawise.org.uk), a spin-off founded by CPBF National Council veteran Mike Jempson in 1993. As a de facto alternative to the industry-oriented PCC, PressWise's focus on the media field (journalism practices) is complementary to the CPBF's policy focus; it assists people (like refugees and asylum seekers) subjected to media intrusion. A visit by Jeff Cohen to CPBF also helped inspire him to establish the media monitoring organization FAIR in the US, sometimes described in *Free Press* as CPBF's 'sister organization'. Moreover, CPBF has also collaborated with other liberal and progressive media policy advocates on specific issues. Although more middle-class in base and middle-of-the-road in politics, other organizations have overlapping interests in defending public broadcasting in particular. One especially relevant network of groups, each with a distinct niche, clusters around volunteer organizations in civil society. Under the rubric of the advocacy coalition Public Voice, these organizations – including Voice of the Listener and Viewer, 3WE (the Third World and Environment Broadcasting Project), Media Trust, Campaign for Quality Television, and Community Radio Association – have helped gain impetus for some of the CPBF's issues. But they are also inevitably sometime-rivals within the political space available for media reformers in the UK – if not for funding, then for standing with the media and policymakers. In that regard, the Public Voice cluster has apparent advantages – a reputed 'canniness' about framing its policies in language (like notions of 'citizenship') that resonates with policymakers; policies of incremental change rather than fundamental structural reform; the support of non-partisan charities; and a measure of 'realism' and credibility given its standing within both the NGO and media fields.

Hasn't the CPBF also made friends and influenced people in the media field? Of course. From the start, the CPBF had many journalistic members and supporters, including 'stars' like Pilger and Palast, and a base in the NUJ and media unions. But its foot in the newsroom door is somewhat like Media Alliance's before 1996. Its supporters tend to be progressives and union militants. Neither has necessarily been at the centre of post-Thatcher, post-Wapping British newsroom culture since the 1980s. In pubs and booklined studies, several British journalists and academics told us off the record of the challenges CPBF has faced in bringing rank-and-file journalists into a media reform coalition. While the regime of objectivity characterizes British broadcasting more than the conservative 'quality' dailies or (especially) the raunchy, sensationalist tabloids, mainstream journalists feel brickbatted from all sides, and are afraid of being associated with an 'agenda', particularly one seen as left-wing. Media management has been more sensitive and responsive to criticism from the right than from the left. As for NUJ, the journalists' union, while it has been a bulwark of democratic media advocacy it does not ideologically reflect the industry workforce, or even its own members. Indeed, during the 1990s, the NUJ itself worked to become a more bread-and-butter union, focusing on protecting its members during contract disputes, especially in financially besieged regional newsrooms like the commercial ITN network.

Like the Media Alliance, the CPBF faces the dilemma of offering sharp critiques of actually existing media, while seeking alliances with working journalists. As British cultural industries become more commercially driven, as media culture shifts towards market populism and away from a public service ethos, the gap between the CPBF's policy principles and media realities widens. While the CPBF has retained credibility on ownership issues, and while it has shifted its language over the years in response to the times (from a socialist critique of class bias in the press, to a defence of public service broadcasting more akin to public sphere liberalism), some not otherwise unsympathetic observers belittle its grasp of newsroom processes, and its perceived inflexibility of rhetoric and perspectives. It risks becoming a 'sideshow' on the impotent fringes, said one, although he added semiapologetically that perhaps critics like himself 'accept the status quo too much'.

So, while it has a foothold on the journalism field, the CPBF's main political horizons were constituted by the Labour Party, albeit without any formal connection, and by the trade unions, particularly the print unions in the early years, and the NUJ, and BECTU – the Broadcasting Entertainment Cinematograph and Theatre Union, whose articulate president Tony Lennon has also served as CPBF Chair. Granville Williams asserted that, while the CPBF has always maintained its autonomy, it could not have survived without a union base, a link which characterized the Campaign as 'old Labour' – and 'we've not been ashamed of this label'. The Labour Party itself, during its wilderness years in opposition during the 1980s, incorporated some of the CPBF's policy challenges to the corporate media giants (right of reply, ownership divestment, reform of periodical distribution) in its programme.

But Labour has never unequivocally backed such a challenge. Britain's first majority Labour government appointed the first Royal Commission on the Press in 1947, but it sought to avoid further press hostility, given its wide-ranging programme of economic and social reform, from the nationalization of selected industries to the creation of the National Health Service. To the extent that the media have appeared on Labour's policy radar screen, voices other than radical reformers have often predominated, including those of journalists and industry interests. And strategies other than structural reform have been touted and pursued at different periods: direct ownership of pro-labour newspapers, the profession- alization and self-regulation of journalism, a 'social market' approach of public subsidies for socially valuable but commercially unviable minority media (Curran 2000), and a non-legislative approach of massaging media coverage through professional spinmeisters.

By the early 1990s, the Labour leadership was getting cold feet about radical democratic media reform. In 1992, Labour attributed its fourth consecutive elec- toral defeat in part to the influence of the Tory press – and indeed, polling research suggested that the vitriolic hostility of the Murdoch tabloid *Sun* had swayed enough voters to tip the balance (Hackett and Zhao 1998: 179). Through a 1994 confer- ence well attended by industry heavyweights, and more pointedly through new Labour leader Tony Blair's well-publicized 1995 handshake with Rupert Murdoch at an Australian island resort, Labour signalled a retreat from its previous media policies. 'There has to be a loosening of ownership rules', asserted Labour's parlia- mentary Heritage critic, while Blair declared himself for 'an open and competitive media market' (O'Malley and Soley 2000: 94). In the debate on the 1996 Broad- casting Bill, Labour's leaders actually took a position on cross-media ownership to the right of the governing Tories, arguing for loosening restrictions.

After its long electoral drought, Labour returned to office in 1997. Fuelled by resilient hopes of reform, CPBF's membership temporarily surged. Some initial signs were momentarily encouraging. Chris Smith, the new Heritage minister (responsible for communications policy) and a supporter of right of reply legislation while in opposition, consulted with the Campaign. And Labour did move to improve BBC funding, and to strengthen privacy rights via the ECHR. But on the more fundamental democratization of state and corporate media power, deeper and darker currents were at work. It soon became apparent that meaningful freedom of information, right of reply and anti-concentration legislation was not on the agenda. To the contrary, New Labour's communication policies were heading down the neoliberal road, albeit one adorned with a succession of discus- sion papers and consultations.

As the Labour government moved towards a new Communications Act, combining five previously separate media regulators into a single Office of Communications (Ofcom), the CPBF mustered whatever resources and allies it could, and lobbied for several years in reaction to this impending legislation. The CPBF mounted a cogent critique in the pages of *Free Press* and other publications, public talks, parliamentary hearings, and meetings with sympathetic MPs. The proposed bill, it said, opened the door to US and other foreign ownership of broadcasting channels, and to greatly increased cross-media and concentrated ownership, including the expansion of Murdoch's empire. It could put British broadcasting on the road to an American-style commercial system, with public service requirements on private broadcasters minimized, programming dumbed down in the competition for profits and cheap ways to grab audiences, regional production decimated, and the BBC left as a public service ghetto catering to minority audiences. The proposed Ofcom itself would be overly centralized, to the detriment of the UK's internal regions and nations (Scotland, Wales, Northern Ireland); its board would be government appointees rather than democratically nominated by broadly-based civil society organizations; its mandate is to promote economic competition and to allow self-regulation within media industries, to promote the values of consumerism but not citizenship, and to replace 'positive' with 'light touch' regulation.

Beyond specific criticisms, fundamental ideological differences were at work. New Labour had converted to a market liberal paradigm, and was indeed bent upon spreading market principles to all areas of public life, accepting 'virtually the entire legacy of the Thatcher and Major years – "pro-business" trade union and employment law, privatization, a "marketised" public sector, a no longer universal welfare system, privatised housing, the neutering of local government' (Leys 2001: 42–3).

Ultimately, the Communications Act was passed in 2003, with relatively minor concessions to public interest campaigners. While the Campaign still has friends on Labour's backbenches, its position vis-à-vis the government has become increasingly adversarial, with no obvious openings for policy influence.

The CPBF's ambiguous impact

The CPBF's trajectory is a reminder that while we make our own history, it is not under conditions of our own choosing: its fate was tied to much broader political forces and currents. The CPBF was premised upon widespread discontent with existing media, which certainly existed in 1979, and which the CPBF sought to translate into concrete, progressive policies to be implemented by a political agent (the Labour Party) with the necessary will and ability. Those were not unreasonable assumptions at the time. But they have not materialized. Why not?

First, the power and militancy of British trade unions, CPBF's main wellspring in civil society, have declined since 1980. The Thatcher government's rejection of the postwar 'deal' with organized labour (social welfare programmes, consultation on policy issues) was combined with an attack on unions' legal rights, resulting by 1997 in what Tony Blair approvingly called 'the most restrictive trade union laws in the western world' (Leys 2001: 39). Union assertiveness has been further undermined by long-term shifts in employment away from sectors with strong traditions of collective militancy (coal-mining, engineering, docks, public transport), by the defeat of the print unions over technological change in the press, and by higher unemployment and falling membership. Arguably, many unions have also shifted from an adversarial to a 'partnership' approach to industrial relations. By 1997, only 130,000 workers were involved in industrial disputes, compared to an annual average of 1,658,000 during the late 1970s (Hyman 1999).

Such relative quiescence has meant that compared to the winter of discontent, or the miners' strike of 1984, the right-wing tabloids have turned their machinery of vilification away from unions (and often towards more marginalized scapegoats, like immigrants or refugees). In the absence of industrial conflict, workers are less likely to perceive a problem with the capitalist press, suggested one CPBF activist; many of them bought into the New Labour political project, and/or they have shifted their priorities from political engagement to bread-and-butter issues. Similarly, their communications strategies have shifted from confronting to massaging the media; as Davis (2000: 173) notes, the British trade union movement during the 1990s 'widely adopted professional PR practices and personnel as an alternative means of influencing corporate and political decision-making', and sometimes with notable influence on media frames, such as the communications unions' successful 1994 campaign against post office privatization.

Second, the prolonged neoliberal assault has put not only unions but the political Left on the defensive, forcing it to engage in reactive campaigns, and undermining confidence and vision – a process sometimes palpable within the CPBF too. When Labour was finally elected after an unexpectedly prolonged stay in opposition, its leadership not only *abandoned* democratic media reform; it *intensified* the media's democratic deficit, both through formal legislation and through the techniques of political spin, using operatives like Peter Mandelson and Alastair Campbell to influence daily coverage and intimidate critics. None too subtle threats to privatize the BBC or to share its licence fee with commercial broadcasters were widely seen as payback for what the government perceived as critical coverage of its Iraq war policy. As University of London communications lecturer Des Freedman described Labour's media policies (*Free Press*, March/April 2004):

> Ofcom's light touch regulation is accompanied by the highly interventionist and politicized role of government in influencing both long-term policy and everyday media content. It's not just the spin and constant harassment from Number Ten [the Prime Minister's official residence] that should disturb us, but the more profound alliances between Blair and the media establishment.

The New Labour leadership has insulated itself not only from radical reformers like CPBF, but also from its own party membership. Tony Blair's transformation of Labour between 1993 and 1996 created a new political landscape for Britain, and not least the CPBF. Until then, the CPBF had an open door to the Party at two levels. It had open relations with key spokespeople in the parliamentary caucus, including shadow ministers (the opposition party's Cabinet-in-waiting), and a number of backbench MPs, some of whom had sponsored the CPBF's Right of Reply bills. And the Campaign appealed to Labour Party activists. Many of them attended the CPBF's 'fringe' meetings (unofficial events for specialized groups and issues) at the Party's annual conference. Some Labour constituency associations were affiliated to the CPBF.

Both those links eroded rapidly when Blair and his 'New Labour' supporters refashioned the party. Their centralization of policymaking and professionalization of election campaigns made it more difficult to motivate branch-level activists, whose numbers at party conferences dwindled (while those of corporate operatives increased) after 1996, thus shrinking further the organized potential support base for media reform. Meanwhile, Blair began casting his own shadow over the selection and pronouncements of Labour's parliamentary leadership. The CPBF began to feel that it was swimming against rather than with the flow of Labour's policies.

Looking back over the past century, James Curran (2000) concludes that press reform in the UK is a history of failure. The social market approach (of subsidies to maintain diversity against commercial pressures) has declined in the era of neoliberal ascendancy, and would now be nearly irrelevant, in that (unlike Norway or Sweden) there are few progressive or labour newspapers left to save. Nor has the strategy of professionalization and the development of public service culture within press journalism taken hold. While there is public anger and elite fear of press abuses, this could as easily generate authoritarian restrictions as democratic structural reforms. So, while the CPBF has identified the press's partisan bias, concentrated ownership, and poor standards as important democratic deficits, and while it has tapped into real grievances, there is a lack of political opportunity to pursue reform: the unity and power of press owners, the strength of libertarian ideology, and the weakness of reform movements have historically combined, argues Curran, to sideline it.

Progressive reformers have more to cheer about, historically, in the broadcasting field. Compared to the US, British broadcasting policy has successfully fostered pluralistic, innovative and quality programming which meets many of the criteria of public sphere liberalism; partly for that reason, British public service broadcasting (PSB) – which includes regulated commercial channels – has proved remarkably resilient even in the face of Thatcherism. The CPBF and other public interest voices could claim some of the credit for blunting neoliberal assaults on PSB, although of course broader forces were at work – the popularity of public service television, a collectivist streak in British political culture, the BBC's reputation for independence, and support within the political elite for the 'quality' that PSB is held to provide (Curran 2002: 202). PSB's strength, therefore, is not only a resource for media democrats (there is an institutional and popular base for public service principles, and a valued and working model to defend) but also a handicap to mobilization, in that relative success can generate complacency. In the absence of conflict as galvanizing as the Pacifica board 'coup', or the dramatic deterioration of programming fare, the threats which CPBF identified in its campaigns around Ofcom, the BBC's periodic charter renewals, and other regulatory retreats towards neoliberalism, may seem too remote, hypothetical or incremental to rouse mass protest. Even in the national daily press, notwithstanding the right-wing tabloids' viperous political influence, the *Guardian* and *Independent* arguably offer enough diversity to blunt potential protest about lack of 'consumer choice'.

A final factor in the CPBF's policy isolation derives from the ecology of British media advocacy groups. CPBF is distinct and nearly alone in offering a radical democratic critique of both commercialism and concentrated ownership, though less often than in its early years, of capitalist ownership as such. It has won respect for its commitment and expertise on ownership issues. But industry and foundation funds, and policymakers' ears, are more attuned to non-partisan service organizations, or at most, to more centrist policy groups, like the 'Public Voice' defenders of PSB, and to freedom of expression groups like Article 19, Index on Censorship, or PEN International. As one CPBFer put it, those latter groups are 'narrowly focused – they work in a safe area, stay there, and don't make the connections' with corporate control. By contrast, 'CPBF is dangerous because it *is* making the connections'.

To put it in terms of the typology outlined in Chapter 3, CPBF has sought to challenge the 'system' in both the media field (particularly news representations and practices), and its environing conditions (mainly, state policy); but it has not since the 1980s been able to tap into sufficiently strong counterhegemonic cultural currents in the lifeworld, including the subaltern public spheres of alternative media and social movements, to make that challenge more effective.

The CPBF has also at times (most notably, as in the community radio and mandate retrenchment debates in the 1980s) stumbled across a fault line, a tension between supporting independent media, and supporting public broadcasting – and perhaps more broadly, between public sphere-oriented strategies for change (in this case, building public service broadcasting), and strategies that emphasize counterhegemony, through the independent media's amplification of subaltern counterpublics. Perhaps these tensions were exacerbated by a certain dogmatism within the CPBF, and by a government pursuing a divide-and-rule strategy – for example, by offering community radio activists part of what they sought – to further both its own market liberal agenda, and the interests of media capital more generally. But perhaps these dilemmas have more fundamental roots in the constitution of the media and political fields within contemporary capitalism, such as the division between salaried employees of market- or state-financed media institutions, and community activists 'self-exploiting' their labour (Atton 2003: 63) to meet non-commodified communicative needs.

Given its lack of policy victories after 25 years, a cynic might sneer at the CPBF as a failure. But that is much too summary a judgement. Institutionalized reforms of the system may be the most important form of success, but not the only one. The CPBF's achievements are subtle but multi-dimensional.

First, it has contributed significantly to defensive policy victories, resisting the further encroachment of the system logics of commercialization and political censorship in the media field. The CPBF was amongst the groups preventing further privatization of the BBC by the doctrinaire, market liberal Thatcher government; and it took a lead role in the repeal of the broadcasting ban against Sinn Fein.

Second, organizationally, the CPBF has directly nurtured spin-offs like PressWise, and has inspired media activists in the US and Canada, notably FAIR, Free Press, and the Canadian CPBF.

Third, CPBF campaigns have demonstrated the broad-ranging coalitions which can be built around media democratization, and like Media Alliance, it has sometimes played the valuable role of mediator between diverse interests within that coalition – even those once as far apart as unionized media workers and community radio activists (Richardson and Power 1986: 206). And it has raised consciousness about democratic communication among its own broad constituency, especially the parliamentary Left and union movement.

Finally, arguably its main achievement has been to sustain a level of activity, publication, and core support, in a hostile political environment. Beyond sheer organizational survival since 1979, itself a significant accomplishment, the CPBF has helped set terms of debate on press standards, and has kept its issues alive and circulating in the public sphere far more than would otherwise have been the case. Its success in popularizing strongly reformist measures like Right of Reply, and even getting them onto Britain's parliamentary agenda, is remarkable by post-Reagan US standards.

Of course, that is not enough. It is impossible to imagine overcoming media's democratic deficit without changing the rules enforced, and resources allocated, by the state. In the UK, that struggle probably requires finding fresh constituencies, dynamics and strategies, while building upon the valuable experiences and connections of the CPBF and other progressive, campaigning organizations. In the next two chapters, we consider respectively the obstacles and the opportunities for that kind of struggle in the North Atlantic societies.

7 Challenges for media activism
Obstacles and opponents

This chapter and the next one distil many of the insights that media activists based mainly in the United States, United Kingdom and Canada shared with us in a series of nearly 100 in-depth interviews conducted between 1998 and 2004. These conversations offer practitioners' views of the problems and the promise of democratizing public communication. In this chapter, we focus on the problems: the obstacles and challenges that in many respects have consigned democratic media activism to the margins in the wider political field – the factors that activists identify as inhibiting the successful democratization of the media system, or more immediately, popular mobilization towards that goal. In the next chapter, we strike a more optimistic note, exploring sources and resources, including viable strategies and coalitions, for moving media democratization from the margins to the centre of political contention.

A serviceable analytic framework for these companion chapters is the resource-mobilization perspective we introduced in Chapter 3. This approach views movements pragmatically, as rational collective actors pursuing shared objectives in strategic interaction with other groups and institutions. It attaches importance to the 'framing processes, mobilizing structures, and political opportunities' that enable movements to form, to act, and to have effect (Cormier 2004: 10). It is through framing – the construction of schemata of interpretation – that grievances are understood as both unjust and remediable. It is through mobilizing a constituency for action that a movement develops collective agency. It is in taking advantage of openings and opportunities (which includes constructing workable alliances and exploiting opponents' weaknesses) that a movement creates change.

If these factors help specify the requisites for an effective movement, they also point implicitly toward some of the key obstacles and challenges. It is no small feat to create frames that resonate with potential participants and allies, that open up resistant identities, and that suggest productive political strategies. Clearly, in the struggle to democratize communication, the hegemonic power of the dominant media system looms large – not just as a target but as a barrier to change. Unlike some movements (e.g. Greenpeace, Live 8), whose sensational events attract coverage that boosts corporate media revenues, media activism challenges the legitimacy of the corporate media system and faces difficulties both in framing its project and in conveying it to the wider public. The incipient movement has also encountered specific problems in mobilizing its constituency with coherent strategies. Although digital communicative innovations have opened certain opportunities for media activism, in other ways the movement has been stymied by both an array of entrenched opponents and a relatively weak set of alliances with kindred political interests.

Framing challenges

Movements construct collective action frames out of a sense of grievance and injustice, and the mass media's democratic deficit would seem to furnish plenty of raw material. Yet action frames are not simply cut from whole cloth; they are assembled on the basis of the philosophies, metaphors, imagery and common sense already in circulation, and to be effective they must resonate with the sensibilities and aspirations of the people they address (Snow *et al.* 1986). What we might term a discursive structure of 'cultural opportunities'[1] defines and delimits the horizon for political vision, within which framing efforts occur.

One of the most significant barriers to activism in general, and media activism in particular, is the cultural matrix within which activists must fashion their frames. Two powerful and inter-related forces are at work here: the political and ideological hegemony of market liberalism, and the 'naturalization' of an increasingly commercialized media system. As a result, what media activists see as a democratic deficit becomes simply an ineluctable element of everyday life and common sense for the general public. The media's failure to constitute a public sphere and to maintain healthy communities and political cultures, its complicity in maintaining inequality and in contracting the public commons, its role in homogenizing public opinion and other aspects of the deficit tend to be cognized as uncontestable 'facts of life'. Our respondents confirmed that the hegemony of market liberalism and the naturalization of the corporate media system present profound barriers to democratizing public communication. Many lamented a general lack of awareness by the public (including activists in other movements) of deep flaws in the media system. Cees Hamelink, an originator of the People's Communication Charter, sees the insufficient recognition of media as a political issue as indicating a lack of political literacy. Philip Lee at WACC observed that as media become like the air we breathe the media's connection with oppression or with state power becomes imperceptible.

Even among activists who perceive news coverage as rotten, 'the idea of actually trying to organize to do something about that is not a very widespread idea', says Canadian professor Marc Raboy. In Britain, Arun Kundnani of the Institute of Race Relations agrees: 'People shy away from looking at media as something that can be changed because you run up against a freedom of speech argument.' That barrier is most formidable in the United States, a bastion of liberal individualism. Most Americans have no idea that the public owns the airwaves, or that stations are licensed, argues Herbert Chao Gunther, of the Public Media Center in San Francisco. Indeed, media lead people to feel unqualified to make policy decisions. American media reformer Robert McChesney believes that the public largely does not understand that they have the right and power to determine their media environment and 'the corporate lobbies understand this and work incessantly to make sure that people never understand that they actually have a choice'. But he sees an enormous silver lining: 'If we get this on the political agenda, if we make it an issue so it's actually talked about, we'll win.'

How to get on the political agenda is indeed the nub of the issue, but as we saw in Chapter 4, media activists are themselves not in agreement as to exactly what to *put* on the agenda: how the movement should be framed as a political project. Besides the lack of consensus as to what the movement is about, a number of respondents agreed with Kim Deterline of the non-profit media training centre, We Interrupt This Message, that media activists are 'not framing issues in a way that most people can understand'. Mark Lloyd of the Civil Rights Forum says it is difficult to reach beyond the media field in the US, because activists have their own language. Scholars, activists and NGO employees express similar frustration at the international level, where the lack of a common and effective frame is multiplied by cultural, historical and political as well as sheer linguistic differences.

Mobilization challenges

Mobilization is what transforms a group or interest from passive spectator to collective actor (Tilly 1978). It is a multifaceted phenomenon that includes recruitment of participants and supporters, amassing of other necessary resources (such as funds, means of communication, skill and leadership), and creation of organizations and networks through which collective action can be sustained. Our overview of types of democratic media activism in Chapter 3 established that DMA organizations have been proliferating in the Anglo-American heartland at least since the 1980s. Yet the challenges are many. The current wave of DMA occurs in the context of a weakened Left, ravaged by the apparent triumph of globalized capitalism and its political programme of neoliberalism. This in itself limits the discretionary resources that can be diverted from the defence of past gains to emergent issues such as the democratization of public communication. Respondents in both the US and Britain, implicitly assuming that the Left would be the main standard-bearer of democratization of and through the media, noted the Left's weakness as a major impediment.

More specifically, in analysing barriers to mobilization it is helpful to distinguish between shortages of 'objective' resources, notably staff and money, and problems that stem from the practices of advocacy groups themselves. The latter include alienation from dominant values, poor organization and coordination between groups, lack of common focus or strategy, and problematic attitudes towards, or practices of, leadership.

Resource shortages

Funding is a perpetual problem for most progressive, public interest advocacy groups. Our interviews suggest a strong correlation between financial constraints and limitations of energy, morale and scope of activity. Funding, of course, can mean organizational life and death. Volunteers have certainly added to the energies of many media democracy groups, particularly in response to crises like the 1991 Gulf War, but few organizations can survive strictly on the basis of unpaid effort.

Funding constraints contribute to staff shortages relative to mandates, to low pay and high workloads, and thus to high staff burnout and turnover with the attendant costs of discontinuity. Jeff Perlstein of Media Alliance suggests that this is a 'really deep dilemma', even a 'crisis'. The difficulty of making a living doing progressive media work explains why so many activists are young people without families to support. To the extent that younger people are less oriented towards policy advocacy and more towards alternative media and direct action, the relative absence of older activists may have unintended political and strategic conse-quences.[2] Money problems force decisions about programme priorities which can be internally divisive, as the example in Chapter 6 of the CPBF's crisis in the late 1980s demonstrates all too clearly.

Funding constraints also place advocacy groups in competition with each other, especially in the US where media democracy groups are highly dependent upon the same small pool of liberal foundations. These foundations tend to fund specific projects rather than supply ongoing operating funds, forcing activist groups to invest substantial time in generating and writing grant proposals. By contrast, wealthy conservative foundations have invested in long-term institution building. To add insult to injury, some organizations, like Media Alliance and alternative media, spend time training people who are eventually seduced by the higher sala-ries of mainstream media.

Dependence on foundation or (in Canada) government grants also raises the dilemma of funder influence on recipient agendas. It is a constant struggle to main-tain organizational objectives and resist being swayed by funders. Some activists conceded off the record that their choice of projects to pursue is influenced, or even determined, by what will receive funding. Foundations should also make their own agendas clearer so that 'we don't have to waste our time if we don't fit', notes Kim Deterline.

Resource constraints need not be regarded with undue pessimism. While most media democracy groups are underfunded and understaffed relative to their mandates and ambitions, some like FAIR in New York, and the Independent Press Association in San Francisco have enjoyed periods of impressive expansion,. Like the stock market, many of them experience 'bull' and 'bear' fluctuations in funding fortunes. Marc Raboy argues that there is 'a movement based on a limited number of people with limited energies' who can identify problems and solutions, but who lack the strength and numbers to sustain the pressure. However, he argues, this is typical of the early stages of movements; it does not preclude eventual success.

Self-marginalization: the Left needs to get its act together

When asked about barriers to successful movement mobilization, activists had no shortage of comments on their own collective shortcomings. Clearly, there is a perception within the Left that it contributes to its own marginalization and therefore the marginalization of media democratization initiatives. Several themes emerge from our interviews.

Alienation from dominant values

In the US, where corporate hegemony is arguably most ensconced, 'you have to embrace uncomfortable realities', says Mark Lloyd. Rather than constantly challenging mainstream lifestyles and values, most people enjoy watching TV and trust the local news. The American Left's oppositional mentality alienates it from what Herbert Chao Gunther of the Public Media Center calls 'the fundamental sense of patriotism, the sense that America is an incredibly powerful experiment in democracy'. As Gunther stated at the 1997 Media and Democracy Congress, 'we reject the very values that, in fact, are the motivating force of the ideals we carry'. 'You hear the phrase "sterile oppositional culture",' said Fred Stout, formerly with the Media Alliance. 'We're against everything and we're loud and articulate about it. This marginalizes the politics of the Left.'

Indicative of the US Left's identity crisis, the 1997 Media and Democracy Congress saw the Left being described by Michael Moore as representing 'the majority of the country' while another speaker accused the Left of 'constantly trying to pretend to be more normal than it is, and constantly looking around for a popular thing and trying to hitch a ride on it'. In contrast, Kim Deterline suggests that conservative groups concerned with media issues are actually more media literate and in tune with popular culture than their counterparts on the Left.

Poor organization and coordination

Key to any mobilization process is 'becoming organized', so that human and material resources can be effectively deployed. Among our respondents, the need for better networking and coordination was a repeated theme. This difficulty can easily become a vicious circle. Lack of awareness of what similar groups are doing precludes the groups from developing a common strategy or focus. Lacking common ground, groups do not devote resources to collaborative campaigns, and when they do collaborate, they may have difficulty getting along. It is not necessarily a question of antagonism or rivalry, but sometimes a simple lack of coordination. 'There's a lot of people doing tremendous work, and it's very hard to know who's doing it,' says Aliza Dichter.

Lack of coordination and networking can often be traced to insufficient resources. 'Look at what we're fighting, we're up against this model and we're all just basically holding down jobs and trying to keep this all together,' says Richard Edmondson of San Francisco Liberation Radio. On the other hand, 'there's a fair amount of territoriality', says Dorothy Kidd, an alternative media activist and professor at the University of San Francisco. Rose Dyson of C-CAVE laments that we 'never really get very far because there's so many people who want to do their own thing; unlike the Right, we have a lot of difficulty cooperating'.

Speaking in the wake of the divisive Media and Democracy Congress in 1997, Media Alliance's Andrea Buffa observed that the problem with US media activism is a lack of common projects, and of any mechanisms to stay in contact. A disconnect between Washington DC-based public interest advocacy groups, and grass-roots activists around the country was also noted. The former's 'underdog' lobbying work with Congress and administrative agencies is generally admired, but 'they don't have the resources, skills or orientation to be organizers of the mass movement', said one respondent. Internationally too, 'each NGO is fighting in its own corner', noted Philip Lee at WACC. 'They can agree on principles in abstract, but coordinated action is a different matter.'[3]

Lack of common focus and strategy

To some extent, non-collaboration between media activist groups can be related to different, and sometimes seemingly incompatible priorities and strategies. As we have argued in previous chapters, media activism does not cohere around a single strategy. This does not necessarily create a barrier to mobilization – a division of labour can be quite productive. But it could be problematic if activists dismiss or denigrate others' work, to the extent of precluding collaboration. The lack of a common action frame increases this possibility.

Such dismissals seem to be frequently directed at the idea of structural media reform, from those who approach media instrumentally as a by-product of advocacy on other social justice issues. Kim Deterline concedes that a media and democracy movement 'can be useful', but so long as it is unduly 'separate from other kinds of activism, it will be incapable of building bridges'. There are also activists who instead prioritize building alternative media. It is pointless to try and pressure the corporate media, argued Greg Ruggiero, of Seven Stories Press. What is needed instead is the creation of 'sovereign media'. 'Media wealth is too concentrated, too solidified, and too integrated into the corporate-government elite to make social change within the existing system possible,' writes the director of Project Censored (Phillips 1999: 131). Similarly, John Anner, of Independent Press Association, offers a commentary worth quoting at length:

> Unfortunately, when you're faced with ... these giant conglomerates, the amount of resources that you can bring to bear in your strategic opportunities are so limited by comparison that simply proclaiming that it's bad – you might as well form the anti-earthquake committee and claim that you've succeeded as long as there aren't any earthquakes. It just doesn't seem to me to be something that you can go up against ... You have to pick your fights ... Besides, it's a moving target. These corporations are engaged in such tremendous levels of deal-making ... that no matter how many limbs you chop off this octopus, it isn't going to get any weaker, it's just going to grow new limbs in other directions ... We can't possibly beat AOL and Time/Warner at this game. By the time we figure out what to do about it, they've already morphed into something else.

And yet, exclusive reliance on constructing a parallel field of alternative media also has its limits: it can blind activists to the need for structural reform. 'You have at some point got to engage with (dominant media),' said Kathy Lowe of CPBF, 'and also contest what is being said and done in your name in them.' Even those who are trying to establish alternative media are self-critical of their endeavour. The IndyMedia Centres tend to be 'endlessly self-referential', suggests a veteran organizer. The established alternative press, like *Utne Reader*, *The Nation*, and *Mother Jones*, is a 'conversation among elites', albeit left-leaning ones. As well, the gay 'alternative' press, argues Don Hazen, of the Independent Media Institute, has been coopted by dependence on advertising, which has weakened its political punch.

In addition to the distinction between media reform and building alternative media, Hazen sees a related kind of division – between those who want to move towards the mainstream in order to expand the audience for progressive messages, and those who fear that orienting towards wider audiences would mean watering down their ideas. This distinction overlaps with a perceived generation gap, separating older activists from younger activists involved in initiatives like the IndyMedia Centres.

Certainly media activists have no shortage of critical observations about the approaches taken by other groups. Many respondents critiqued other organizations for lacking a constituency, for not filling a particular niche within the organizational ecology of media reform, for not translating mandates and rhetoric into effective action, or for being unable or unwilling to help forge coalitions. There is little doubt that very real political differences are at play. The tension between 'free press' and 'media justice' action frames is visceral in the insistent demand from ethnic and gender minorities that their identities and priorities not be submerged in a process of building mainstream coalitions.

Outright antagonism can pose a problem for mobilizing media reform. Many respondents noted 'turf wars' between organizations competing for a limited supply of funding and recognition. This especially rings true in the US, where the organizational ecology of media activism is arguably the densest.

Similar tensions appear within groups. Larry Bensky of Media Alliance refers to internal disputes concerning whether membership and staff were sufficiently diverse. Several of the women we interviewed noted that trade unions and progressive alternative media are heavily male-dominated. Yet, particularly when it challenges hierarchy, conflict itself need not be destructive, as demonstrated in Chapter 5's example of the 1996 Media Alliance board election, which revitalized the group. As well, for the overall media reform movement, such critiques are not necessarily paralysing or debilitating. Conversely, they may well indicate the health of the movement: people are aware of its diversity, and of how they differ from other groups and why they have chosen to occupy a particular niche within it.

Strategy, however, is essential to maintaining a movement's momentum. 'We need vision, something to strive for,' argues Don Hazen, 'but visions lose their luster if there's no pragmatic path to reach them.' As John Anner puts it, if you can't tell me where the resources are going to come for that [long-term] fight, who the constituency is ... how you're going to engage that constituency and what your likelihood is of winning, who your allies are, who your enemies are, what's the strategic handle that's going to allow you to move this thing, then you don't have a strategy. All you have is a vague idea that you're doing the right thing.

Activists interviewed criticized the focus on short-term tactics, such as trying to change mainstream media coverage of a particular issue, at the expense of long-term campaigns to achieve structural change in the media and state policies. At the international level, Cees Hamelink noted a tendency for people to get excited about producing a manifesto to launch a movement but then not to stay involved in its development and promotion.

Leadership problems

A challenge for any movement whose prime object is democratization is to devise forms of leadership that prefigure a democratic future. The fissure between future and present was acknowledged in what some respondents called a 'strong founder syndrome', whereby an organization revolves around an individual, typically an 'alpha male' with energy and vision.[4]

Successful organizations need to grow beyond the founder. Part of the reason that FAIR has flourished for two decades is because of a conscious strategy that enabled founder Jeff Cohen to step back and delegate authority to the strong staff team that had been built. By contrast, the Cultural Environment Movement, an ambitious effort to create an ongoing organization working to humanize the media system, foundered, partly because it was unable to grow beyond the public profile and personality of its chief founder, communication scholar George Gerbner.[5]

Apart from the 'strong founder syndrome', media democratization has struggled with the issue of effective leadership. The ambivalence around leadership is partly a generational division of political style, between an 'old guard' Left which tends to centralize power within organizations, and 'the younger generation of activists' that is 'profoundly phobic on leadership' and hierarchy, suggest Linda Jue and Jeremy Smith at the Independent Press Association. The struggle to reconcile democracy with leadership continues.

Opportunities: missed and blocked

As William Gamson (1987: 2) points out, the field within which a movement moves is not inert: it is comprised of social forces actively striving to direct, influence, contain, or destroy the movement. In this guise, the field for collective action presents a dynamic 'structure of political opportunities' – a multi-organizational field containing both supportive and antagonistic sectors. Bert Klandermans (1992: 95) refers to the first as a movement organization's 'alliance system' – the groups and organizations that support it – and to the second as its 'conflict system' – its opponents, including countermovement groups: 'Alliance systems provide resources and create political opportunities; conflict systems drain resources and restrict opportunities.' Put concisely, democratic media activism has been stymied by a weak alliance system and by a very strong conflict system centred on the corporate media. Below, we consider two potential allies whose ties to DMA have not grown to the extent they could – labour and journalists, and then turn to the conflict system arrayed against the movement.

Building coalitions is an inherently challenging process. Media reformers face a challenge to persuade potential allies to move beyond focusing exclusively on trying to change mainstream media coverage. 'It is a tough problem,' notes Media Alliance's Ben Clarke, 'because on a daily basis, what people need is to insert their message in the mainstream, but that can be done successfully only on an intermittent level.' In 1998, John Anner suggested that, by and large, minorities and the poor were not engaged with media and democracy organizations, because 'there is no base building strategy on the part of the movement ... If the people who you're claiming are being screwed over by the way the media operates are not being engaged by your organization, then it's hard to see how you're having a movement.' There are signs of such engagement, however. As we saw in Chapter 5, Jeff Perlstein at Media Alliance has recently outlined a strategy for encouraging minority youth activists to move from producing their own media, to engaging with media policymakers, at least at the city level where cable TV franchises and related access policies are negotiated.

Missing partners and cultural divides

A significant missing partner for media reform in the US, and relatively by contrast with Britain and Canada, is the labour movement. Peter Phillips notes that Project Censored gets support on a local basis from trade unionists, but that there is no larger coalition in the works at this point. McChesney and Nichols (2002a: 127) identified organized labour, along with teachers, librarians, civil libertarians, artists, religious denominations and civil rights advocates, as 'natural allies' who have been 'absent for far too long'. American unions are not looking seriously at the media environment or investing in policy for media change, lamented Andrea Buffa.[6] American labour 'is too diverse to get them all onside at once, there are real rifts within it', noted a Bay Area activist. Moreover, during the Clinton administration, 'they had a vested interest in the status quo and some access to power'.

Arguably though, more historically rooted factors, as discussed in Chapter 2, are at work. Labour's relative absence bespeaks the legacy of Cold War conservatism within US trade unions, as well as an historic split within the American Left. The Vietnam war era, when anti-war students and blue-collar workers were at loggerheads, may well be echoing still. While the mainstream British Left was nurtured within the working class, the contemporary US Left springs from outside 'middle America' – ethnic minorities, students, academics. As a result, the alliance system for media democratization in the United States is chronically impaired by the lack of a labour left. Jeremy Smith of Media Alliance argues that historically, the labour movement was behind most progressive legislation in the US and 'once that went, we lost a base that I think left the rest of the activist movement kind of floundering'. Janine Jackson notes that American unions are reluctant to be seen as critical towards media for fear of jeopardizing their prospects of positive coverage.[7]

While the UK labour movement has historically been far more involved in pushing for media reform, younger activists nowadays see trade unions as old-fashioned and are not joining either unions or the Labour Party as much as they once had, argues Kathy Darby of the CPBF. Her colleague, Kathy Lowe, notes that many young people in the UK reject the existing political system, creating a division between radical and more reformist strands. Barry White, also with the CPBF, agrees that a libertarian ethic, disinterested in policy debates, is developing among British youth, but he expresses more concern about youth activists' narrow focus on individual concerns at the expense of 'a much wider picture'.

Perhaps there is some justification for the reluctance of young people to join labour unions or pursue traditional reform measures. A British trade unionist observed that it is frustrating to be calling for democratization of the media without also calling for democratization within the labour movement. Even the National Union of Journalists (NUJ) is losing members and is not really representative of its members, said one observer off the record – although an NUJ official claimed that to the contrary, membership is rising. Paradoxically, the CPBF may sometimes benefit from the relative lack of union democracy, in that it receives funding from unions whose members were not actively involved in deciding to support the Campaign, according to one sympathetic academic.

A particularly fateful gap separates journalists from media activists outside the newsroom. As potential change agents, journalists have more leverage than do most outsider groups. In the erosion of their working conditions and professional status and ideals, journalists bear the brunt of corporate concentration, rationalization, and workforce casualization in the media field. However, those very processes also erode journalists' power and make resistance more difficult. Moreover, although North American journalism's 'regime of objectivity' has progressive aspects, it generally works to obscure the integration of news production with commercial imperatives, to reproduce hegemonic definitions of reality in news narrative, and to dissuade journalists from ideologically challenging corporate control of the media or working with progressive groups who do (Hackett 2000: 69; Hackett and Zhao 1998; McChesney and Hackett 2005: 229).

Part of the difficulty of building alliances between journalists and democratic media advocates is that the latter sometimes critique the very practices that journalists see as a hallmark of professionalism. Journalists and activists may well have in mind different models of what constitutes professional, democratic journalism. Journalists learn a bureaucratic, top-down style of journalism in journalism schools, says Janine Jackson of FAIR, so they may not perceive the need to include the perspectives of those on the receiving end of policy. In short, the ethos of objectivity is an important barrier to political involvement by journalists. To some extent, it is imposed from above, as many news organizations set explicit limits on public advocacy or civic engagement by their journalists. 'I don't want any of my reporters going down to City Hall and testifying at some committee about an issue, I don't think it speaks well with the paper, our objectivity,' said an editor at a San Francisco daily. 'Journalists are very sensitive to being seen as biased,' argues Media Alliance's Andrea Buffa, 'especially if it's a bias towards the Left.' The idea of 'associating themselves with an organization that actually takes strong political positions on media issues ... scares away journalists'. Buffa noted that Media Alliance is in 'a kind of a bind' because it publicly identifies itself as a progressive organization but does not want to risk 'completely losing the journalists' who are in it.

In Canada, a CBC reporter noted that CBC management was 'quite hesitant to be seen as being involved or associated with any sort of coalitions outside of oneself', and thus was reluctant to cover protests by the Friends of Canadian Broadcasting against cutbacks to CBC. But journalists themselves typically endorse objectivity as a hallmark of professionalism.[8] The situation may not be much different in Britain, where union activism amongst journalists has declined. While many journalists might join the NUJ because it is linked to professional ethical concerns, they stop short of joining the CPBF because they see it as too political, claims Darby. Their aspirations to independence and professionalism discourage British journalists from joining unions or engaging in politics, laments an NUJ official.

In Vancouver, David Beers, the founding editor of the online journal *Tyee*, expressed concern that the very culture of journalism has 'atrophied', as a result of its 'reward and punishment system'. Journalists are 'a miserable bunch' because their initial high civic ideals, and their expectations of reward for initiative and creativity, run afoul of the market-driven realities of their workplace. But they fail to translate their discontent into mobilization, because they are already 'self-selected to not be that sort of person; those who are ... have tended to walk already'. Furthermore, many of the young journalists in corporate media may be coming not out of journalism but business schools, Beers suggests, so criticism simply 'doesn't register on their radar'.

The kind of people attracted to journalism, *Vancouver Province* editor Mike Walsh suggests, are 'lone rangers':

> This inhibits too much passing of information back and forth when you're on a story, because after all you're in competition ... It also inhibits getting too close to coalition-building ... because you don't want to be perceived as being anyone's cat's paw.

Peter Murdoch of Canada's CEP union comments that journalists are more attuned to worrying about state intervention in the newsroom than 'the long arm of corporations'. 'The elephant is in the room and they can't see it,' says freelance journalist Frances Russell, or they are just too fearful of losing their jobs to say anything.

Activists at both FAIR and Media Alliance noted the difficulty of balancing carrot and stick, insider and outsider strategies vis-à-vis news media. 'We have to be working with journalists and work inside these institutions and not just write them off,' says Jeff Perlstein. There are signs that rapprochement is possible. Jeff Cohen comments that journalists are unwilling openly to identify with FAIR, but will privately express appreciation for FAIR's work and will accept its support when necessary. Granville Williams acknowledges that the CPBF is critical of journalism, but notes that the Campaign has earned journalists' respect to some extent, because it has defended them from government attacks. The nature of their alliance will shift with each issue, he says.

On the other hand, some activists are sceptical of placing too much emphasis on coalition-building. Fred Stout said that the idea of making coalitions 'with guys who wear thousand dollar silk suits and ride around in limousines, which is the leadership of organized labour' is the road to cooptation. The executive director of the Praxis Project, Makani Themba-Nixon, considered it preferable for multiple organizations to 'chip away' at the media system from a variety of angles. Indeed, she argues intriguingly that a movement does not have to be cohesive, that the 'chaos and conflict' of the Media and Democracy Congress 'freaked out a bunch of people' but usefully exposed the 'false unity' of media work, replacing it with the realization that the movement is huge and that 'nobody owns any of it'. Long-term coalitions may be less appropriate for media democratization, compared to other movements. Janine Jackson notes that most of FAIR's partnerships with other groups are short-term and focused on single issues, partly because media issues are variegated and changing, by contrast with the relative constancy of (for instance) environmental issues.

Arguably the most momentous cultural divides are those of race and gender. Like the proverbial elephant in the living room, these issues appeared to be difficult for activists to raise or discuss, at least with white, male interlocutors. Some, like Aliza Dichter, did emphasize the need to re-centre the 'incredibly fundamental' issues of race and gender, as well as class, not just in the media but in the movement's practices as well. Such entrenched hierarchies of material and cultural status, and the tensions and responses to which they give rise – their 'pertinent effects', including so-called identity politics – form a subterranean fault line underneath most progressive social movements, particularly in the US (Gitlin 1995). The framing, coalition-building and leadership challenges facing media democratizers are undoubtedly exacerbated by these broader social cleavages.

Opponents of media democratization

A more obvious blockage to democratic media reform comprises the vested interests who stand to lose power or profits from their control over public communication. From a global pulpit, the world's largest communication conglomerates preach the gospel of privatization and the belief that 'people cannot be trusted to make sound ... decisions about their own lives' (Hamelink 1995: 32–3).

Media democratization's 'conflict system' extends beyond the media field per se, to struggles over media representations of other social justice issues, and related policy outcomes. Norm Solomon of the Institute for Public Accuracy, cited 'the dominant role of major think tanks in the US, like the Heritage Foundation, American Enterprise Institute and the Cato Institute'. Trade unionists at the Media and Democracy Congress spoke of the National Labor Relations Board, and companies that can spend thousands of dollars per vote to defeat union organizing drives. Public health and anti-violence community activists identified the tobacco and alcohol industries, the government and its agencies, fast food chains, and the National Rifle Association. Overall though, the core opponents, whom Dutch communications professor Cees Hamelink (1995: 31) identifies as 'the enemies of the democratic ideal', are media corporations, their associations, and their political and intellectual allies.

Internationally, the size and power of the opponents of media democratization are exponentially greater than they were during the NWICO debate of the 1970s. Then, 'we were very impressed with the power of organizations such as the United Press, International Press, which are bankrupt today', says Hamelink, but 'now we face a company like AOL-Time-Warner, with stock value comparable to the entire Dutch economy'.

Media corporations make formidable opponents, for many reasons. First, they control significant financial resources, which gives them many strategic options. For example, corporate takeover has not been adequately contested because there has been a conscious strategy, through agencies like the AOL Foundation, to coopt people by funding digital divide research rather than issues related to control, ownership and vision. The success of these organizations in marginalizing broader debates about the role of media and information technology in society was highlighted by Pradip Thomas at WACC, who mentioned that those who question information technology, which is a prime focus of the private sector and many governments, are immediately dismissed as Luddites. Marc Raboy notes that there is a 'move' on the part of pro-globalization forces to 'contain' information sources that come out of the independent media movement. 'Look anywhere in the world and you will not find democratization of communications,' adds Philip Lee at WACC. 'In fact, the trend now is towards entrenching the powers that be, the owners and the whole system.'

Moreover, more than other corporations, media companies directly control publicity that can promote their own positions, or denigrate or intimidate those who dare to challenge them.[9] Their influence in politics and government is a further dimension of media corporations' power. In Canada, NDP MP Wendy Lill notes the donations by CanWest Global and BCE to the governing Liberal Party, and the influence of corporate lobbyists in government. In the US, respondents cite as evidence of corporate media's political power the fact that since 2000 Congress has rolled back many of the advances of the microradio movement. Furthermore, the (ab)use of the First Amendment to push the notion of corporate personhood has made media accountability more difficult. In Britain, Barry White notes 'a general understanding between the government and the media owners', which prevents media policy from coming up in enquiries. He instances the agreement before the 1997 general election between Rupert Murdoch and Tony Blair, whereby Murdoch agreed to lay off critical press coverage in exchange for Blair retreating from Labour's commitment to democratic media reform.

Another dimension of corporate media power is its domination vis-à-vis its workforce. A Canadian media unionist notes that it is difficult to gain much bargaining leverage with media conglomerates. During a strike at the *Calgary Herald*, for instance, Hollinger brought in strikebreaking workers from the US. Moreover, with ownership concentration, a media company can make it difficult for an employee to find work elsewhere in the industry if s/he 'runs afoul' of the employer.

Some respondents also define 'politically organized conservatives' as opponents of media reform. Conservatives have been remarkably successful in creating their own media. Thus, a progressive communications lawyer in San Francisco notes that with the partial legalization of microradio far more conservative religious groups have applied for the new licences than have activist community groups, because 'they're better organized, and they've got more money to get the word out'. Another potent weapon of the American Right is the myth of the 'left-liberal' media. Intellectually, that myth has feet of clay; it assumes that journalists control the news, are politically left-of-centre, and are willing to abuse their power to advance their politics rather than report 'objectively', i.e., in accordance with their conservative critics' worldview (McChesney 2004). Such assumptions are sharply challenged by the research summarized in Chapter 2, but the myth persists through its persistent and active promotion by well-funded political conservatives – including institutes devoted specifically to critiquing the media's alleged 'left' bias.[10] Interestingly, few respondents cited either the myth or the right-wing institutes as obstacles to media democratization, indicating perhaps little direct contact between the two sides. Nevertheless, the political consequences of the left-liberal myth are clear: mainstream American journalism has become much more timid in reporting critically about conservative positions and politicians, and the public's perception of 'the problem of the media' has been skewed by the inaccurate but politically useful conservative critique; thus, a 2003 survey found that 45 per cent of Americans considered the media 'too liberal', compared to 15 per cent 'too conservative' (McChesney 2004: 114).[11]

Post-9/11 political climate

The changing political climate after 9/11, with the Bush administration's 'war on terror', military adventures abroad and the Patriot Act's new regime of domestic surveillance (including the criminalization of dissent), reconfigured the conflict system for media democratization. The impact on news media has gone well beyond the boundaries of the United States with Barry White describing what he calls 'a militarization of reporting' in Britain. However, there was also vigorous criticism in the UK press, especially the *Guardian* and the *Daily Mirror*, of American policy and British involvement in the 2003 invasion of Iraq.

North America presents a somewhat different picture. In Canada, David Beers saw a new McCarthyism in press reaction to an October 2001 speech by feminist professor Sunera Thobani vigorously denouncing US foreign policy. Led by the right-wing *National Post*, columnists across the land denounced not only Thobani but also federal Cabinet minister Hedy Fry for being in attendance at the speech. Such trends, of course, ran much deeper and longer in the American media. The *San Francisco Chronicle*'s removal of Stephanie Salter, its most progressive local op-ed voice, was seen by the Media Alliance's Jeff Perlstein as 'part of a broader trend ... around the silencing of journalists post-9/11 who are creating space for thought-provoking discussion of the war on terrorism'. Another prime example was the firing by ClearChannel of Bay Area disc jockey Davey D, which we discussed in Chapter 5.

One should not exaggerate the political constraints created by 9/11. In Iraq, New Orleans, and elsewhere, the Bush administration has burned some of its political capital in the years since. At the same time, 9/11 and especially the political uses made of it by conservative forces, have changed the landscape for media democratization. A climate of fear undoubtedly helped Bush win re-election in 2004, despite a stumbling economy and an unpopular war. Years of uncritical coverage, or no coverage at all, in domestic media about the repressive and violent aspects of US foreign policy have helped pave the way for conservative political dominance. While there is dissent in the US press over Iraq policy, it is 'still a far cry from democratic journalism; it's still handcuffed by what people in power are communicating to journalists' (McChesney and Hackett 2005: 232).

Looking at the big picture internationally, Aidan White argues that 'democratic states have begun to pull back the liberties and fundamental freedoms that seemed so important such a short time ago', in both the European Union and the US, including a 'rush of legislation, phone-tapping, police surveillance, encryption technology, detention of migrants, patrol of the internet, [restrictions on] freedom of movement'. Moreover, such repression has a multiplier effect, as the 'war on terrorism' reinforces autocratic regimes' cynicism about Western commitment to human rights, and provides the occasion to launch 'a fresh round of media oppression in countries that routinely victimize and intimidate journalists'.

In sum, 9/11 may have reduced the space for political mobilization to reform the media, but it has also increased the democratic deficit of state policies and media structures –and the urgency of addressing them. In the next chapter, we consider resources and strategies that can provide openings for a media democratization movement.

8   Springboards for media activism

Opportunities, resources, strategies
and allies

Having surveyed the blockages to remaking media, we must now acknowledge a
dialectic between obstacles and openings. Social movements are catalysed and
defined by what they perceive to be obstacles to valued goals. The identification of
a villain or opponent responsible for perpetuating a state of injustice is an important part of the collective action frame through which movements are mobilized.
The ways in which the media system contradicts democratic values and frustrates
the goals of social movements are precisely the motives for engaging in media-oriented activism. For some, such blockages are energizing. Mark Lloyd of the Civil
Rights Forum argued that many Left activists in the US work best when they have
something concrete to oppose.

Of course, if obstacles are overwhelming, other responses become more likely –
ranging from accommodation (especially for the materially privileged) to resigned
acquiescence (Gaventa 1980), despondency, cynicism, and even the social implo-
sion found in impoverished and violent margins of the current global order.

Societies dominated by social alienation and disintegration may lack the reservoir of civic energy required for movement formation. But if there is a rough
balance between obstacles and openings, then the media's democratic deficit – the
very factors which hinder social movements in achieving immediate political goals
– can also be a catalyst for action. This appears to be the case in the Anglo-American democracies.[1] In this chapter, we explore what media activists see as the key
springboards and strategies for a movement to democratize communication.

Hot pokers: prods to activism

Much as a hot poker on the derrière provokes a reaction, political events with negative consequences can stimulate activism. Our respondents identified a number of
such hot pokers. The broadest is the triumph of neoliberalism. 'The increasing
globalization of capital, the privatization of public institutions, all form a context
for us,' explains Jerry Starr, of Citizens for Independent Public Broadcasting. 'Our
driving notion is to promote the forces of democracy in a mass society where
government is increasingly dominated by corporate interest.'

A sharp prod was George W. Bush's disputed electoral victory in 2000. The election
debacle showed people how media access and campaign finance issues are linked,

argues Holly Minch at SPIN. More subtly, for many progressive groups, including labour, Bush's 2000 victory destroyed the Clinton-era illusion of having a seat at the table, which had made them less reluctant to publicly oppose the government.

Those employed by media industries have their own hot pokers prodding them into action. Journalists and union officials in Canada and the UK mentioned layoffs and commercially motivated threats to editorial integrity. The advent of the McNewspaper, a management model in which news is driven explicitly by commercial imperatives, was a catalyst for union organizing in Canadian newsrooms, according to a CEP official. As well, heavy-handed editorial intervention by owners, such as the Asper family's imposition of centralized editorials on their CanWest newspapers, provoked a response from some of its newsrooms, particularly those with a history of dissent.

Activists we interviewed spoke of specific events as catalysts, as well as broader shifts in the media environment. In Canada, the regulatory award of one of the new pay-TV channels to Playboy in the 1980s galvanized feminists' attention to media issues. In the US, our respondents mentioned the corporate abuse of copyright, televised commercials in school classrooms, the distribution barriers to new and independent magazines, the Telecommunications Act and deregulation paving the way for greater media concentration, poor regulation of advertising, the FCC's repression of low-power FM radio, the loss of local radio, cutbacks and privatization of public broadcasting, the inability of journalists to pursue stories they feel to be in the public interest, and the marginalization of labour in mainstream media. These grievances, though seemingly disparate, are all instances of capitalism's political economy of communication.

Writer Barbara Ehrenreich described the mainstream media's disconnection from 'the great majority of Americans' as 'our opportunity'. People 'do not see themselves or their concerns or struggles reflected in the media', she said at the Media and Democracy Congress. Robert Bray at SPIN asserted that surveys repeatedly show that 'Americans feel they're not getting the news they need to make decisions that affect themselves, their families and their communities'.

Of course, history offers no guarantees. In a consumer society, audiences dissatisfied with the dominant media are more likely to turn to alternative media, which at least offers immediate relief, than to media reform activism. Perhaps even more likely, the media's democratic deficit cultivates apolitical ignorance and indifference – to reconfigure the 1960s acidhead slogan, people turn off, tune out, and drop out. Still, growing public awareness and discontent over media issues in general are trends conducive to media activism.

Social movements are typically founded by those groups most negatively affected, argues Linda Jue of Independent Press Association (IPA). In the media field, these would include consumers and social activists, but without an alternative reference point the former group may not be aware of the deficiencies and omissions of corporate media. That situation, however, may be changing. The struggle over low-power community radio has provided an opportunity to give the issues of media consolidation and diversity a face that is easily understood, according to professor Andy Opel. The microradio movement derives energy from its connection to basic needs – like keeping African-American residents informed of police brutality in their housing complex. As well, the decimation of local programming following the expansion of national radio giant ClearChannel in the US was so blatant that it fuelled the 2003 popular revolt against the FCC's proposed liberalization of (already weak) concentration and cross-ownership rules. For many people, ClearChannel concretized the case for media reform.

As theory on collective action frames predicts, mobilization is facilitated when a villain can be identified. In Canada, Conrad Black put an easily vilified face on the issue of corporate concentration. As head of Hollinger Inc., his takeover of the venerable Southam newspaper group in 1996 triggered the formation of the Canadian CPBF, a common front which launched a court challenge to the takeover on the grounds that it violated freedom of the press, as guaranteed in the Charter of Rights. While predictably the Federal Court rejected the challenge, the initiative succeeded in creating a network of groups with a common interest in opposing media concentration.

If anything can trump a good villain as a catalyst for mobilization, it is the threatened loss of a valued media service, as we saw in Chapter 5 with the attempted transformation of Pacifica Radio. This struggle encouraged media activists throughout the US, argues IPA's John Anner, because it engaged them in a meaningful fight for something concrete, and showed that they have a constituency.

It is not surprising that a major long-term catalyst for media activism is the frustration of other social movements in dealing with media. The large number of people already involved in anti-WTO activism is a springboard, argues Professor Marc Raboy, as 'they will come to realize the limitations of the media with respect to those issues'. By the same token, ethnic groups have become more active due to their exclusion from the dominant mass media. Mark Lloyd thus argues that media reformers should look to diverse ethnic groups searching for equality under the law. As if to verify his point, the demonization of Arab-Americans in the wake of 9/11 created a new constituency for Media Alliance and its strategic communication training.

As we suggested in Chapter 4, the movement to remake media lacks a unifying action frame and thus a clear collective identity. But as we have seen, there are many tangible grievances galvanizing various groups to take action, and it is through action that frames begin to take shape. Similarly, despite the limitations on available resources and opportunities noted in the last chapter, media democratization can draw upon certain sociopolitical assets and conducive aspects of the social environment, including a promising set of possible alliances. Below, we provide an overview of these, before turning to the crucial issue of strategy.

Positive springboards

Structural conduciveness

Openings for a new social movement take different forms. The field of media activism is conditioned by political, cultural, technological, economic and spatial factors, some of which render a situation opportune, or 'structurally conducive' (Smelser 1962) to movement formation.

The political system can provide openings for activists pressing state-centred claims. British and Canadian political systems are more receptive to third parties than the US system, allowing more points of entry into parliamentary debates. Canadian media reformers find a relatively receptive hearing in the left-of-centre New Democratic Party, with its concerns about Canadian sovereignty and excessive corporate power. Public enquiries and parliamentary committee hearings provide a further avenue for public interest advocates. In Britain the Labour Party leadership has retreated from previous commitments to democratic media reform, but the CPBF still has supporters in the party's caucus and the government has been less hostile on some issues, such as financial support for BBC, compared to its Tory predecessors. Even though it is a virtual two-party dictatorship, with big money dominating elections, the US political system also allows openings for media reformers. From his experience lobbying in Washington DC, Mark Lloyd holds that there are sympathetic people in Congress and the FCC, but their political hand would be strengthened if they heard more often from progressive groups.

Dominant media organizations offer their own openings. 'Media are not monolithic', as Janine Jackson of FAIR put it: 'It's not the case that nothing critical or progressive ever gets through.' Journalists do have a certain amount of autonomy, creating 'a lot of give in the system' for groups who understand their internalized roles, adds her colleague Jim Naureckas. Even if they are reluctant to join explicitly political campaigns or groups like Media Alliance, their professional concerns, such as free speech, do overlap with those of more militant media activists.

Nor are the pressures of commercialization monolithically homogenizing. Providing specialized or 'non-mainstream' programming for affluent niche markets can be quite profitable. In television, 'market forces in some ways help diversity efforts', says an academic with San Francisco's Center for the Improvement and Integration of Journalism, 'because people will tune out eventually if they don't see themselves represented'. That argument, however, applies only to cultural needs and target audiences which can be served profitably – which may help explain why the media image of affluent gay males outshines that of less well-heeled African-Americans.

Casting envious eyes across the Atlantic, a leading UK scholar sees a vigorous tradition of media criticism within American universities, by contrast with the near absence of British public intellectuals. The case should not be overstated, given the industrial orientation of journalism schools, their pursuit of corporate media funding, and their immersion in the 'regime of objectivity'. But a vital strand of media criticism has emerged from journalism schools like Columbia, and universities have provided important bases for media monitoring projects, like Project Censored in California and its northern counterpart, NewsWatch Canada.

The rise of digital media, as discussed in Chapter 3, must also count among the openings for media activism. As baseball legend Yogi Berra once allegedly said, 'When you come to a fork in the road, take it.' With respect to digitalized communication networks, media activists are branching off in both directions: using the internet, and trying to democratize it. On the one hand, our respondents discuss the sense of empowerment that it brings as a tool for connection and cost-effective movement building. In a wired world, a successful campaign or inspiring model may have more immediate resonance, sparking others to imitate or join it. On the other hand, activists also speak, however haltingly, of the internet as a part of the overall media system, a site of policy struggle. As a contested space, the internet is raising new issues of access, control, and its relationship with social, political and economic inequality (Patelis 2000), but the internet also constitutes a new field of social action for a younger generation of activists. In the US, observes Kathryn Montgomery of the Center for Media Education, youth are making effective 'civic use' of the web, especially in the wake of 9/11, creating new and oppositional sites. 'It'll be a force for good' notes Vancouver Province Editor Mike Walsh – *if* it survives 'the attempt to turn it into a shopping mall'. However, Liza Dichter, now with the Center for Independent Media Action, worries that if people become too excited about the technology, or simply take it for granted as they use it for their own purposes, then policy work addressing conventional media's ownership concentration and representational biases will be abandoned.

Some see the general 'mediatization' of economic, social and political processes as an opening for media activism. Marc Raboy argues 'more people are going to want to get involved in issues related to the media and communication as they begin to recognize the centrality of this to everything else that's going on in their lives'. As formal media education and the proportion of the workforce in the 'knowledge industry' both increase, popular scepticism towards the media is on the rise – even if this has not yet translated into a sophisticated understanding of media's political economy and 'what can be done from a citizen's point of view to respond', argues a Vancouver journalist. A good number of our respondents were turned on to media issues through post-secondary education courses in gender issues related to pornography and media violence, or through journalism, political science and communication/cultural studies degrees. The spread of higher education, and the mediatization of society, are trends likely to nourish future media activism.

Although often seen in its capitalist mode as a threat to human welfare and democracy, globalization also has created openings for media democratization. Transnational movements against corporate-driven globalization have been a driving force for alternative media. While disavowing neoliberal economics, some activists, such as WACC staffers in London, concede that globalization can link up communities, with 'people for the first time having a sense of being one world'. Also globalization can introduce Westernizing norms that could benefit the status of women in some countries where 'women do not have a voice'.

Finally, among the factors enhancing structural conduciveness is the role that certain global cities have played as 'incubators' for activism – sites where alternative media and media activism can flourish. San Francisco (as discussed in detail in Chapter 5) is a key example, though we shall see in Chapter 9 that Vancouver has played a similar role.

Resources

Social movements are built not by abstract forces but by people making sense of their situation and striving to influence it. What experiences, incentives or motives draw citizens to become personally involved in media activism in the first place and to remain engaged? What resources are available for media activism? While our interviews are hardly exhaustive, they suggest several paths to such involvement.

Despite scarcities noted in Chapter 7, our respondents described a variety of resources directly available to their organizations. Such resources – economic (money, staff), psychological (enthusiasm, confidence), and cultural (expertise, credibility, recognition) – can be deployed to create collective organization, to launch and win campaigns, to provide incentives for participation (reducing the 'free rider' problem), to punish or defeat opponents, and to achieve influence vis-à-vis other social actors within both the media field and the broader field of power.

Probably the most useful starting point is to consider who butters the bread. The political economy of neoliberal capitalism systematically overcompensates the owners of capital, encourages the production and individualized consumption of commodities that often have massively harmful social or environmental impacts, and under-rewards activity pursuing collective and non-commodifiable benefits – like democratic media. In such a system, how do public interest groups survive, let alone succeed?

For media democrats, the inventory of funding sources is all too small. It includes grants from a handful of left-liberal philanthropic foundations (especially important in the US), and or large-scale memberships and subscriptions from trade unions (more common in the UK). In Canada and the UK, more than in the tax-phobic US, progressive local or national governments and their agencies have sometimes contributed to cultural democratization projects. The Greater London Council in the 1980s, as noted in Chapter 6, is a prime example. In Canada, in the 1960s and early 1970s, the federally funded National Film Board undertook projects in local communities 'to use film as a tool for social change' (Henaut 1991: 48). More recently, the early 1990s NDP government of Ontario gave the Friends of Canadian Broadcasting $20,000.

In all three countries, membership dues and donations from supporters are an important funding source. These can be divided into altruistic donors (particularly important during stages of organizational start-up or financial crisis), and those who are paying for a benefit such as a magazine, classes or even health insurance. In the era of right-wing fundamentalist Christianity, it is easy to overlook religious organizations as a resource for progressive activism; but Protestant churches in the global North and the US Catholic Conference of Bishops have helped fund the WACC and the Civil Rights Forum respectively.

Some media activist groups have successfully found a niche within the political economy of capitalism, generating a revenue stream through commodified services or products. Most obviously, 'alternative' media from magazines like *The Nation* to Michael Moore's commercially successful documentaries have tapped a market for oppositional ideological weaponry. By providing marketing and distribution services for independent/alternative magazines, John Anner's Independent Press Association grew visibly between interview visits in 1998 and 2001, from a staff of two in a dingy upstairs office to a staff of seventeen in a spacious, sunlit building. The IPA by then had amassed a $500,000 revolving loan fund for individual magazines to meet their capital needs, and sufficient resources to begin advocacy work (over issues like magazine postal rates, for instance) on behalf of its members. FAIR has likewise found a commodity-based (but advertising-free) revenue stream through its magazine *Extra!*, with about 16,000 paid subscriptions by 2000.

Against the temptation and logic of capital accumulation, some groups like Media Alliance, as previously discussed, use such revenue streams to cross-subsidize organizing work. For instance, in addition to foundation funding to launch the Praxis Project, Makani Themba-Nixon used consulting contracts with those who could afford to pay to subsidize advocacy work on behalf of those who couldn't. Such market-generated revenue sources have reduced dependence on foundations or unions, though not on the requirement of producing a marketable commodity and finding a profitable niche. However even with cross-subsidization, the financial resources of media democracy groups are minuscule compared to the aggregated billions of dollars available to advertisers, media corporations, and other political actors in the field. Media Alliance's dues from its 3,000 to 4,000 members, the £56,000 income during the CPBF's heyday in 1986, even FAIR's US$800,000 budget or the Can$1.6 million raised by the Friends of Canadian Broadcasting in 2000 – all pale next to the budgets for government information departments, corporate public relations, or national political party campaigns. The discrepancies in resources translate more or less directly into disparities in cultural reach. Typically, the efforts of media activists do not enable even successful alternative media, or system-challenging media reformers, to project their voices far beyond the choir. The 5,000 circulation of the CPBF's *Free Press*, the 16,000 readers of *Extra!*, the 20,000 members of the CEP union, even the Friends of Canadian Broadcasters' impressive 51,000 direct mail donors in the year 2000, are but a tiny fraction of the audience for a prime-time 'reality TV' programme.

Securing financial resources is important, but group survival and influence depend critically on people's energy and commitment, on networking and mutual support, and on leveraging existing resources. The old adage – organized money can be challenged only by organized people – is confirmed by the collective experience of our interviewees. Many successful initiatives have built upon existing institutional resources and networks – foundations, universities, trade unions, or established movement organizations with compatible objectives.

In other cases, groups have been built almost from scratch, on the backs of one or a few extremely dedicated and skilful activists. Jeff Cohen describes launching FAIR in the 1980s through Los Angeles friends who helped scrape together air fare for a few round trips to New York, where he worked 80 hours a week for months, sacrificing a social life, meeting potential funders, using his own savings and friends' donations, working with a small and mostly volunteer staff, including Andy Breslaw, an intern whose inheritance enabled him to work without pay. While

FAIR has grown well beyond its original founder, it would likely not exist without his initial sacrifices. Similarly, other groups would likely have been stillborn, or foundered later in their trajectory, but for the energies of people like Granville Williams and Tom O'Malley in CPBF, and Andrea Buffa at Media Alliance – activists who have earned the admiration of their peers.

For many, media activism was an extension of their previous political commitments. Their media activism grew out of a radical habitus (Crossley 2003) – in feminist communities, in struggles for social justice in the health care system and disability services, in opposing cuts to the arts, in opposition to the Vietnam war, in environmentalism, in Third World development and (in Britain) in trade unionism. Some people dealt with the media on behalf of these specific causes; others saw involvement in the media field (whether as journalists, producers or critics of media) as an expression of more general values. Growing up in America during the Vietnam war led Vancouver freelance journalist David Beers to understand from an early age that there were 'big struggles underway, and it could be an interesting and very rewarding life to be somewhere involved in those'.

It is not surprising that much media activism derives from those who feel that their causes or communities are under- or mis-represented in the media. KPFA broadcaster Larry Bensky's words bespeak the energy of outrage: the corporate media are closed 'to telling the truth about political, environmental and social issues', and thus contribute to 'a planet … and a society that is disgracefully unequal as ours … filled with discrimination and conditions that drive people crazy and poison them mentally and physically'.

In the US, the media activists we interviewed were more likely to have a background in 'alternative' than 'mainstream' media. But in Canada and the UK, media unions have been more directly involved in coalitions challenging corporate media power. Britain's stronger union and socialist traditions explain some of the difference; some leading members of the CPBF have had formative experiences in both journalism and socialist or Marxist political parties. Others, particularly in Canada, appear to have arrived at union activism through disillusioning workplace experience.

As with many movements, media activism typically entails low or no pay, long hours, daily confrontation with unpleasant political realities, and very uncertain political outcomes. What factors help people to sustain their involvement? At the organizational level, groups like Media Alliance could not have survived for decades without providing incentives for membership – from its social activities in the early years, to professional support for journalists and freelancers, to material incentives – classes, access to job listings and health insurance. A good board–staff relationship, participatory decision-making, a clear political vision, and an ongoing public profile, including public events on topical issues, also help to maintain morale and commitment. Of course, positive and visible achievements, like the defeat of the Pacifica 'coup', certainly galvanize an organization. But in a climate of neoliberal hegemony, such victories are not plentiful; by contrast with the 1960s and 1970s, the Left in the North Atlantic has little sense of being carried by the tide of history. Other incentives must be found. At the personal level, the feeling of 'being part of something worthy' helps one cope with the demands of activism, according to a Media Alliance staffer. One media reform veteran, a retired professor in his sixties, explained that political outcomes are usually ambiguous at best, so his continued activism depends on enjoying the organizing and campaigning process itself.

Allies and coalitions

The formation of alliances and coalitions expands the reach and scope of media activism. Although, as we saw in Chapter 7, the movement has been hampered by its weak ties with social forces that should count among its constituents, our respondents pointed to numerous possibilities in the emerging situation for coalition formation. Many respondents proclaimed support, at least in principle, for inter-organizational and professional alliances. Groups most often mentioned included journalists, alternative media producers, academics, unions, public interest policy advocates, grassroots social justice groups, and the broader community. To be sure, sentiments expressed in words do not necessarily translate into action. Nevertheless, the kinds of coalitions being proposed are indicative of at least the desire for a broad-based social movement with staying power.

We asked respondents to identify groups they regarded as *actual or potential allies*. Of course, the question of whom 'we' should ally with presumes a conception of who 'we' are. The allies any particular group will seek are partly determined by its position on the social and political 'map'; a map which is itself constituted through a web of relationships. But the answers are in fact *not* all over the map; they break down into several fairly cohesive clusters.

Other media activists and communication-oriented groups

Frequently media groups complement each other, either in terms of geographical location, or particular focus and expertise. A case in point: the relationship between microradio activists and progressive lawyers, people with vastly different backgrounds but with a shared commitment to free speech and citizens' access to the airwaves. Even groups with similar 'organizational repertoires' (Mueller *et al.* 2004: 19) may collaborate on different aspects of the same project; thus, the Berkeley Media Studies Group and the Public Media Centre both work on health advocacy through the media, but the latter specializes in paid advertising.

Partnerships between organizations with a history of 'turf wars' are probably less likely. Groups that continually compete for the same project funding and clientele are likely either to die, or to shift their mandate to a less contested organizational niche. This conclusion, though speculative, is reinforced by the observation of Mueller *et al.* (2004: 25) that the political and economic environment in the US – the limits of human and financial resources, and of public attention to communication policy issues – can currently support a 'population' of not much more than 100 national public interest groups in this field. On the other hand, such a view may be too static, leading to unwarranted zero-sum views of strategy. Holly Minch at

SPIN argues that 'the task is so great that there's going to be work for all of us for a long time to come', and that by sensitizing other social justice groups to communication issues, SPIN is actually increasing the demand for the services of other media-related groups, like Communication Works. As a movement gains momentum in public and political agendas, the number and size of related SMOs may well increase.

Non-media advocacy groups in civil society concerned with progressive social change

In the US, activists concerned with public interest policy reform cite as allies a range of NGOs, particularly in the fields of the environment, civil rights and women's equality: the Leadership Conference on Civil Rights; National Organization of Women, unions, church groups (including the US Catholic Conference which is conservative on other social issues); the Unitarian Universalist church; pediatricians; public health groups; disability advocates; 'mainstream educational and cultural organizations' like the national PTA, National Education Association and National Council of Churches; Washington-based policy advocacy groups like the Consumer Federation of America and the Center for Digital Democracy; progressive policy research institutes, like the Center for Policy Initiatives, foundations and institutes seeking investment in childcare, or the prevention of violence or drug and alcohol abuse; associations of African-Americans and Latinos; neighbourhood associations and local coalitions; and in the words of Peter Phillips at Project Censored, 'anybody concerned with human rights and social justice'.

Trade unions

Considered in the previous chapter as a weak link in the system of alliances in the US, unions have several potential motives for supporting media democratization. When they represent workers inside media industries, they have a stake in job security, working conditions, and (to some extent) the integrity of journalism and the protection of individual journalists' autonomy in the face of ownership, state and commercial pressures. Unions outside the media industries have often been frustrated by their mass-mediated image, though other priorities and their investment in public relations have diverted energies from sustained media reform campaigns. A major exception was the anger of public sector workers and striking coalminers at their treatment by Britain's rabidly right-wing, pro-Thatcher press in the 1970s and 1980s, anger which fuelled the CPBF in its early years. To the extent that trade unionists think of themselves as part of a broader movement, they have a third reason to favour media reform – principled support for social change.

Governments, political parties and state agencies

Cees Hamelink argues that some long-term coalitions might well include governments, which may sometimes have coinciding interests with media democrats. He himself has worked on media education promotion with the Swiss government, which seeks a distinctive role within the United Nations system.

Often political parties, whether governing or not, provide portals to the state. In Britain, the CPBF had long regarded the Labour Party as its primary political ally. In Canada, the federal NDP provides a voice for democratic media reform within the parliamentary arena, even if it does not give media issues as much priority as some of its own members hope for. A Vancouver reporter mentions the broadcast regulator CRTC, not as an ally but at least as 'a place you can go to complain if there's a problem', by contrast with 'press councils that have absolutely no teeth'. In the US, while the 2000 Ralph Nader-led Green Party made media reform a major plank in its platform, media activists have generally had to appeal to individual politicians rather than parties. The two Democratic members of the five-person FCC, Michael Copps and Jonathan Adelstein, were instrumental in the anti-media concentration 'uprising' of 2003 (McChesney 2004: 261–4). While some Democrats, like Jesse Jackson, addressed the 2003 National Conference on Media Reform in Madison, Wisconsin, Republicans were conspicuously absent. Still, the Democratic Party as a whole is hardly a unified force on media reform, and American media activists do not appear to be aligned with it as an organizing venue.

Tactical alliances with media industry groups

Sometimes, advocacy groups find themselves siding with commercial interests on specific issues. Ian Morrison says the Friends of Canadian Broadcasters will 'do business' with the Canadian Association of Advertisers on the issue of preserving CBC regional news programmes, even though 'we don't share their values'. The two groups also have a common interest in opposing CanWest's attempts to obtain regulatory approval for increased minutes of ads per broadcast hour. The Friends are concerned about excessive commercialism; the advertisers worry about 'diminishing the quality of the contact with viewers'. Media activists are also at times aided through corporate philanthropy. George Soros' Open Society Institute and its support for political and media democratization in the former Soviet bloc is well known. Youthful dot.com millionaires in Seattle, who are credited with helping finance the launching of the IndyMedia Centre at the 1999 WTO protests, are another example.

Sometimes helping young upstarts is plain good business. John Anner is proud of a deal his IPA achieved with Barnes and Noble to give major display to IPA periodicals under the marketing rubric of 'Independent Magazines for Independent Thinkers'. For commercially-distributed alternative media, making deals within the media industry is a direct outgrowth of their mandate, a reminder that market forces can support diversity, if only to the extent that it is profitable.

Tactical alliances with conservatives

Such alliances may be practicable on libertarian/free speech issues or in opposition to the excesses of commercial imperatives in broadcasting – excessive violence, poor children's programming, and so on. In pressuring local county commissioners to make more community access programming a condition of a renegotiated local cable TV franchise, an activist at the ACME Summit described 'conservative radio, anti-government types' as among 'our biggest allies', lending legitimacy and leverage in negotiations. Gerry Morrissey of Britain's BECTU union mentions the socially conservative pressure group MediaWatch UK: 'We wouldn't contact them on every issue, but there are certain issues that we sing off the same hymn sheet and we can work together.'

The importance of social and/or economic conservatives as tactical allies was amply illustrated during the 2003 anti-FCC 'uprising', when influential right-wing groups like the National Rifle Association helped flood Congress with three million messages of outrage. Conservative beefs included the decline of competition and of local ownership and programming. They shared 'public distaste with the vulgarity of radio and television'; vulgarity that was 'exacerbated by media concentration, because huge firms provided the cheapest fare possible and were unaccountable to local communities' (McChesney 2004: 280). Perhaps some conservatives also believed their own myth of the 'left-liberal media' and feared media concentration as a vehicle for pinko newscasters and media moguls.

Alliances in perspective

This review of alliances and coalitions suggests several points.

First, in responding to our questions, *activists understood 'alliances' along a spectrum*, from coincidental alignment on the same side of an issue, to short-term cooperation on a single project, to long-term working relationships, to mutual solidarity and automatic reciprocal support. There was little evidence of the last. In the UK, the CPBF has some very longstanding patrons amongst the trade unions. But in the US, long-term partnerships seem no easier in progressive media activism than in personal life. As Janine Jackson says of FAIR, most alliances are short-term and focused on single issues, and collaborating with other groups is hard work. The efforts of the Media Democracy Congress and CEM to bring a variety of groups into the same tent for more than a two-day conference failed miserably. John Anner declares as one of IPA's mottos, 'No permanent enemy, no permanent friends.'

One could read these responses as a legacy of the divisiveness of 'identity politics' in the US over the past twenty years, or a by-product of the territoriality inspired by the predominant organizational form of US public interest activism – the foundation-funded advocacy group. But other reasons are also plausible: activist groups' commitment to their own mandate or principles, combined with (as Janine Jackson suggests) the multiplicity and abstractness of media issues. Whatever the reason, in the US communication policy field, public interest advocacy groups – by contrast with trade and professional associations – have tended to die out rather than merge or adapt mandates, as the issue-focus shifted to include digital media (Mueller *et al.* 2004: 28).

Second, our respondents' aggregated list of allies helps to outline, albeit hazily, *the shape of a potential media democracy coalition* – as well as the missing partners and connections needed to bring it to life. Although several respondents, like Robert McChesney, counted 'political people who call themselves conservatives' as potential allies, there is little indication of a willingness to exploit divisions within corporate capital and the state. When asked to identify groups that could be *potentially* mobilized for media reform, our informants essentially reproduced the roll call of existing allies, with perhaps an added emphasis on religious, anti-globalization and academic groups.

Considering their proportion of the population and their historical marginalization, gays and lesbians appear to be under-represented in media democracy campaigns. Speculatively, the relative improvement of gays' representation in popular culture (think of *Ellen, Queer as Folk, Queer Eye for the Straight Guy*), the strength of urban weeklies oriented towards the affluent gay male market, and the success the Gay and Lesbian Alliance Against Defamation (GLAAD) has enjoyed through working with rather than against media giants like Disney, have reduced the incentive for 'moderates' in the gay rights movement to critique corporate media. Also dissatisfaction with the priorities of other progressives may have reduced their willingness to enter coalitions centred on structural media reform, which is not perceived as addressing gays' particular grievances. 'Why has Chomsky never written about homophobia in the media?' one activist plaintively asked.

Revisiting the late 1990s, there was another missing link: few of our respondents mentioned collaboration between civil society groups working on national communication policy and those working at the international level (like the WACC). But with events like the WTO protests in Seattle, and the (debatable) political opportunity presented by the first World Summit on the Information Society in 1993, public interest media groups working nationally have begun to turn attention to international communications policy as an increasingly crucial field for intervention (Ó Siochrú 2005a, 2005b).

Third, whatever the limitations of existing collaborations, there was nevertheless a widespread acceptance of the *need for coalition building*. Indeed, a number of successful partnerships, and a willingness to cross the boundaries from familiar strategic repertoires into important but less comfortable terrain when circumstances demanded, were evident in the interviews. Two examples of such bridge building are worth recalling here:

- FAIR helped catalyse a coalition around the apparent mainstream media cover-up of Gary Webb's 1996 exposé of connections between the CIA, the illegal funding of Contra insurgents in Nicaragua, and the cocaine trade with its devastating consequences in black communities. Called 'Snow Job', the campaign involved blacks and Central American solidarity groups who had not previously worked together, demonstrating the potential of media activism to build bridges between different stakeholders. FAIR activist Tom Blazer at the Media Democracy Congress noted: 'It was easy to get support from other groups; whenever we generated a particular issue, we were able to get attention because everybody knows that what we were doing was important to their cause.'

- The Canadian CPBF 'common front' against press concentration included the major anglophone media unions (CEP, GCIU, Canadian Media Guild, Newspaper Guild); some major public sector unions, including several provincial teachers' federations, postal workers, and CUPE; a major private sector union (Canadian Auto Workers) and two provincial and one national labour congress; research and advocacy groups concerned with media issues (Friends of Canadian Broadcasting, MediaWatch), and other progressive advocacy groups – Rural Dignity, National Farmers' Union, Jesuit Centre for Social Faith and Justice, National Anti-Poverty Organization, Action Canada Network; and the country's largest progressive umbrella group, the Council of Canadians. While the rank and file of these organizations were not particularly involved in the campaign to stop Conrad Black, it does suggest the potential for broad organizational support for media reform.

Fourth, the picture emerging in this chapter and the last one suggests a *revision of the concentric circles of media democratization constituencies* outlined in Chapter 3. At the centre, we had suggested, were journalists and other workers in media industries who had a daily stake in challenging the exploitation of labour, the stifling of creativity, the downsizing of resources, the undermining of autonomy and 'objectivity' which underpin journalists' claim to professional status. But the main energies for democratic media activism flow, arguably, not from those at the centre of the media field (whose ambivalence was discussed in Chapter 7) but from those in the second of our concentric circles: social groups and individuals with some degree of social and cultural capital (education, skills, networks, political analyses) who need but are constrained in their access to the machinery of public representation. As with many other social movements, the impetus for system challenges derives neither from the very top or bottom of the social hierarchy, nor from the centre or the outermost margins, but from the most privileged of the marginalized.

Strategy

As outlined in Chapter 3, democratic media activism comprises several different strategic vectors – direct challenges to the dominant media system and its political/economic framework through legislative reform or strategic communication, or building alternatives in the 'lifeworld', notably alternative media. In this section, we present a composite action repertoire, drawn from interviews with activists, as a basis for considering whether different strands of DMA are working in competition, isolation, or synergistic collaboration with each other. Our distinction between initiatives centred on the political-economic system and those centred on the psycho-cultural lifeworld enables us to highlight the strategic importance of several forms of activism. These include 'insider' actions *within* the corporate media (e.g. by journalists), alliances that *transect* system and lifeworld, and media education, culture jamming and related practices that create a radical habitus for reception and production of alternative media.

Building alternative media

As a panellist at the Media Democracy Congress noted, alternative media have a dual role: first, to expose and fill the blind spots of mainstream media; and, second, to arm their audiences 'to take action on various issues' by supplying them with 'mobilizing information' – the details and context that enable readers to become actively involved in the issue being reported (Stanfield and Lemert 1987; cited in Atton 2002: 86). These roles approximate respectively the distinction between democratization *of* and *through* the media.

   Our interviews did not focus on alternative media, but it seems that the potential for challenging the credibility and audience share of corporate media is far from being realized. Alternative media do not necessarily have counterhegemonic or system-challenging ambitions. In Britain, they seem oriented towards defending the interests of particular communities, such as the 'Undercurrents' project teaching hundreds of grassroots organizations to use cameras to inhibit police violence, or an organization like Public Voice advocating for the interests of charities and volunteer organizations in broadcasting. There is nevertheless a current of activism that sees building independent media as the best route to challenging the corporate media's domination of public consciousness. Peter Phillips of Project Censored hypothesizes that once 5 or 10 per cent of the population obtains 'real news' from independent media a widespread clamour for media reform will follow. Certainly alternative and non-corporate media are more likely to give favourable attention to media reform initiatives. In Vancouver, the independently owned weekly *Georgia Straight*, with a tradition of 'alternative' journalism, has probably devoted more columns to NewsWatch Canada and Media Democracy Day than both corporate dailies combined.

   Alternative media take in a wide range of communication technologies. Media democracy groups have creatively integrated new digital media with conventional mass media. Print publications such as *Extra!*, *Free Press* and *Media File* remain a core activity for many groups, as do assemblies which emphasize interpersonal communication – notably conferences, and Board and membership meetings. Some groups, like FAIR, produce radio programmes for both conventional and web-based broadcasting. Norm Solomon writes a newspaper column of critical media analysis, syndicated to about 15 dailies; and his Institute for Public Accuracy coordinates a network of progressive sources for newspapers and other news media.

Media education, culture jam

Forms of lifeworld-centred activism, such as critical media education, foster the cultural sensibilities necessary for a media democratization movement to thrive.

Activists explicitly emphasized media education's critical component (to 'challenge media in our daily life'), as well as its importance within and beyond the context of formal schooling.

Public events – talks, celebrations, conferences – are opportunities to raise public profile and activist morale, and build personal and organizational links between the diverse groups with a stake in media democratization. They also create a sense of belonging to a larger whole. Such was the purpose of the Media and Democracy Congresses and the Cultural Environment Movement in the 1990s, and the National Conferences on Media Reform in the current decade. Moreover, perhaps inspired by Nichols' and McChesney's (2000) call for a media reform equivalent of 'Earth Day', activists in Toronto and Vancouver organized a Media Democracy Day in October 2001. IndyMedia Centres circulated the idea globally and by October 2002, Media Democracy Day T-shirts were being sold in Barcelona. While it has not remained a global phenomenon, it has become an annual tradition in Vancouver, with support from the city's library, major unions and educational institutions.

Other strategies for building critical consciousness use spectacle and humour to make a point in a way that attracts positive attention. Examples abound. In March 2002 protesters dressed as angels and sang parody hymns like 'God bless ye bold commissioners' to satirize FCC Chair Michael Powell's statement that no 'angels of the public interest' spoke to him opposing his deregulation policies. Similarly, after San Francisco PBS station KQED refused to air a series on opposition to the 1991 Gulf War, activists promised to get the programme 'on' KQED – so with a film projector they screened it onto the side of the station's building!

Taking on corporate media

Mainstream media presents a vast and uneven terrain of struggle for activists. One important means of engagement has involved careful *monitoring and documentation* of media practices and products. Critical academic research can encourage people to 'look' at media as an object of intervention and political activity. Documenting media's democratic deficit, as in Rocky Mountain Media Watch's statistical analyses of local television news content, can generate public reports which in turn earn the credibility to influence at least marginally media practices and policy outcomes. Progressive media monitoring groups (which several respondents suggested should be made permanent at local levels, and where possible involve journalists them- selves) have reported favourable responses from media outlets when they present concrete suggestions for content or programming changes.

But mainstream media can also be challenged, often subtly, by 'boring from within'. Journalists themselves can employ *insider strategies* to expand the news agenda, and even shift newsroom culture. Tactics our respondents suggested included pursuing smaller-scale stories, engaging journalists in media analysis and critique, organizing caucuses, and 'mouthing off to management'. A Vancouver CBC journalist sees three potential ways for journalists to be active: first, through the stories they cover and the sources they access; second, through their unions and collective agreements in the workplace; third, through coalition-building with other groups in campaigns outside the workplace. More ambitiously, some journalists and academics have talked of building entire new paradigms of journalism, such as the public journalism and peace journalism movements discussed in Chapter 3 and David Beers' proposed Alternative Futures journalism (to consider 'how things might go right tomorrow' rather than 'how things went wrong yesterday').

Activists positioned outside the mainstream, instead of resorting to confrontation, may *massage the media* by cultivating relations with journalists and other insiders. Indeed, surprisingly few media activists reported negative relations with news media. We infer two reasons for this. First, policy-oriented media reform receives so little press attention that there is little basis for friction; media activists may have simply resigned themselves to the reality that 'press coverage will always be the weak part of this social movement', as McChesney told us. Second, a great deal of media democratization energy is invested in exploiting openings in the media system for progressive messages. Projects like SPIN and FAIR sometimes function, in effect, as mediators between social activists and working journalists. Our interviews were replete with tactical recipes:

- establish dialogue with individual reporters;
- build relationships with them;
- speak in their language (objectivity, balance, completeness);
- provide them with evidence that coverage is slanted and suggest how it could be more balanced;
- educate them on specific issues.

Such recipes can be realized through conferences, demonstrations and handbooks, targeted at journalists. Activists might co-sponsor conferences that appeal to journalists' 'professional' concerns, or better still, have such forums run by journalists (although Jeff Perlstein of Media Alliance, for one, confesses uncertainty on how to make these both a political space, and one hospitable to mainstream journalists). Also an 'information subsidy' (Gandy 1982) can reduce the coverage threshold by supplying journalists with research and documentation. Following the Berkeley Media Studies Group, activists might produce handbooks as resources for journalists covering issues like violence from a public health perspective. 'Mainstream' journalists can also be granted free subscriptions to alternative magazines, like Saskatchewan's *Briarpatch*. Or demonstrations can be organized with a humorous or newsworthy hook. Finally, like FAIR does, activists can support journalists in cases of apparent censorship, often 'behind the scenes' to avoid compromising working journalists with their employer.

Awards that recognize outstanding journalism are also effective 'carrots'. GLAAD, by 2000, generated a reported one-third of its annual $2 million budget through annual awards for gay-positive media. In a similar vein, Media Alliance's Meritorious Achievement (MAMA) awards for investigative journalism were coveted by Bay Area journalists during the Alliance's earlier years. Such awards can be effective when they are consistent with both media organizations' recognized professional criteria, and the donor group's social or political objectives.

A number of groups, however, *combine carrots with sticks.* The latter are directed in particular at media management and ownership. FAIR makes a crucial distinction between working journalists and media ownership. They continue to critique the latter, and 'when we go after the big fish [media management], it's through shame and embarrassment', for example, through criticizing television in major dailies: 'The best way to get under the skin of the powerful is to embarrass them in news outlets they care about.' Such confrontational approaches include exploiting rivalries between different media outlets, especially television and newspapers; organizing protests at media outlets' doors; focusing on local media outlets that are more economically dependent on the local community than are national media; using professional organizers to run media accountability campaigns; and taking advantage of news organizations' economic interest in 'looking objective'.

Creative confrontations like protest rallies, marches and town hall meetings can earn media coverage, and force media corporations and governments to pay attention to a grievance. Canada's CEP union's tactic of buying one share of Hollinger, the company employing many of its members, in order to raise issues at annual shareholders' meetings, fits under this rubric. Such confrontations can also assist activists in publicly and selectively defining opponents, as a means of framing and broadening a campaign – in the spirit of Oscar Wilde's injunction that people cannot be too careful in choosing their enemies.

A final strategy for taking on the corporate media involves cultivation of *strategic communication skills* – teaching members of social movements how to improve their press coverage. At a concrete, tactical level this can mean supplying potential allies with templates for letters to the press or politicians. More strategically, Robert Bray explains that San Francisco-based SPIN Academy teaches groups how to work with the press, be better spokespeople, write news releases and op-eds, stage media events and brief journalists. SPIN not only effectively creates community media activism, which 'strengthens the ability of community members to speak out on their issues, but also brings different grassroots organizations together in a new way. From the viewpoint of media democratization, the long-term result is that progressive groups will have a better analysis of the media system, and that media relations will be part of their strategic plans, not just an afterthought.

Ultimately, strategic communication requires not only technical skill but political savvy: the capacity to challenge and shift media frames on vital issues. An example is the successful campaign by 'We Interrupt this Message' and allies in San Francisco, following the killing of Erin William, to shift the media focus from the alleged criminality of the victim to the brutality of the police. Strategic communication often means consciously framing stories to appeal to media's appetite for news angles, humour, human interest and sensationalism.

Changing the rules

Many activists, especially but not exclusively older ones, advocate using established judicial and political channels to achieve reform. This may involve lobbying government both to raise the priority of media issues in the legislative agenda, and to promote progressive democratic positions on such issues as public broadcasting, freedom of expression, children's privacy on the internet, and public access to cable TV and the internet. Robert McChesney feels it is necessary to 'make all political candidates, whatever their party, whatever the office, answer to media reform questions. Make it a political issue.'

Interestingly, few media activists in either the UK or US saw political parties as their primary domain of action, probably reflecting widespread disillusionment within the Left with the direction of the 'new' Labour and Democratic parties respectively. Activists do have contacts with sympathetic politicians within these parties, but there appears to be no systematic caucus to develop or prioritize a progressive media reform policy.

By contrast, in Canada's federal NDP, a grassroots membership caucus was launched in 1995 with precisely that objective. Moreover, partly as a way to high-light media issues, several Canadian respondents stood as candidates in federal elections, either for the NDP or for the Progressive Conservatives – a party that until its amalgamation into the Conservative Party in 2004 had visible nationalist (i.e., independence from the US) and socially progressive wings. Notwithstanding the electoral disincentives for political parties to antagonize media corporations, NDP MP Wendy Lill, the party's communication critic, could say credibly in 2002 that 50 or 60 New Democrats in the House would make media reform 'an issue that they would have a lot more trouble pushing off the agenda'. And yet the low salience of media issues in the NDP's recent election campaigns, and the related frustration of the media caucus's founders, may illustrate the reluctance of competitive political parties to challenge media corporations.

In the US, Henry Kroll of the Democratic Media Legal Project argues for 'a legal front to reclaim the media', to be developed in tandem with political pressure, since courts do not operate in a political vacuum. One successful example saw the Committee on Democratic Communication of the National Lawyers Guild advise microradio broadcasters on their legal rights, and thereby helped reframe the issue as one of constitutional rights rather than 'piracy' of the airwaves. 'We can help use the courts to create space for social movements to grow to the point where they are effective ... We helped legitimize [microradio] ... It grew to the point where the FCC had to recognize it,' said one CDC member.

Extending and deepening social justice struggles

Much of the strategic advice our respondents offered fits within our typology of modes of media activism, but one crucial theme exceeds those categories. If there is to be a 'deep media democracy movement', argues Dorothy Kidd, independent media need to follow the lead of social movements rather than vice versa. The point, observed Liza Dichter, is to build a constituency for media reform by listening to other social movements and figuring out how 'the media piece' fits into *their* agenda – a principle embodied in 'The Listening Project' (available at www.omgcenter.org/listen/, accessed October 2005).

By 'listening', media activists can extend their struggles beyond the media field per se. For this to happen, several respondents emphasized, activists must start with concerns on the ground, as in attempting to engage groups not currently involved in media reform campaigns, like minorities that would benefit from an improved media system, or churches that have 'larger value concerns'. Providing services and advocacy for a group is a good way to win a constituency – just as freelance journalists in the Bay Area looked to Media Alliance 'to be their institutional voice' in dealing with local newspaper companies.

Concomitantly, activists like Dichter emphasize the need to re-centre the 'incredibly fundamental' issues of race, class and gender, as they bear upon media democratization. Such entrenched hierarchies of material and cultural status, and the unresolved tensions to which they give rise, including 'identity politics', form a subterranean fault line underneath all progressive social movements, particularly in the US (Gitlin 1995). As noted in Chapter 7, many public interest groups in the US are led by an 'alpha male' and staffed disproportionately by women who feel that their contributions are not always sufficiently acknowledged. The management of corporate newsrooms is also often disproportionately male. But there are some hopeful signs within media activism. Women are forming caucuses, networking, holding their own conferences, even starting their own organizations. Some media reform groups have consciously sought to promote gender equality and women's voices. FAIR, whose director is an African-American woman, has a women's desk project. The British CPBF, whose activists are overwhelmingly male, consciously seeks to recruit women to its National Council. Microradio has more women's programmes than commercial radio, according to Greg Ruggiero of Seven Stories Press, and the IPA's stable of alternative magazines includes many with strong pro-feminist perspectives.

Parting observations

Our overview of strategies supports three general observations on the current state of media activism and its apparent trajectory. First, the strategies in play are consistent with the schema outlined in Chapter 3. Some focus on the field of media production, content and distribution – building alternative media, or challenging and shifting media frames. Other strategies intend to change the environing conditions, particularly the rules and resources dispensed by government and its agencies. Most actions intended to raise public awareness are also meant to stimulate public engagement in challenging and changing either media content or state policies. Second, the choice of differing strategies is not simply a division of labour within media activism: it is motivated to some extent by differing political judgements, styles and sensibilities. Third, notwithstanding the contrast between civil society and state-oriented strategies, and between confrontational and consensus-building approaches, the overwhelming sentiment favoured diversity, and sometimes coordination, between complementary strategies.

One should not exaggerate. Jeremy Smith of IPA recognizes that the different strategies could complement each other, to form the nucleus of 'a very good media democracy movement'. But so far, 'everybody tends to be doing ... their own little thing'. Yet recognition is apparently growing that different constituencies and actions should be combined into coherent campaigns. In 1998, John Anner argued for the need to identify specified problems and clear goals: 'You have to pick your fights', build on a string of smaller victories, and have goals more concrete than 'media democracy'. He lamented that there was little evidence of such strategizing. But by the time of the FCC campaign in 2003, it appeared that US media activist organizations had become increasingly adept at combining tactics and adapting them to circumstances.

American media activists have accumulated not only a repertoire of actions but also knowledge of what is most likely to succeed. At FAIR, Peter Hart commented on the need to employ both bridge-building and confrontational approaches:

> It's something we have to evaluate and re-evaluate ... because we want the editor ... to view us as a credible group that's critiquing them on solid ground [but also] we want to have the option of organizing people in the street ... in front of the *New York Times*. But the moment you do that ... you lose a certain amount of credibility. So it's a constant balancing act. We can fulfill both roles.

Thus, the movement's sustainability hinges on combining multiple approaches. Or as Jeff Cohen puts it: 'If you can build a big enough coalition, you can have some groups doing the militant actions, and another being sources for the media.' At Media Alliance, Jeff Perlstein sees a 'stepwise progression towards broader engagement' with policy issues on the part of local community and alternative media groups, in which the 'process of education ... and activism is transformative'. As the movement builds capacity to act within the media field and upon its environing conditions, barriers can indeed become springboards.

9 Movement formation and counterhegemony in a global city

If Chapters 7 and 8 enquire into the general conditions for its success, in this and the next chapter we ask about the distinctiveness and the political character of democratic media activism. We draw upon a set of interviews conducted in Vancouver, Canada – a self-consciously 'global' city of over two million inhabitants, a major trade, investment and immigration gateway between Asia and North America, a scenic playground for jet-setters, and a bastion of some of the previous century's most significant social movements. From the 1930s Vancouver was an urban stronghold of labour militancy and socialist advocacy in Canada (Phillips 1967). During the 1970s it gave birth to Greenpeace, arguably now the world's most influential environmental organization (Dale 1996); yet in the same years Vancouver became the home of the Fraser Institute, one of the most successful neoliberal advocacy think tanks. In the 1980s the city hosted the largest annual peace rallies on the continent (Hackett 1991) and was also the site for an urban reform movement that gained strong representation in city government in the mid 1980s and in 2002 helped elect a left-wing council (Vogel 2003). Studies of activism in Vancouver in the 1990s documented affinities and differences between 'new social movements' and the labour movement (Carroll and Ratner 1995); they explored the network of 'cross-movement' activism in terms of differing social visions (Carroll and Ratner 1996); compared the media strategies of Greenpeace with those of the leading local anti-poverty and gay/lesbian/bi/trans groups (Carroll and Ratner 1999); and documented the persistence of distinct 'oppositional cultures' within movements (Carroll and Ratner 2001).

Vancouver, like San Francisco, has been an incubator for media activism. It is home to a number of alternative media, including Co-op Radio, a listener-supported station closely identified since the 1970s with critical social movements. It is the birthplace of *AdBusters*, an internationally-known anti-consumerist magazine, and was one of the first Canadian cities to create an IndyMedia centre following the 1999 'Battle in Seattle' at the WTO Summit. For all these reasons, the city provides a propitious locale for exploring the formation of a movement to democratize public communication.

This ethnography of the Vancouver scene is based on 54 in-depth interviews conducted in the closing months of 2001, supplemented by observations from the field and documents (including websites) from key media-activist groups. We interviewed Vancouver-based activists who seek to transform the media field, as well as activists in 'other' movements (e.g. environmentalism) whose political communication practices might bring them into contact and sometimes conflict with media. Our sample is made up of 30 informants whose activism is primarily focused around issues of media democracy and 24 whose activism is primarily focused elsewhere.[1] No comprehensive listing of groups and individuals active around media issues exists for Vancouver. We chose our respondents on the basis of our own informed judgements about the organizations and activists who play leading roles on the Vancouver scene; i.e., our research employs a purposeful sample, not a probability sample.[2] Each respondent was questioned about her or his political background, activity, vision and strategy, about the group at the centre of her or his activism, and about participation in and contact with other activist groups.

We begin with an overview of the key media-activist organizations, then present sketches of eight key groups, and finally consider the Vancouver scene as a social network of activist groups. The network analysis highlights the *social organization* of media activism. By analysing relationships between media-oriented and other activism, we can assess the extent to which a distinct media democracy movement has emerged, even if only incipiently, or alternatively, whether media democratization seems destined to remain an adjunct, a supplement, to other movements.

The Vancouver scene: a local field of media activism[3]

Table 9.1 (p. 181) summarizes findings from our interviews as they pertain to respondents' judgements about the most important Vancouver groups active on mass media issues. Our 54 respondents made a total of 296 specific nominations of key media activist groups. In all, 93 distinct groups were nominated, but 63 received only one nomination each, while another 11 received only two nominations each. The table lists the 19 groups that received three or more nominations.[4] In the judgement of activists themselves, these are the important agencies of media democratization in Vancouver. The ten groups that each received 10 or more nominations, accounting for 54.4 per cent of all nominations, have an especially high profile within DMA in Vancouver. A remarkable 34 of 54 respondents nominated IndyMedia as a key group, demonstrating the salience of internet communication and of the project of open journalism in the minds of activists.

The 19 groups can be loosely categorized into the four quadrants of a simplified version of our typology from Chapter 3, contrasting on the one hand *lifeworld-centred* activism with *system-centred* activism and, on the other hand, activism that focuses on the *media field* with activism that focuses on environing *conditions* for that field (see column A of Table 9.1).

Beginning with alternative media, i.e. *lifeworld-centred praxis that focuses on changing the media field*, we find the largest clutch of activist groups. Seven of the top 10 and 11 of the top 19 nominees are primarily involved in producing and sustaining, within the lifeworld, democratic communications media. These include direct producers of independent media in various forms (e.g. IndyMedia, Co-op Radio, *Columbia Journal, Latin American Connexions* and *Redwire* – print, ICTV and Working TV – television), as well as three groups involved in building capacity for production (Pacific Centre for Alternative Journalists (see below), Tao.ca, an anarchist collective dedicated to 'organizing autonomous telecommunications', recently re-launched as Resist!ca (resist.ca), and Vancouver Community Network, a freenet (www2.vcn.bc.ca)). The production of independent media clearly occupies a major region of Vancouver's field of media activism.

Among groups that focus on the *environing conditions for lifeworld transformation*, we have categorized Adbusters, the third most-cited group, as an organization devoted primarily to transforming those conditions by inculcating a more literate and critical audience, but of course Adbusters is itself the most widely circulated alternative magazine produced in Vancouver. That is, while Adbusters's project is one of culture jamming in the service mainly of anti-consumerism, it accomplishes this by being a major producer of independent media. A much smaller, local group, Guerilla Media (ranked 12th), has specialized in a direct-action style of culture jamming, doctoring billboards and spoofing the product of the local newpaper monopoly, both in print and on the internet (globalbs.8k.com).

Two other organizations, whose activities are not primarily focused on democratic media activism, also figure in this quadrant. Five nominations were directed toward Check Your Head, a youth-driven popular-education group, well known for the workshops it conducts in high schools on globalization, sweatshops, the commercialization of education and media awareness (www.checkyourhead.com). Although not itself a media activist group, the School of Communication at Simon Fraser University has played a catalytic role in nurturing the development of activists and activist organizations on the Vancouver scene (several of our respondents had taken courses, graduated from, or taught there). Like other academic units such as the Birmingham Centre for Contemporary Cultural Studies (Richard Hoggart, Stuart Hall and others) and the Boston College Media Research and Action Project (William Gamson and Charlotte Ryan), the School has built capacity for production of independent media while also contributing to enhanced media literacy. Moreover, some of its faculty members (including this book's first author) have spearheaded groups such as NewsWatch Canada (which remains housed at the School) and the Campaign for Press and Broadcasting Freedom. Although not a DMA group per se, the School of Communication has contributed to all four quadrants of media activism in Vancouver. With one foot in the lifeworld – raising critical consciousness – and another in the system – training and credentializing members of the salariat – it occupies a unique place in the activist field.

The Vancouver scene contains far fewer organizations whose praxis is targeted primarily at hegemonic institutions and *systemic* threats and barriers to democratic communication. Moreover, two of the five groups with a 'system' focus are not primarily 'media activist' organizations. Each of these two groups attend to both the media field – offering critiques of the corporate media – and its environing conditions. The Canadian Centre for Policy Alternatives (CCPA), established in 1980 and the fourth-most cited media-activist group, is Canada's main left-wing think tank. Its monthly publication *The Monitor,* an important instance of independent media in its own right, is distributed to its 10,000+ members. Although the CCPA has provided low-key logistical support for the CPBF and its Media Democracy Day (discussed below) its main function is not media activism but policy-oriented research. It produces a steady stream of research-based publications (most of them available *gratis* online at www.policyalternatives.ca), running the gamut from aboriginal issues and agriculture to tax policy and women's equality. The BC office, located in downtown Vancouver with a staff of nine, was established in 1997. It issued 360 studies and reports between January 1997 and April 2005. Integral to its practice is a highly proactive media strategy that strives to obtain extensive coverage of CCPA perspectives in the mainstream media. In this sense, the CCPA's media politics is oriented mainly to influencing the content of mainstream media. Much the same can be said of the Council of Canadians (www.canadians.org, established in 1985), a broadly based coalition of the democratic left that maintains extensive contact with both mainstream and alternative media but is not primarily engaged in democratic media activism – even if it did play a crucial role in the original formation of the Canadian CPBF. The fact that our informants nominated these two groups illustrates the hazy boundary in activists' minds between the savvy media strategies of groups such as CCPA and the Council and the actual practice of DMA.

Among the 19 high-profile groups in Vancouver, only three (each of them profiled below) could be described as media activist organizations that target hegemonic institutions ('system'), with the aim of transforming the way they function. Both IMPACS and Newswatch focus on attempting to influence mainstream media production. The Vancouver chapter of the Campaign for Press and Broadcasting Freedom, a Canadian group inspired by the venerable British organization of the same name (see Chapter 6), is the one media activist group that pursues a strategy of media reform primarily through state regulatory practices and corporate media coverage.

Below, we provide sketches of eight of the groups that have been integral to the field of DMA in Vancouver, beginning with three groups whose work focuses on producing alternative media.

Co-op Radio

Vancouver Co-operative Radio is an organization that strives to provide the programming and voices missing from the mainstream media. Founded at the tail end of the wave of 1960s activism, in 1974, the station is non-commercial, cooperatively-owned (by 30,000 shareholders), listener-supported, and operated by more than 400 volunteers plus a small staff. Its signal is broadcast throughout greater Vancouver, carried throughout British Columbia on cable, and available online (www.coopradio.org/listen/index.html). Co-op Radio assembles a wide spectrum of alternative and left communities as audiences for its mix of public affairs, arts, music, and multicultural (minority language) programming. As one informant told us,

> We provide a forum or ... a voice for people. We are a medium that people can use to get their ideas out there. Whether it's somebody that is involved in alternative music or in experimental sound, or ... in politics, or whether it is somebody from a refugee community ... or somebody interested in labour issues who wants to get ideas around that out, or people from the gay and lesbian community. A really wide variety of people with a very wide variety of interests can come here and get their ideas out into the world and we give a voice to the voiceless.

The mandate, then, is to be a community radio station yet also part of a democratic movement 'putting forward a view that is really underrepresented, terribly, in corporate controlled media'. Another informant observed that

> democracy is a commonly used term, but it's not practised very much and when it is, it's very rudimentary or very limited. The whole idea of expanding democracy is giving people more information. Not only that, but letting them have access to have their point of view ... come out. And that's what we're there to do in a practical way ... And I think that is the ultimate role of any media – the free exchange of information and ideas and viewpoints with the goal of public education and developing cooperation and mutual respect.

Co-op Radio is run by a board of directors elected by the membership at the annual meeting, but apart from elections, members have little input into the running of the station. Management is fairly decentralized and nearly devoid of clear editorial control. Show developers – volunteers from constituent communities – decide on their own content based on the primary aims of the programme. In this sense, the station's *practice* exemplifies the participatory-management model of alternative media proposed by Downing *et al.* (2001), while its *content* exemplifies their notion of alternative media as purveyors of counterinformation.

IndyMedia

The Vancouver Independent Media Centre is part of a nationwide Canadian IMC project and a worldwide IndyMedia movement. The Vancouver branch describes itself as 'a non-commercial and non-profit democratic collective of Vancouverite independent media makers and media outlets', whose mission is

- to cover, on the internet, local events that are ignored or poorly covered by corporate media;
- to encourage, facilitate, and support the creation of independent news gathering and organizations;
- to offer community classes in internet and media skills;

- to provide links to alternative media, activist, and research groups;
- to offer 'coverage underscoring the global nature of people's struggles for social, economic, and environmental justice directly from their perspective'; and
- to encourage a globalization based on diversity and cooperation rather than 'homogeneity and exploitation'.

(vancouver.indymedia.org/process/about.php)

As one informant told us, IndyMedia is about 'putting the power in people to say what they think is important, instead of being told what is important. To put the responsibility back into the people, ... through saying, "you create the media, we'll facilitate, we'll help, we'll assist, we'll support you ..."'. There is irony in the 'anti-globalization' framing that dominant media have typically employed in discussing groups like IndyMedia. As one respondent suggested, although IndyMedia is often characterized as part of an 'anti-globalization movement', in fact, the group is deeply committed to globalization – *from below* (Brecher *et al.*, 2000): 'We want democratic media to roll out across the globe as quickly as possible, and to provide an alternative which activists and others concerned about globalization ... can share and exchange and in some cases organize and coordinate their activities.'

Integral to IndyMedia's democratizing praxis is its policy of 'open journalism', which has been discussed at length by Downing (2003). This involves 'facilitating spaces that allow for people to tell their own stories, rather than ... the centralized bureaucratic structures you find in the mainstream media, where journalists are story tellers, and they rely on expert knowers to deliver a picture of "reality"'. All three of our informants at Indy emphasized that IMC does not try to impose one version of 'truth'. In opposition to the mainstream media system, IMC allows just about anything to be added to the conversation, although it does sometimes submerge or 'hide' material that is overly offensive or incongruent with the stated mission.

IMC Vancouver was re-launched in March 2005 as BC IndyMedia, a collective effort of media activists in several cities (bc.indymedia.org). It continues to be organized as a collective committed to reporting local events within a global context, and to fostering political discussion across a wide range of issues and perspectives. One of our informants explicitly likened this commitment to the Habermasian project of building a democratic public sphere 'where people can come and discuss and debate the issues – knowledge and information being the lifeblood of democracy'. IndyMedia does indeed exemplify the Habermasian moment in DMA. It does not necessarily push an editorial or 'expert' line on members and contributors. One respondent described Indy as

> an experiment in democratic media where people – you, me, everybody, expert or not expert – are empowered to tell their own stories and to raise up their own skills through the process, and to understand the world themselves, so that it becomes meaningful to them and they can actually talk to other people about it.

In accordance with its emphasis on empowering people to 'be the media', the group has produced several workshops on the production of alternative media. Notwithstanding concerns that gendered inequities are reproduced in a malestream pattern of participation (Rodgers 2004), Indy's internal practices and organization are self-consciously democratic:

> Everything is geared towards collective decision making. What that also means is consensus building, and consensus creating ... Our minutes are posted online, so that people who can't make it to the meeting can contribute whenever they can.

If this decentralized structure makes IndyMedia particularly democratic, it also creates ongoing tensions with the environment that surrounds the group, which one informant describes as imbued with hierarchy, competition and the power that accrues to expertise. IndyMedia's challenge is to maintain its practice of openness and democratic collectivism while operating effectively within a system organized along quite different lines.

Pacific Centre for Alternative Journalists

The Pacific Centre for Alternative Journalists (PCAJ) is a non-profit collective whose half-a-dozen core activists focus on media skills development at the grassroots level. Formed in 1998 by individuals from Co-op Radio and the SFU School of Communication, the group orients itself to alternative media, but attends to the task of building capacity. According to one informant, the group's main focus is 'skill-building and media literacy' at the grassroots, rather than 're-tooling the emphasis of the elite'; that is, PCAJ's praxis is lifeworld-centred both in its sources and target. Its project includes the development of critical media audiences (some of its workshops have focused on media literacy), but centres on 'providing low-cost, accessible media training for alternative media workers, community groups, and other interested individuals' (Abbs 2000: 2). Not only has PCAJ emphasized training to improve writing, editing, reporting, production and fundraising skills, it has sought to promote discussion within the activist community of 'a philosophy and practice of alternative journalism' (Abbs 2000: 3).

To achieve this goal, members of PCAJ have held workshops on democratic and alternative media production, as well as more relaxed 'café' meetings. End Legislated Poverty, Latin American Connexions and various anti-globalization and environmentalist groups have all attended PCAJ conferences. At the time of our fieldwork, PCAJ was planning a café on alternative media solidarity with indigenous struggles, at which people from aboriginal communities could talk to alternative journalists about how alternative media could support their struggles. The group has also provided grassroots groups with training in media relations, to improve their capacity to gain strategically advantageous coverage in the mainstream media, and has produced a widely distributed handbook for alternative media groups. PCAJ functions as a resource for various critical movements that builds skills and helps develop solidarity, illustrating the extraverted character of democratic media activism.

Adbusters

Adbusters is based *in* Vancouver, but it is not *of* Vancouver. Through its glossy magazine, whose circulation tops 120,000 worldwide, Adbusters Media Foundation (which includes the magazine, a 'culture jammers headquarters' website (adbusters.org) and an advocacy advertising agency named Powershift) has since its founding in 1989 gained a global profile on the cutting edge of culture jam. Although Adbusters Media Foundation is reader-supported and non-profit it is organized hierarchically, with founder Kalle Lasn occupying the position of sovereign. As one Adbusters insider told us, 'it's not an activist organization in the sense that it doesn't run on consensus; it's not driven entirely by its volunteers and so on. It's more driven by a sort of creative struggle among the people who are most intimately involved with its actual products.' Still, Adbusters does, through its culture jammers website, support a vast, decentralized network of media activists, giving them resources to produce their own local events that may then be discussed in the magazine or in forums on the website. The culture jammers network currently has 75,000 subscribers worldwide, who are sent strategic updates, campaign materials and other information on a regular basis. The relationship between Adbusters and its cybernetwork is reciprocal: Adbusters furnishes important cultural and strategic resources to activists but at the same time it is the network of activists that enables Adbusters to enact its campaigns. In the words of one of its most prominent activists,

> this network now allows us to really launch international campaigns, like Buy Nothing Day ... suddenly we have about one hundred and fifty organizers all around the world who are organizing stuff in their cities, who are coming up with their own posters or using our images to help them come up with posters. They are organizing bicycle rallies, critical massing rallies or (store) invasions or credit card cut-ups ... and many of them are also very articulate spokespeople who will then go on radio or TV.

A glance at the campaigns detailed on the Adbusters website – Slow Down Week, TV Turnoff Week, and so on – gives a sense of how Adbusters strives to transform lifeworlds by criticizing the norms of consumer capitalism and by supporting alternatives. As 'the journal of the mental environment', *Adbusters* invokes a 'cultural environment' frame (as discussed in Chapter 4), likening the culture of consumer capitalism to a matrix of pollutants whose elimination will require a 'new ecology of mind', in Lasn's terms. At the core of the project is a critique of mainstream commercial media that addresses two issues in the commodification of everyday life: the role of advertising in driving media content and the media's general celebration of consumerism as an ultimate lifestyle.

Although best known for its spoof ads – which are now classic exemplars of culture jamming (see adbusters.org/spoofads/index.php) – Adbusters' assault on commercial media has also involved recent court challenges to the sovereignty of commercial media. In 2004, after repeated unsuccessful attempts to buy commercial time on mainstream television networks in the US and Canada for its subvertisements and uncommercials, Adbusters began its Media Carta campaign, a four-step programme for media democratization. The first step is to press for abolition of the 'corporate advertising monopoly', which censors critics like Adbusters while reserving the airwaves exclusively for corporate sponsors whose celebrations of consumer capitalism are no less ideological than are Adbusters' critiques. In the earnestly optimistic narrative of the Media Carta website, this first step will prepare the way for more radical moves to re-regulate commercial media in ways that open up access for citizens and break up corporate monopolies:

> after we've cracked the corporate advertising monopoly, won free airtime and gained control of our media system, we'll take our most important step towards media democracy. We'll enshrine a new human right for our information age: the Right to Communicate – the right of every person to meaningful access to the world's most powerful communication media.
>
> (adbusters.org/metas/psycho/mediacarta/4step/4.html)

The Media Carta campaign has taken Adbusters beyond its longstanding repertoire of action (which aimed to reform the lifeworld through culture jamming and production of alternative media), to the use of the legal system in opening new political space. In another shift, Adbusters started accepting orders in 2003 for its Black Spot running shoe, an anti-branded commodity meant to 'uncool' Nike and other corporate fare. Thus began the extension of Adbusters to the capitalist economy itself, a venture in 'antipreneurialism' that intends to transform the market system from the bottom up:

> We're talking about a new breed of bottom-up enterprise that does things differently: promotes ethics over profit, values over image, idealism over hype. A brand of grassroots capitalism that deals in products we actually need – and believe in. No sweatshops. No mindfucking ads. Just sustainable, accountable companies. Run by us.
>
> Imagine a chain of restaurants serving only locally-sourced food. Or an artist-controlled radio network. Instead of Nikes? Blackspot Sneakers. Instead of McDonald's, Warner Music and Microsoft? Tell us in the forum.
>
> (adbusters.org/metas/politico/antipreneur)

The radical character of this initiative has been questioned by Joseph Heath and Andrew Potter who suggest that with the creation of its own Black Spot (anti-)brand, Adbusters has not only 'harnessed the entrepreneurial spirit' (Adbusters' own self-description) but has followed the general movement of countercultural politics, from criticizing 'the system' to *being* the system:

there never was any tension between the *values* of the counterculture and the functional requirements of the capitalist economic system. The counterculture was, from its very inception, intensely entrepreneurial. It reflected, as does *Adbusters*, the most authentic spirit of capitalism.

(Heath and Potter 2004: 3)

Certainly, there has been a qualitative shift at Adbusters from the critique of the advertisements that promote consumer capitalism to the production and marketing of commodities (using Portuguese unionized labour) whose conspicuous consumption is meant to signify resistance. Despite possible cooptation on this front, Adbusters continues its educative project through its magazine, website and associated campaigns challenging commercial values and consumerism as a way of life.

Guerrilla Media

Although they share a similar location within the field of media activism, Adbusters and Guerrilla Media (GM) are otherwise quite different entities. In contrast to the large, professionalized, well funded, hierarchically organized and globally oriented Adbusters, GM is a small, semi-underground cell, with two core activists and a wider surrounding network; it runs, in fits and starts, on a volunteer basis and with no defined organization, let alone hierarchy; and its focus is provincial and occasionally national. The contrast extends to strategy, with GM positioning itself more clearly on the left. As one GM activist put it:

> I think they've [Adbusters] got a very consumer sovereignist kind of approach and when you start talking about I guess left politics, that's where we part company. Our analysis of power differs from theirs. Theirs lies in the individual making decisions and ours is a lot more complicated than that ... we're both satirical, and some of their work I like a lot, it's very good, but overall, I think the projects are very different.

Using satire as its main political tool, GM creates and distributes parodies of daily newspapers, government press releases and other 'official' discourse, in print and online (globalbs.8k.com). Its praxis is that of conjoining humour to popular education around social justice issues, in ways that reach people who might not otherwise search for such critical analysis. One informant explained to us that 'the mandate is to preach to the non-converted wherever possible'. GM is 'reaction based' in the sense that its campaigns take shape in response to events that present themselves in the media. The group's most well known product is its 'wraps', broadsheets that closely resemble the local Vancouver newspapers (the *Sun*, and *Province*, both owned by the same corporate parent) and are distributed to thousands of unsuspecting readers at strategic conjunctures, such as the beginning of an election campaign.

Among the political parodies GM has created since its founding in 1993 are

- critiques of the way corporate news media have represented environmental protest and social welfare (e.g. the *Providence/Province* welfare-bashing wrap, 1994);
- parodies of the practice (until banned by the federal government in 1998) of tobacco companies sponsoring cultural events, as in du Maurier's Vancouver Jazz Festival;
- satirical coverage of the Vancouver APEC conference of 1997, which Indonesia dictator Suharto attended and at which protestors were pepper-sprayed in what became a dress-rehearsal for the 1999 'Battle in Seattle';
- a five-part internet cartoon called Daywatch, starring the leader of Canada's right-wing populist Alliance party, Stockwell Day, as lifeguard to the rich (2001);
- a sporadic series of newspaper parodies, flagging issues of corporate concentration and ideologically saturated content.

GM's interventions, while often hilarious, are seriously strategic. They are engagements with 'the great middle' of the political spectrum, active neither on left nor right; they are efforts to put alternative ideas into the public sphere. In the words of its core activists,

> [GM] attempts to engage people with critical ideas about the nature of the world in which they live, to increase their horizon of expectation, to expose the contradictions within corporate capitalism in their lives. And just to say, here's what we see – does this resonate with you? If it does, maybe there's something you can do.

> The core mandate [is] presenting alternative ideas in the public sphere – in a sense, undermining the mainstream media homogeneity and hegemony. Having fun is part of the core mandate. That's why we can do it with all volunteers and be working full time on top, and so on and so forth, … what's the famous Emma Goldman quote 'a revolution where I can't dance isn't my revolution'.

NewsWatch Canada

As we discussed in Chapter 3, democratic media activists have devised several strategies for reforming or transforming the *system* of mediated communication. Some focus on directly influencing the media field, others on reforming the field's environing conditions– in particular the state's regulatory framework. The local Vancouver field includes two organizations of the former type but, again, these are of quite different scale and scope. NewsWatch Canada, established in 1993 and co-directed initially by Bob Hackett and Donald Gutstein (since joined by Shane Gunster) at the SFU School of Communication, mobilizes academic resources in a project of media monitoring that was originally inspired by US-based Project Censored. NewsWatch 'undertakes independent research on the diversity and thoroughness of news coverage in Canada's media, with a focus on identifying blindspots and double-standards' (www.sfu.ca/cmns/research/newswatch). The group has relied on university students enrolled in a critical media studies course to undertake media-monitoring research on a continuing basis, focusing on patterns of under- and over-reporting. The methodology identifies contemporary national or international news stories that, although of major significance and interest to a large proportion of the population, received minimal coverage in the mainstream media. By documenting patterns of bias and censorship, media monitoring pressures the mainstream to be fairer, and lends support to progressive journalists who work within dominant media institutions. NewsWatch's monitoring is also a form of media education: it raises social consciousness about the democratic deficit in mainstream media, and the need for reform.

The publication of *The Missing News: Filters and Blind Spots in Canada's Press* (Hackett *et al.* 2000), consolidated into one volume many of the insights gained through NewsWatch and associated ventures in the 1990s. More recently, in 2003, NewsWatch published an insert in the CCPA *Monitor*, reporting a content analysis of Vancouver's largest newspapers that documented extensive right-wing bias. Also included in the insert was an essay that raised the 'top ten' unexamined questions about dominant US media coverage of the 'war on terrorism' and an article analysing the agenda-setting role that Canada's CanWest-Global media empire has played in attempting to recruit popular support for privatizing public education under the cover of a 'school voucher' system. These kinds of analytical exposés are NewsWatch's bread-and-butter, but a spin-off of the group's praxis has been the training of media activists and analysts, contributing to the formation of a radical habitus for democratic media activism. Various undergraduate and graduate Communication students have passed through internships at SFU and gone on to contribute to groups such as PCAJ, IndyMedia, TAO, and the Campaign for Press and Broadcasting Freedom.

The Institute for Media, Policy and Civil Society

Established in 1997, the Institute for Media, Policy and Civil Society (IMPACS) is a registered Canadian charity whose mandate is to strengthen communication between not-for-profit organizations, government and mainstream media, both in Canada and internationally. One of our respondents described as the group's core mandate, 'to increase the effectiveness of civil society organizations to engage in public policy', in large part through improving their effectiveness in working with media. IMPACS is system-focused: its work with not-for-profits aims not so much to renovate the lifeworld toward greater communicative democracy, as to improve the *coverage* activist groups receive in the dominant media, thereby reshaping those media while enabling civil society to thrive. Unlike other groups on the Vancouver scene, IMPACS has worked largely within the political system to enhance the media's role in the process of democratic development, good governance and public sector accountability. This emphasis on 'working from within' is also evident in IMPACS's funding sources (the group has received extensive funding from the Canadian International Development Agency – CIDA) and in its mode of governance (it is run by a board of directors that one informant described as a 'self-perpetuating' oligarchy, including 'key players' in the three major national political parties). IMPACS does not have a membership base reaching much beyond its board of directors, and it relies on a paid professional staff of 14. In lieu of membership, it maintains a roster of 130+ 'media practitioners' with extensive professional experience in journalism and related fields such as media and elections, media and law, media management, and strategic communications, whose specific training and journalistic skills IMPACS matches 'to complex media environments around the world' (impacs.org/media). IMPACS' myriad ties to 'the system' – through its networks domestically and internationally, through its funding and board and through its campaigns – enable it to exert influence upon media content by holding educative discussions with mainstream media insiders:

> On the media front, we have developed a very strong network of relationships across the country with media … because many of these media folks have worked with us. So then when we convene a round-table to look at race issues in the mainstream press … we get senior representation from editors and others and we have some really good discussions about the issues … I mean, there are hundreds of people in the media that are behind the scenes whose names will never appear on an IMPACS document who are assisting us. They'll come down, they'll come for martinis, and they'll give us a sense of how to structure a campaign on the grizzly hunt or on westcoast or on childcare issues, or anti-poverty issues.

The IMPACS project is actually broader than media democratization per se, yet the latter occupies a central place in the group's efforts 'to create an environment in which democratic values can thrive' (impacs.org). On its website, IMPACS describes two ongoing campaigns that fall within the realm of DMA:

- providing communication training and services to not-for-profit organizations, 'helping them become more articulate about their causes and more effective at telling their stories';
- supporting and building programs 'to facilitate the emergence of free, open and accountable media in countries in transition to democracy'.

Through the online workshops available via its Communications Centre, IMPACS offers public relations training to increase the visibility of NGOs and activist groups. The emphasis is upon improving the media strategies that enable activist groups to reach audiences through the mainstream media. That emphasis on strategic communication carries over to the Communications Centre's 'leading-edge services' for not-for-profit clients. Available services include Strategic Communications Planning and Implementation, Media Relations, Issue Advertising ('we will develop a high impact marketing campaign for communicating your issue to the public through print, radio, television, web and outdoor advertising') and Branding ('IMPACS will help you change, improve or strengthen the public perception and/or position of your organization') (impacs.org/communications/CommunicationsServices).

Clearly, IMPACS's Communications Centre works within the logic of the dominant media. It does not challenge that hegemony but seeks to shift the balance of power within civil society so that its clients can reach larger publics more effectively. In doing so, it takes for granted, and may even reinforce, hegemonic practices such as elitism (the cultivation of a communications elite), instrumentalism (prioritizing the marketing of information over dialogical aspects of communication) and commodification (the emphasis upon 'branding'). Inevitably, Audrey Lorde's question – can the master's house be dismantled using the master's tools? – must be raised. IMPACS exemplifies a pragmatic approach to media activism, which may sacrifice utopian vision for the sake of realism and immediate effectivity.

IMPACS' Media Centre extends its activism onto the field of international media development, where it co-exists with other international groups such as the Communication Initiative (www.comminit.com) and PANOS (www.panos.org.uk). It offers training and support to journalists and other media practitioners in countries 'in transition to democracy', in two areas: 'media and peacebuilding' and 'media and elections'. IMPACS believes there is a connection between levels of media literacy, media training and ethics, and human rights conditions, including increases in democratic forms of government. As an informant related, knowing what is going on is integral to democracy: 'What's really important in the democratic society is that people be aware of what's going on around them, and as much as possible, be aware of the issues that are affecting them or at least know that there are issues out there that are affecting them.' However, the extent to which the group's international initiatives are driven by its financial dependence upon CIDA is a legitimate question. What is clear is that IMPACS advocates a liberal participatory democracy that falls far short of the vision of radical democracy we traced in Chapter 4.

Campaign for Press and Broadcasting Freedom

The Canadian Campaign for Press and Broadcasting Freedom (CPBF) was initially established in 1995 as an Ottawa-centred national alliance of media unions, the Council of Canadians and other progressive groups. Its first initiative was a court challenge to Conrad Black's takeover of the Southam Press newspapers. After the Federal Court rejected the challenge, the national CPBF became dormant. In 1999, however, a group of Vancouver activists took up the name, optimistically describing itself at the time as a common front of 'readers and viewers, those working in the media industries, and labour and community groups concerned about the increasing concentration of media ownership in Canada' (www.presscampaign.org/vancouver.htm). Two years later, a Toronto chapter was formed, now operating under a different name.

The Vancouver chapter's first project was a web-based media review featuring articles by media analysts, comments from local media workers and consumers, and updates from local supporting organizations. This was followed by a content analysis of political bias in the editorial pages of the Vancouver *Sun* and *Province*, culminating in a meeting between a CPBF delegation and the *Sun*'s op-ed page editor; a brief and intervention to the BC Press Council, urging it to broaden its mandate and its independence from the industry; and, starting in 2001, the annual organizing of Media Democracy Day.

CPBF's core goals, which resemble those of its British namesake, are to raise awareness of problems in the current mass media system and to press for reforms and alternatives. The group, whose active membership has varied from half a dozen to several dozen, has been focused more on reforming system than on transforming lifeworld. However, its 'common front' organization has lent it a major role in *integrating* the local field of media activism (including the more lifeworld-focused groups) through Media Democracy Day – which has won support not only from movement groups and independent media but also from the Vancouver Public Library, the BC Library Association, post-secondary institutions and trade unions.

More than any other Vancouver-based group, the CPBF places media democratization at the heart of its project. Its approach is not to call for the elimination of corporate ownership but, following Curran (2002), to advocate a more pluralistic media system in which the power of corporate media is constrained both by state regulations and by a revitalized public sphere that holds news media to high standards while supporting a greater range of progressive perspectives. The Campaign sees the lack of alternative perspectives in the mainstream media as a basic aspect of the democratic deficit. Key to its political objectives is the use of the state's regulatory power in limiting and reversing media ownership concentration, in encouraging diversity of media ownership, and in promoting corporate responsibility and diversity of content.

An illuminating example of the CPBF style of activism could be found in the representations that its members made to the Senate Committee on the Canadian News Media upon its visit to Vancouver in March 2005. These were crystallized in an 'open letter' that various activists forwarded electronically to the Committee via the CPBF's website as well as through that of a local alternative newspaper, the *Columbia Journal* (www.columbiajournal.ca). The appeal outlined five 'first steps' as well as a final course of action – all of them imbued with a vision of democratizing the media through limiting corporate power and encouraging plurality:

1   'establish a market domination cap' and create legislation to reduce media concentration and cross-ownership where it is unacceptably high;
2   'maintain Canadian ownership requirements' to check domination by foreign corporations, which have little interest in representing the democratic interests of Canadians;
3   'enhance the role of the public broadcaster', the CBC;
4   'put communities in charge of community media funding and programs', as in transferring responsibility for community television from cable companies to local community organizations;
5   'foster community media' by providing tax incentives and other supports 'to cooperative and member-based media ownership, to community media philanthropy, and to programs for media literacy'.

As a final and all-important course of action, the CPBF called for a deepening civic participation in the Canadian media system: 'only when citizens have the tools and the power to understand, to access, to hold accountable, and to create news media will we be assured that this most recent federal study will amount to more than another forgotten report'.

Alongside such state-centred initiatives, the Campaign works closely with other media activist organizations in what one respondent called a 'loose network', maintaining ties to most other groups on the Vancouver scene. In effect, the CPBF is situated within a nexus of other organizations and movements, including, through CEP, organized labour. It functions as a loose coalition with members from many different groups, who do not formally represent their 'home' groups, but who can draw upon those resources as needed. Its work has been volunteer-based and project-driven, and thus quite variable in intensity; yet one project, mounted on an annual basis, has become an integral aspect of the Campaign's local identity, while also diffusing to other urban locales. The Vancouver CPBF group, and its allies in Toronto, were key initiators for the idea of an annual Media Democracy Day each October, and a conference combined with an alternative media fair (an increasingly important focus for the group) has been held annually in Vancouver and other cities like Chicago and Toronto since 2001. The slogan on the 2004 promotional poster read, 'Know the Media, Change the Media, Be the Media' – an encapsulation of Media Democracy Day's three themes: Education (understanding how the media shape social life, including democracy), Protest (dissenting from a media system based on commercialization and exclusiveness) and Change (creating independent media, and pressuring for media reforms that promote diversity and ensure community representation and accountability: see www.mediademocracyday.org).

Media activism as a political field: a network analysis

The eight organizations profiled above illustrate the diversity of a movement in formation. They differ in scale – from groups like Guerrilla Media and NewsWatch Canada that are centred on several individuals – to well-resourced mid-sized organizations like Adbusters and IMPACS. They include various kinds of structures – informal partnership (Guerrilla Media, NewsWatch), cooperative (Co-op Radio), collective (IndyMedia, PCAJ), coalition (CPBF), formal organization (Adbusters, IMPACS). They embody a diversity of projects that converge upon a politics of democratizing public communication. In effect, the groups occupy distinct *niches* in a complex division of activist labour:

- IndyMedia, Co-op Radio and PCAJ (among others) focus on the revitalization of the public sphere (and cultivation of alternative public spheres) through production of independent media;
- Adbusters and Guerrilla Media foster the kinds of literacy needed to decode dominant media in resistant and oppositional modes;

- NewsWatch and IMPACS endeavour to influence, or (for NewsWatch) at least critique, dominant media content and practices;
- the CPBF pursues the cause of state regulation to render the media system more pluralistic and accountable, while also providing a nexus for a range of local media democracy groups.

It is difficult to resist the inference that these intersecting and overlapping forms of democratic media activism add up to a local instance of a social movement in formation. Certainly, the Vancouver scene is replete with innovative groups that directly respond to the grievances comprising media's democratic deficit by mobilizing a wide range of resources in campaigns and activities that take advantage of emergent opportunities for media activism – whether globally (e.g. IMPACS, IndyMedia, Adbusters) or locally (e.g. PCAJ, Co-op Radio, Guerrilla Media). Yet a movement is more than a series of responses to grievances, more than a mobilization of resources, and more than a seizure of opportunities – as important as these factors may be (Klandermans 2001: 276). As Charles Tilly (1978) has noted, movement formation entails the attainment of certain 'catnet-ness' – a combination of the creation of the *categories* through which activists construct a collective identity and the *networks* through which they become integrated into a whole that is more than the sum of its parts.

How is media activism embedded within the larger activist field? One way to explore this question is through a network analysis. Social networks exist by virtue of various kinds of social relations, but one basic criterion is whether activists in one group have some kind of *contact* with activists in another. When asked which groups, out of those they had nominated as key media activist organizations, they were in touch with as part of their own activism, our 54 respondents cited a total of 199 connections spanning the various groups. These links vary in intensity and institutionalization: 55 (18.6 per cent) involved only occasional communication; 19 (6.4 per cent) involved regular communication; 28 (9.5 per cent) involved one-off collaborative projects; 43 (14.5 per cent) involved ongoing collaboration; 15 (5.1 per cent) involved sharing resources; and 31 (10.4 per cent) involved joint memberships or interlocking boards. Column C of Table 9.1 shows the total number of links 'received' by each of the 19 most prominent groups. The distribution of incoming ties ('in-degree'), a measure of centrality in the activist network, matches the distribution of nominations, with one major exception: Adbusters, ranked as the third most *prominent* media activist group, ranks only eighth in actual *centrality*. Evidently, Adbusters – both as a magazine and as a web-based 'culture jammers headquarters' – is hooked more into an international network than into the local Vancouver scene. By the same token, however, the eight incoming ties that embed Adbusters within the local network also draw Vancouver activists into a more 'global' field of cultural politics.

All told, the 199 linkages bring 71 movement organizations into a single connected network; however, 35 groups each participate in the network through only a single link, and another 15 occupy relatively marginal locations. The network is centred upon 21 SMOs that include the 19 listed in Table 9.1 plus the

Table 9.1 Key Vancouver-based activist groups around media issues

	A	B	C
Name of group	*Type of activism*	*Nominations*	*Incoming ties*
Vancouver IndyMedia	Lifeworld, media field	34	24
Co-op Radio	Lifeworld, media field	21	19
Adbusters	Lifeworld, conditions	19	8
Canadian Centre for Policy Alternatives (CCPA)	System, mixed*	17	15
Campaign for Press and Broadcasting Freedom (CPBF)	System, conditions	15	11
Columbia Journal	Lifeworld, media field	12	9
Independent Community TV (ICTV)	Lifeworld, media field	12	10
Working TV	Lifeworld, media field	11	9
Pacific Centre For Alternative Journalists (PCAJ)	Lifeworld, media field	10	5
Tao.ca	Lifeworld, media field	10	8
NewsWatch	System, media field	9	6
Guerrilla Media	Lifeworld, conditions	7	6
IMPACS	System, media field	7	4
SFU School of Communication	Mixed, mixed*	6	3
Latin American Connexions	Lifeworld, media field	5	5
Check Your Head	Lifeworld, conditions*	5	3
Redwire	Lifeworld, media field	5	3
Vancouver Community Network (VCN)	Lifeworld, media field	3	3
Council of Canadians	System, mixed*	3	2
All other groups		85	46
Total		296	199

* Groups whose activities and resources are *not* primarily based on democratic media activism.

BC Teachers Federation (sponsor of numerous initiatives in progressive cultural politics) and Mobilization for Global Justice Vancouver (MobGlob), at the time a key anti-corporate globalization group with ties into the media activist sector.

Figure 9.1 maps the links among these 21 core groups. Considering the eight groups profiled above, alternative media producers – IndyMedia and Co-op Radio – are especially central in the network; indeed, Co-op Radio is directly linked to all but one of the profiled groups, and IndyMedia is tied to all but two. As producers of alternative culture and of alternative political perspectives, these groups play a crucial role not only in integrating the field of media activism, but more broadly in progressive community development, i.e., counterhegemonic cultural production. Not surprisingly, they are also connected to groups that are not primarily involved in DMA but that have a strong interest in the project – the CCPA, MobGlob, Check Your Head and the Council of Canadians.

A similar pattern holds for two other producers of alternative media, namely ICTV and Working TV. In contrast, two of the smaller groups profiled above – GM and NewsWatch (each with only two core activists) – are less central, as is IMPACS, a comparatively large and well-resourced organization, but one whose focus is less local and whose strategy more mainstream. Adbusters, rather marginal in the local network, receives nominations only from four of our eight profiled groups, and it 'sends' only a single tie to the CCPA. PCAJ and CPBF – groups thoroughly involved in the politics of media democratization but relatively informal in structure and small in size – occupy fairly central positions in the network, and the latter – true to its 'common front' project – plays an especially integrative role with ties to groups as diverse as IMPACS, NewsWatch, Co-op Radio, Adbusters and PCAJ.

Within the network mapped in Figure 9.1, there is no tendency toward segmentation, although groups with somewhat different political strategies (e.g. Adbusters and Guerrilla Media) may not be directly linked to each other, even if they are involved in similar activities. And although the centre of the network is occupied primarily by media activist groups, two organizations that play a broader role in movement politics are also well connected. But while the CCPA – a leading centre of left intellectual production, with ties to organized labour, environmental and other movements – predominantly *receives* ties, the Council of Canadians – the leading left-oriented citizens group – *sends* ties; i.e., Council activists tend to be well-connected to other movement organizations. The extensive linkages between media activist groups and these broader left organizations suggest that the movement to democratize communication is embedded in, indeed permeated by, a larger field of left activism.

This interpretation, based on our respondents' reports of their *contacts* with various groups, gains further specification when we consider a second kind of link that may exist between two activist groups, that of *cross-membership*. As previous research has shown, activists often participate in multiple movement organizations, sometimes spanning across movement sectors. Such 'cosmopolitan' activists are positioned to play counterhegemonic roles in integrating the field of activism (Carroll and Ratner 1996). This phenomenon has potentially important implications for our understanding of media reform as a prospective movement. Are media activists distinct from other activists in their patterns of cross-affiliation; does their activism tend to reach beyond 'media' issues, to other movements? What we find is a clear tendency for *all activists* to spread their activism

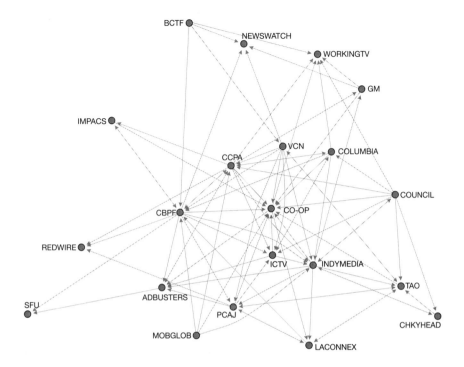

Figure 9.1 The network of 21 key groups in the Vancouver field of media activism

Key:

ADBUSTERS	Adbusters	INDYMEDIA	Independent Media Center (Vancouver)
BCTF	British Columbia Teachers Federation	LACONNEX	Latin American Connexions
CCPA	Canadian Centre for Policy Alternatives	MOBGLOB	Mobilization for Global Justice
		NEWSWATCH	NewsWatch Canada
CHKYHEAD	Check Your Head	PCAJ	Pacific Centre for Alternative Journalists
COUNCIL	Council of Canadians		
COLUMBIA	Columbia Journal	REDWIRE	Redwire Magazine
CO-OP	Vancouver Co-operative Radio	SFU	Simon Fraser University School of Communication
CBPF	Campaign for Press and Broadcast Freedom	TAO	Tao.ca (relaunched in 2005 as Resist.ca)
GM	Guerrilla Media		
ICTV	Independent Community Television	VCN	Vancouver Community Network
IMPACS	Institute for Media, Policy and Civil Society	WORKINGTV	Working TV

across two or more groups – only six of our 54 respondents concentrated their political work exclusively within one group. However, most of the media activists with multiple memberships (19 of 27) are active in at least one group *outside the field of media activism*. That is, over two-thirds of the individuals we identified as media activists are also involved in the politics of environmentalism, feminism, peace, labour, youth, anti-globalization, and so on. On the other hand, most

Table 9.2 Links across movement organizations, categorized by activist sector

Activist's primary affiliation	Activist's secondary affiliation		
	Media activist groups	Other activist groups	Total
Media activist groups	21	41	62
Other activist groups	7	60	67
Total	28	101	129

other activists with multiple memberships do *not* belong to media-activist groups (18 of 22), though many of them are active in multiple movements. In one sense, one could read this difference as a simple reflection of the broader range of activist causes and groups that lie beyond media activism. Yet it also points to a tendency for media activists to be particularly *extraverted*, and cosmopolitan, in the political causes they embrace: typically, their media activism intersects with other struggles.

When we consider the pattern of all cross-membership links across two broad sectors of activism, we find much the same. Table 9.2 cross-tabulates our informants' 129 joint affiliations as to whether each leads from a primary affiliation in one sector to a secondary affiliation in the same or the other sector. Here, the unit of analysis is the link, not the person doing the linking. Many cross-memberships lead from the media activist sector to other activist sectors (n=41), but the reverse flow is relatively uncommon (accounting for only seven cross-affiliations). Whether we consider the individuals or the links that comprise the activist network, the pattern is clear: struggles around media are embedded within the broader activist field largely through the cosmopolitan tendency of media activists to participate strongly and profusely in other social movements.

The local Vancouver network thus has an integrated character, in two senses. The media activist sector is *internally integrated* via key groups occupying different niches in the field (IndyMedia, Co-op Radio, CPBF, PCAJ); but at the same time, the media activist component *reaches out* to other sectors of activism, mainly via the cosmopolitan ties and multiple memberships of media activists themselves. The first aspect of integration suggests an organizational basis for social movement formation, as the various strands of media activism are drawn together across groups, even as each group pursues its unique project. Yet, by embedding media activism within a network of joint affiliations to myriad other struggles, the second aspect may undercut the phenomenal basis for collective identity. Activists who count media activism among a plurality of political involvements may not identify themselves as members of a movement for media democratization. The activist network appears to hold a counterhegemonic potential to weave the strands of activism into a common project of democratizing communication, but that very potential may place limits on collective identity formation.

According to Tilly (1978: 64), a group is highly organized to the extent that its strong internal network promotes a common identity among members (thus, 'catnet-ness'), so that it 'comes close to absorbing the members' whole lives'. By this criterion, the Vancouver media activist network lacks 'organization'. More specifically, it lacks the sort of organization that can provide the basis for a *singular collective identity*, as with the trade union militant whose life is devoted to building a strong activist union. What the Vancouver scene embodies is a different form of organization. Within it, media activism appears as a *nexus*, connecting a whole range of activist struggles – in part through the organizational and individual linkages analysed here, in part through a politics of left and alternative community development that employs various communications media, in part through the coalitional efforts of some groups (notably the CPBF) and the capacity-building work of others.

The collective identities, social visions and strategic frameworks prevalent within that nexus are the topic of exploration in the next chapter.

10 Identity, vision, strategies
Media democratization as counterhegemony

Having mapped in Chapter 9 the *social organization* of the Vancouver activist field, we now consider its cultural/ideological aspects. As argued in Chapters 3 and 4, counterhegemonic politics requires that the diverse movements and subaltern publics that have a stake in radical democratization find common ground. What contribution might media activists make to building such a unity in diversity around an alternative social vision? This is a very big question, and here we can only address one important aspect of it, namely, the extent to which Vancouver media activists share a common identity, vision and strategic framework commensurate with an integrative politics of social justice.

Embedded identities

In the previous chapter we noted the *embedded* character of media activism – its location as a *nexus* situated among various movements. This embeddedness is also evident in the various ways in which our informants described their identities and political trajectories. Some, particularly those active in producing independent media, had gravitated to DMA as a practical extension of praxis within another movement. One activist recounted a trajectory from anti-poverty activism in the mid-1980s, through peace activism opposing American imperialism in Central America in the late 1980s, to producing cable television programmes on global justice issues. A programmer at Co-op Radio observed:

> I guess fundamentally, I'm a labour activist, always have been. [I'm] also active in the cooperative movement, and this is where the media democracy thing mostly involves itself. I've also been active in the more progressive thinking environmental movement … I'm an urban ecologist. Primarily all those three is where I've been … I spent a lot of time in the 80s working against racism and discrimination, and I did a lot of that in connection with the labour movement and the cooperative movement.

Others became active on media issues after brushing up against power/knowledge configurations within dominant institutions. An activist in a feminist media-monitoring group was radicalized by her three-year stint in a public relations agency, generating 'media news coverage of client's products and services for big corporations that had millions of dollars to spend on image' – during which time she came to realize that many news stories are the product of powerful agents' promotional strategies. Another informant recalled how, after an earlier stint with Greenpeace, his work in a large transnational communications-consultancy firm, which was systematically monitoring activist discussion boards and the like on behalf of corporate clients, led him to join IndyMedia. Still others were drawn to DMA through a growing appreciation that, as an activist at Pacific Cinematique put it, 'to think about political activism today, you always have to think about it in relationship to the context of media representation'.

Whatever their routes into media activism, our informants clearly understood their activism on communications issues as embedded in larger projects rather than 'free standing'. When provided with an open-ended opportunity to name the movement within which their activism is located, only three of our 30 media activists actually invoked 'media activism' as an identity.[1] Other respondents mentioned media democracy only to re-position it within a broader project of radical democracy. For instance, an activist in PCAJ stated, 'I'm not sure that I would locate [my praxis] so much in the media democracy movement as in a broader movement for participatory democracy and social activism.' Among media activists the most common way of describing their activism was one or another version of 'anti-globalization' (10 of 30), often problematized with qualifications that acknowledged the difficulties of such an identity. Alternative terms that respondents offered for anti-globalization included 'a social justice movement in an increasingly globalized world', 'reversing what is *seen* as globalization', 'a pro-global democracy movement', 'the movement against corporate greed and for social justice' and 'the global justice movement'. The lack of a shared collective identity among media activists may reflect not only the cosmopolitanism of media activists within the larger activist network but also the movement's germinal nature. In Canada, at least, 'media democratization' has not gained a foothold in public discourse; the movement has yet to become a cultural reality, a collective representation with which one can readily identify.[2]

In contrast, and not surprisingly, activists primarily engaged in other causes made more use of well-established collective identities such as environmentalism, feminism and labour in locating their praxis, yet even among them categories such as 'anti-capitalism', 'pro-democracy' and 'the left' were often invoked, suggesting that they do not experience nor analyse their praxis as being 'contained' within the secure boundaries of singular movements. In short, there was a disposition among the activists we interviewed to identify their praxis within the democratic left rather than within bounded social movements. But it was particularly among our media activist informants that a break from single-issue political identity was abundantly evident. Activists, however, had different ways of describing this break, and of characterizing the role of DMA within a broader activist field.

Some media activists depicted their praxis as *ancillary* to that of other movements, with the latter providing a substantive political basis on which DMA can do its cultural work. Jim Lipkovits, founder of the *Columbia Journal*, commented that the *Journal* and people like myself are carried along in these movements. It's like the anti-WTO people are not – it's not like a sort of monolithic, single, unified movement but the tide seems to be moving in that direction. At least their tide and their efforts are moving in that direction. And I see the *Journal* as moving with them.

For independent media producers such as Lipkovits, democratizing communication involves building a left culture that goes with the flow of grassroots activism. Or, as an activist at Vancouver Community Network put it, 'community media is a movement of its own right, but it doesn't lead social movements; it follows, it's a part of, it's one component of social movements'. Similarly, a member of Guerrilla Media pointed out that the group's methodology is not an end in itself ('we're not doing culture jamming for the sake of culture jamming because we think it's cool') but 'a tool' for helping to realize a larger political vision – a vision that necessitates alliances with a host of progressive movements:

> I can align myself with a lot of movements and groups, but I don't feel that ... I identify with any of them. And that's essentially how Guerrilla Media works: ... we form alliances with various groups for particular projects ... that's one way of escaping the pigeon-holing of being 'just pro-NDP' or 'just left' or 'just union issues' or 'just environmental issues'. We deal with all of those issues and find alliances where we can.

This imagery of alliance and alignment brings up a second way in which media activists conceived of their roles within the larger field: as a *nexus* integrating various movements through the pursuit of a collective good – democratized communication – that is integral to the goals of all critical movements. As a programmer at Co-op Radio suggested, independent media operate not within but 'across movements', and thereby integrate the strands of radical and alternative political culture. This conception of DMA as a nexus was clearly articulated by *Adbusters* editor James MacKinnon:

> Media activism sort of fills the spaces in between the movements. I guess there is something of an activist media movement, but it's probably the least coherent of any of the movements ... the substance of it exists, but it doesn't have any sort of identifiable organizational structure or any sort of coherent structure at all. But it can always be found in the spaces in between the other movements ...

More prospectively, an activist with IndyMedia argued that media activism has the potential to become 'a meta-movement, a movement of movements', precisely due to the strategic centrality of mediated communication in contemporary society. 'The media for me is sort of the catch-all point, where you aren't concerned about biotechnology, genetically modified foods, the environment, social justice, all these sorts of things ... I think where they all sort of coalesce is in the media.' From this vantage point, the challenge for DMA is to build a meta-movement that establishes a 'constant focus', among critical movements, on mainstream media's democratic deficit and on the means for promoting communicative democracy.

Less strategically, and more ontologically, the idea of media activism as articulation, as a connecting-of-the-dots between various progressive causes, was evident in an IMPACS staff person's refusal to locate her praxis within any 'movement':

> No, I wouldn't put it within a movement at all … one part of me would love to be able to split myself into about forty different people and go out and work in every single issue area I'm interested in, and that's simply not possible. So right now I work in a capacity-building role which is to coordinate training for not-for-profits to help them improve their media skills. And the thing I love most about doing that, is the fact that I can support hundreds if not thousands of different individuals and groups to help them do a better job … so this way I can support a whole plethora of issues, which is very important to me … I actually have a greater sense of place by having a finger in a whole bunch of different pies … when I get too far into one movement, I end up feeling really disconnected because I don't know what the rest of the world is doing. I sort of almost end up getting channeled into one very narrow specific thing, which is only part of who I am. And so for me, I feel far more connected when I'm involved in a variety of things and involved in a variety of issues, and can support those, because another one of my deep beliefs is that everything is interconnected.

This informant's capacity-building role places her media activism in an instrumental relationship with other movements, yet her links with those movements sustain a sense of articulation. By empowering diverse activists to interact effectively with mainstream media she plays a role both in democratizing communication and in the concrete struggles that give expression to her own multifaceted identity. This account nicely captures the cosmopolitan, extraverted ethos we found among media activists on the Vancouver scene, while also underscoring the difficulty such praxis poses for the construction of a collective identity that might install media activism, alongside others, as a singular 'movement'. DMA lacks a discursive 'centre', but that is in part because it is spread widely across the field of movement politics, thriving in the empty spaces 'in between', to connect movements communicatively, and thereby strengthen counterhegemonic capacity.

Sociopolitical visions

Whether ancillary or nexus, we found a striking tendency for many of our media-activist informants to share a common sociopolitical *vision* with their counterparts in other critical social movements. When asked whether there is 'an overall vision of a possible future that inspires or guides your activism', the tendency was for activists of all kinds to articulate aspirations for a qualitatively different world, converging upon what might be called a democratic left alternative. Typically, media activists went well beyond a vision of democratic communication in conveying their political aspirations. Only six restricted themselves to the project of democratizing media, while eight presented radical left-wing visions and another 10 evoked imagery that resonated with a 'democratic left' project.[3] Interestingly, our 24 other activists were no less committed to the same sort of vision. Ten of them presented radical left-wing visions and another seven evoked imagery that likewise resonated with a 'democratic left' project.[4] Egalitarian, participatory-democratic imagery predominated among our respondents, suggesting that media activist initiatives committed to revitalizing public spheres, including subaltern counterpublics, might meet with success, if they are able to transcend or finesse the communicative and other barriers to effective coalition formation within the field of movement activism.

Certainly among the Vancouver media activists we found no lack of enthusiasm for building coalitions of one sort or another across movements. In answer to a probe that asked, 'To achieve the kinds of changes you desire, to what extent might it be necessary to build a larger coalition of movements; or, is the yearning for large, durable coalitions perhaps passé, and even part of the problem?' our informants generally favoured coalition formation, a key strategy for constructing a counterhegemonic bloc reaching beyond single-issue campaigns (Sanbonmatsu 2004). Half of our media activist respondents were wholly supportive of this, with most of the others giving qualified support that introduced various caveats, and one rejecting coalition formation as a strategy. Among non-media activists, the picture was more mixed (nine wholly favoured coalitions; five were sceptics; others gave mixed responses) – suggesting that media activists may be among the key agents for possible coalition formation in the broad social movement sector. Activists sceptical of coalitions saw problems in the overly centralized and institutionalized forms that coalitions have taken; the example most frequently given was the Solidarity Coalition in the general strike of 1983, wherein control by the labour movement eventuated in a settlement with the provincial government that marginalized the claims of other coalition partners (Palmer 1987; Carroll and Ratner 1989). These respondents distinguished flexible networks and alliances, which they favoured, from rigid coalitions. As an activist with IMPACS put it, 'I think building alliances is always important. When I think of coalitions, I think of a whole lot of groups with all of their different logos on a single piece of letterhead and they all have to have meetings together.' Put another way, respondents differed as to how durable or situational coalitions – or alliances – need to be, and how explicit the basis of unity. Some saw coalitions as founded on the sort of common vision we referred to above, which can only be achieved dialogically; others had a more conjunctural take. Compare:

> There should be constant, open dialogue between various organizations and movements with the goal of finding as much common ground, and get[ting] people basically on the same wavelength as possible. That should be ongoing and that should be expanding, and that should be reaching out to whoever is willing to listen.
>
> (Co-op Radio programmer)

I think it's very important for all of these organizations to come together. I think we're a bit too scattered right now. I think finding a key where we can all act together is very important now.

(Council of Canadians activist)

The coming together of various movements into a common movement is something that is desirable but will happen in the course of struggle and it's not something that can be done mechanically … it's not something to be done organizationally or formally. It's something to be done in action.

(Mobilization against War and Racism activist)

… when there's an apparent need for a coalition, people know and we come together and we create a big action out of it. But, we will naturally separate and do our things but understand that we're all pursuing the same thing.

(IndyMedia)

Beyond registering this difference in immediacy of action vs. ongoing organizing, activists noted a range of barriers to the formation of a coalition of movements, the chief ones being (1) sectarian tendencies within movements, which limit dialogue across them, and (2) lack of resources, both human (time) and material (money). An activist with Guerrilla Media captured these problems quite succinctly, observing that many activists are

not prepared to compromise and achieve parts of what they want, but not all of what they want. I think there's a real sort of pick-and-choose kind of activism out there that really cuts people off from working with each other, and that's a shame because the right will win if we don't work together, because they have far more power than we do. They have far more money and money will buy you a lot. It certainly buys them organization and we have to engage in organization through relationship building.

Respondents who saw a problem of sectarian division referred *inter alia* to distrust across movement sectors, competitive mindsets and infighting, ego-mania and desires for control, holier-than-thou attitudes, an unwillingness by some activists to view their cause as one among many, and unfamiliarity with consensus decision-making. Some divisions were seen as grounded in differing political projects and modes of organizing, as in the tension between labour and environmental movements: 'The labour movement generally tends to be focused on making better conditions for its workers, and making itself grow. And that might be at times in opposition to the environmental movement' (IndyMedia). As the editor of *Adbusters* told us, a major obstacle to the flowering of independent media as a nexus for coalition formation is the tendency, among some established movements, to orient themselves primarily to the corporate media, creating a 'continued self-interest among activist organizations in the maintenance of the mainstream press'. This observation directs us to the fissure that underlies the distinction between media activism that is lifeworld-centred – that strives to build alternative media and critical audiences – and pragmatic media strategies that work within the logic of mainstream media to secure favourable standing for a given activist cause.

The literature on social movement coalitions generally presents them as having a two-sided impact on the resources available for collective action (Bleyer 1997). On the one hand, coalitions can be effective in creating resources, in part through a division of labour so the activities of different organizations do not overlap but, rather, complement each other. On the other hand, coalitions consume valuable resources, demanding time and energy that could be expended more usefully and successfully within social movement organizations themselves. Our respondents presented both these perspectives while also observing that groups with the most resources (e.g. organized labour) can dominate a coalition, thereby subverting its democratic character. But what preoccupied their reflections on barriers to coalescing was not the distribution but the extent of resources. A good many informants pointed out that they were already stretched to the limit in trying to accomplish their basic goals, so that any *additional* political initiatives were difficult to mount.[5] Given the serious problems that lack of resources poses, it is vital that any potential coalition efficiently create and manage whatever is available. For DMA, this raises special challenges, in light of our finding that *none* of the non-media activists interviewed named media activist groups as important constituents of a potential coalition of critical movements. If media activism has the form of a nexus rather than a movement *tout court*, its amorphous character, betwixt and between more clearly delineated movements, may limit its contribution to counterhegemonic coalition formation. Chronic scarcity of resources can easily translate itself into reluctance by established movements to break from the traditional media strategies in which they have invested and to put effort into the political struggle to democratize communication. In the immediate situation, media activists may need to devise initiatives that do not require much diversion of resources from other struggles but, rather, lower the costs of collective action for the community of critical movements. More broadly, endemic resource scarcity raises the challenge of persuading critical movements that the democratization of communication is a public good worthy of collective effort, on a number of fronts – that media democratization is a necessary component of counterhegemonic politics.

Strategic priorities

Those fronts can, again, be conceptualized in terms of the simplified version of our typology of DMA. We actually presented the four basic categories of that typology to our informants and asked them to comment on their adequacy as a framework for understanding strategies of media reformation and transformation.[6] Their reactions provide some face validity for our basic categorization. All but five agreed that the categories – building independent media, promoting more critical audiences, influencing content and practices of mainstream media and advocating media reform via the state – captured the diversity of strategies and practices in media activism. All activists were asked about the importance of each of these

Table 10.1 Importance of media activist strategies in achieving political goals

	Building independent media		Promoting critical audiences		Influencing content of mainstream media		State reform, regulation, etc.	
	Media activists	Other activists	Media activists	Other activists	Media activists	Other activists	Media activists	Other activists
Important	88	70	83	57	31	75	40	33
Mixed	12	25	17	24	21	12	20	22
Unimportant	0	5	0	19	48	12	40	44
Total: %	100	100	100	100	100	100	100	100
(n)	(24)	(20)	(23)	(21)	(29)	(16)	(25)	(18)

strategies in achieving their own political goals, and media activists were invited to rank them as to 'importance in your own activism' (with tied ranks allowed). While 16 respondents argued that every strategy is very important, most distinguished priorities, and some rejected certain strategies altogether.

It is evident from the ratings of each strategy, shown in Table 10.1, that building independent media is the most predominant media activist strategy in Vancouver. Most of the 44 informants who offered an assessment of this strategy (nine-tenths of media activists and seven-tenths of other activists) judged it as an important means of changing media; only one described it as unimportant. Moreover, when asked to rank the four strategies, 16 media activists ranked building independent media as a top priority. Most of these were themselves active in such media. As a form of activism, building independent media was often deemed to indirectly facilitate other forms of media activism by creating the communications infrastructure of social movements, facilitating the promotion of more critical audiences, and obliging the mainstream media to be more accountable – indirectly influencing the content and practices of the mainstream media. In short, there was a tendency to view independent media as the linchpin of democratization.

A number of informants presented what might be called a dialectical account of cultural production and consumption, with independent media creating the literate audiences whose critical perspectives promote the further growth of democratic media. Indeed, our informants tended to conceive of building independent media as a form of grassroots organizing. As a long-time activist at Co-op Radio suggested,

> I think there is a role for alternative media to challenge mainstream media, to challenge the establishment generally, the people who own the world and run the country, challenge them. And through that continual challenge, you hope to have an influence over what they do and hope to eventually create some changes and hopefully, consequently to influence the content and practices of what they do.

However, this notion of independent media as a *challenge* to entrenched power was complemented by the argument that building independent media is useful in itself for its participatory and pedagogical value as an empowering *alternative*.

> I think it's hugely important. In fact, [it is] probably the most effective one of these [four strategies] because it's also the most empowering. Whether you're participating in it, or on the receiving end of it, you really can see that you just create your own media, and have your message out there, and that's the idea behind democratic media, right?
>
> (MobGlob activist)

While only one respondent outright rejected building independent media as a strategy, others did express reservations. Several of these mainly non-media activists pointed out that the audiences for independent media are often minuscule, raising the question whether such media simply preaches to the choir, without reaching the general public.

The second most cited strategy was promoting more critical audiences through culture jamming or media education. A total of 31 informants, representing 83 per cent of media activists and 57 per cent of other activists, considered this to be important. Fourteen media activists assigned it top priority. Although this strategy was widely viewed as crucial there was an implicit polarization between the two ways of promoting critical audiences that we presented in our question, namely 'media education' and 'culture jamming'. Our respondents overwhelmingly endorsed the former as fundamentally important. Like building independent media, education was seen as necessary in bringing together a constituency for social change that could also push to democratize mainstream media. Culture jamming, on the other hand, was rarely mentioned by respondents, suggesting that many activists share Heath and Potter's (2004) scepticism about the transformative potential of such interventions. Even our informants from Adbusters and Guerrilla Media assigned culture jamming a modest role, as 'one type of tool of expression', 'one arrow in the quiver'. While some argued that culture jamming is 'good for a laugh' and as an 'entry point' for critical consciousness, there did not seem to be a widespread commitment to it as a core strategy. As an activist in End the Arms Race argued,

> I think the media education part is extremely important, through the school system in particular. I think [the] teachers' union plays a vital role in making sure that's happening. Culture jamming? I think it's a fad, to be honest, and not important.

There were some respondents who expressed reservations about promoting more critical audiences. Interestingly, all four of the informants who deemed this strategy unimportant were non-media activists. Three of them were active in the labour/social democratic left; the fourth a leading environmentalist. These sceptics questioned the extent to which the general public has been hegemonized into the grip of a dominant ideology. If the public simply had access to information, they argued, then they would be able to make their own decisions. As Geoff Meggs, the BCFed's Communications Director commented,

> I don't know if it's the circles I move in or not, but I don't think that people are as mesmerized by the mainstream media as we think they are. I think if offered an alternative by someone they have confidence in, they can change on a dime. And I mean that's what we have to [do].

If most Vancouver media activists embraced lifeworld-centred strategies, fewer accorded the more system-centred strategies importance in the struggle to democratize communication. Few media activists saw influencing the content and practices of mainstream media as a viable political strategy; in fact, half of them rejected this strategy out of hand, and less than a third considered it to be of importance. In comparison, three-quarters of other activists, no doubt mindful of the need for their movements to attain standing in the mainstream media, attached importance to efforts to influence the media mainstream. On this issue, our sub-samples of media activists and other activists were remarkably divergent. Among media activists, and particularly those involved with independent media, the tendency was to view mainstream or corporate media as an adversary to be fought. Far from trying to reshape the mainstream, the focus of groups like Adbusters on corporate power in the media led them

> to promote the idea of a certain degree of non-participation in the mainstream media ... The mainstream media is at the forefront of the battle, the army we're up against ... we tend to feel that that's the least fruitful type of media activism.

For many media activists, the commitment to building counterhegemonic, democratic media preempted the possibility of reforming the media mainstream. The four media activists who did prioritize this strategy emphasized the tactical value of media monitoring, writing critical letters to editors, and educating and inspiring individual journalists within the mainstream media structure, but they had no illusions of creating significant institutional change.

For non-media activists, however, mainstream media comprise a crucial conduit for political communication, one with which they must engage if they are to reach wider publics. Understandably, they were much more inclined to view the struggle for fair and accurate coverage as an important front in the overall war of position, with press releases, letter writing, and appearances on radio phone-in shows as part of the day-to-day attempt to get noticed by a general public who continue to have little resort to independent media. Indeed, just as non-media activists sometimes expressed scepticism about the efficacy of independent media, these informants sometimes endorsed pragmatic and traditional media strategies. Compare the analysis of a leading environmentalist with that of a key labour activist, on the value of appearing on Vancouver's most popular talk radio show:

I'm not going to put my money and time and energy into tons and tons of stuff on Co-op Radio if I can get on CKNW. I'll go for CKNW; I'll get it on Rafe Mair. That's just the way it is.

Yeah, that's where our big audience is. Yeah, if we get on Rafe Mair, we have three hundred thousand people for half an hour ... Yeah, we take anything we can get in the mainstream media, because it costs nothing, just staff time.

Pragmatism, however, does not mean pandering. As an activist at CCPA, a left think tank heavily dependent on the media mainstream, put it, infusing critical discourse into the public sphere via dominant media is a complicated strategic gambit:

I think it's a mistake for [progressives] to ignore the mainstream media ... We need to keep on their backs and we need to try and be represented there as much as we can. What we have to do in doing that is be strategic and careful and suspicious of the mainstream media as we do it, because otherwise you get used ... [T]he CCPA allows itself to be used by the mainstream media. They [the media] need the pretence of balance, but that's part of the trade off. We say, okay, fine, but that way we get our message out at least in limited part.

Or, as an activist in the environmentalist David Suzuki Foundation noted,

It's this delicate balance, because it's like, we need these people. So if you also go to them in a critical way, 'look you've got to open up your news hole; you need more of this' – I mean, they're going to say 'hit the road'.

As for our fourth strategy, advocating for policy reform and state regulation of media, media activists were a little less dismissive but other activists tended to reject this route to change or to register mixed assessments (see Table 10.1). This scepticism was, again, fuelled by pragmatism, and specifically by pessimism about the prospects for statist reform in a neoliberal order. While numerous informants acknowledged the need for government regulation, they also observed that neoliberalism's ascendance has narrowed the scope for greater government regulation of the corporate media. Three responses suffice to capture this pervasive pessimism:

I don't think there's any appetite for that these days. The government is so far in the corporate pockets and the regulatory agencies are deregulating like crazy ... So, I wouldn't toss it out, but I say it's not at this time worthwhile to work on that strategy.

(Donald Gutstein, NewsWatch Canada)

I have less hope for advocating for reform of government policy/regulation of media. We don't seem to be in an era where government intervention is accepted unless it's a national emergency.

(Larry Kuehn, BCTF)

Well, I mean I think that's a bottomless pit, to be honest with you ... we know what the Spicer Commission resulted in – oh yeah, we have less corporate control now than we had before? I think it's a dead-end road.

(Ivan Bulic, SPEC)

Those dismissing a state-centred reform strategy did so primarily out of pessimism, not because they rejected the goal of countering private media power through public means. As an activist in the Council of Canadians put it, 'as we stand now, with the kind of government we have, I would see that as very difficult. But it's not something you don't do. I don't think I would put a tremendous amount of energy at the moment in that.' The one category of respondents that actually prioritized state-centred reform was a social democratic current of activists associated with the NDP (itself state-centred in its priorities), four of whom stated this preference, including the Chair and founder of the NDP Media Caucus, Herschel Hardin. As with the other strategies, our respondents sometimes made keen observations on the beneficial impact that democratization in this area could have on other domains. The Director of Communications at the CCPA pointed out that 'if you don't change some of that [the regulatory environment], you can't create alternative media very effectively if there isn't more supportive framework for it to happen'. Similarly, Peter Coombes, Executive Director of End the Arms Race, expressed the view that 'government should be helping civil society groups produce independent media. They should be restricting – putting certain regulations on – business media.'

Another informant, from Guerrilla Media, challenged the adequacy of our fourth strategy in a way that questioned our fourfold typology, arguing that the notion of reform through regulation does not address the 'core issue of private ownership of media'. Along the same lines, Sunera Thobani, former leader of the National Action Committee on the Status of Women, submitted that the four strategies for change do not add up to the radical transformation of social and political relations that is needed, in order to democratize public communication:

I see these as all sorts of reforms, little reforms which are not going to fundamentally transform. And I don't know any other way of putting it – the transformation of the media without seeing it as part of the larger social transformation of the society and a transformation of power in this society.

Other respondents who problematized our fourfold categorization suggested that our terminology – the language of audiences, media content, government policy and the like – did not fully capture some of the most important democratic possibilities implicit in media activism. Particularly underplayed in our four-fold schema is the promotion of an inclusive and participatory approach to media: a broad revitalization of civil society that would sustain an ongoing process of political education. As one media activist insisted, missing from the schema is the promotion of 'a different civic approach to media, a different civic understanding of the role of the media, and the need for the citizen to be involved in that idea of media'.

These reflections press beyond the notion of media activism as a specific movement, or even nexus, to the relations between communication, power, democracy and citizenship. We take our respondent's point: ultimately, it is not sufficient for DMA to dwell in the realm of the media, even if we conceptualize that realm broadly as a field. To democratize public communication is to renovate 'media' *politically*, as part of a broader social transformation. Our Vancouver informants thereby return us, equipped now with a sense of media activism as a *nexus* of movements, to the connection between democratizing media and democratizing society, and the closely associated issues of counterhegemony and the public sphere.

11 Conclusion

Media activism as movement-nexus?

In this book's Introduction we argued that mass media in the Anglo-American heart-land are plagued by a chronic democratic deficit, to which media activism can be read as a critical response. The deficit is multifaceted; it derives not only from media's failures in constituting a democratic public sphere, in sustaining healthy communities and political cultures, and in stimulating diversity in public communication, but also from media's complicity in maintaining inequality, in diminishing the public commons of knowledge and in excluding the public from shaping the mandates of the cultural industries. In subsequent chapters, we detailed a range of media activist campaigns and projects as diverse as the component parts of the democratic deficit. Activists have taken up the struggle to democratize public communication in a great range of contexts that are coextensive with the vast terrain of the media field itself; they have framed their political projects in different ways and have adopted a variety of strategies and of organizational forms. The upshot is a fledgling and inchoate, yet rich, politics of communication, directed both at the institutions of corporate capitalism and at civil societies and everyday worlds.

Whether such collective action constitutes an emerging social movement, and what its conditions of survival and success might be, have been the broad questions posed in this book. If social movements are 'crucibles' for emergent publics (Angus 2001: 83), is media activism developing as its 'own' movement – its own crucible *alongside* other critical movements? Or is media activism more a catalyst increasingly efficacious *within* various movements? Or, again, does media activism, while it may have some of the characteristics of a movement, also emerge as a nexus – a point of articulation *between* movements, transforming and lending coherence to the broad field of movement activism as a counterhegemonic formation? And if, as we have found, this 'movement-nexus' scenario seems the most plausible, what strategic implications might be drawn from this diagnosis? What lines of collective action offer the most promise? To begin these prognostic and strategic reflections, let us revisit our starting point.

The media field as a site of struggle

The idea of a media field as a distinct sphere of legislative/state regulation, and reformist political action, emerges historically along with communications policy, modern mass media, and the interventionist state. Every radical movement of modernity has introduced new communicative patterns and occasionally innovative communications practices as part of its political and cultural struggle, but only in the twentieth century was media/communication recognized as a site for political contention and transformation. The first 'media reform' movements emerged, in the US and Canada at least, in the 1930s around public broadcasting. More recent waves of activism recounted in Chapter 5 – from the political-cultural upheavals of the 1960s through the 1970s/1980s struggle for a New World Information and Communication Order and the post-Communist media reform initiatives after 1989 – evince a coming-of-age of media democratization as a collective project. The current wave is considerably more diverse, as it contends with complex communications technologies embedded in the political economy of advanced capitalism, and with a democratic deficit that has been in recent decades exacerbated by neoliberal political policy, by the increasing concentration and global reach of capital, and by the ongoing corporate colonization of lifeworlds.

How does the structure of the media field condition the tasks, strategies and opportunities for DMA? In the first place, differing histories of the Anglo-American formations have shaped the field in specific ways. In the UK and to a lesser extent Canada, a labour left, contributing to a social democratic political culture, helped instil public-service broadcasting traditions. In these countries, media activists struggle to maintain and enhance a public-service tradition that was never strongly established in the US. The American labour left was never politically influential and a culture of possessive and 'rugged' individualism limited prospects for a strong public-service current. If the disorganized state of the working class ceded much of the media field to private corporate interests, the more recent deflection of New Left politics into expressionist identity issues further divided the opposition (cf. Sanbonmatsu 2004). Yet these political disabilities have a provocative side. In the US, media democratization is now propelled by an urge to overcome fractures of identity politics and postmodernist localism, by the shortage of other venues for progressive groups to come together in a common project, and by indignation at a particularly egregious democratic deficit, as news media morph from watchdogs into lapdogs.

In all three countries the media field is 'weak' – it is porous and vulnerable to influence from political and economic fields ('power through'). Yet it also shows a high capacity to intrude upon other fields ('power of'). In a field whose boundaries are permeable, media's democratic deficit cannot be disembedded from other political-economic issues, and media activism cannot be easily detached from other movements. The field's permeable boundaries and high capacity to intrude on other fields have rendered DMA dependent on the ebbs and flows of broader political tides, but have also conferred on media reformers a capacity to conscientize and help shape agendas and strategies of allied movements, in recognition of the media field as site of struggle. The field's porosity also contributes to media activism's secondary character compared to other movements. Many activists identify primarily with ecology, anti-capitalism or other movements, and see themselves only secondarily as media activists. Yet the high capacity of media to intrude upon other fields helps explain why so many movements now recognize media as a necessary site of struggle. The nexus-like character of DMA is in these ways inscribed within the media field.

As we suggested in Chapter 2, journalism's position in the field has had telling implications for media activism. Journalism's limited autonomy from state and capital places severe constraints on the strategy of reform from within, in the absence of strong allies without – witness the trajectory of Media Alliance from 'insider' to external critic and the recent withering of the US public journalism movement. Given the strategic importance of media to the legitimation, publicity and marketing needs of corporations and governments, effective media reform campaigns are likely to bring capital and the state into the fray, probably as opponents. Conversely though, struggles against the power of capital and/or state on non-media fronts will likely overlap with the 'contestation of media power' (Couldry 2003: 39); thus DMA has beneficiaries, and potential allies, among other social movements. Given all this, one might expect media reform to face an especially strong conflict system, centred on the corporate media, and this is indeed the case. One might also expect the movement to benefit from a good many allies, yet we have found DMA to be stymied by a weak alliance system, especially in its ties to the journalists at the centre of the media field.

The *specificity* of the media field suggests the need to develop capacities and strategies suited to mobilizing constituencies in ways that enable media power to be challenged. The media field creates a plethora of constituencies for DMA, yet only certain groups have been drawn into struggles to democratize communication. Our interviews with activists led us to conclude that the energies for DMA emanate not from those at the centre of the field but from the semi-periphery: social groups and individuals with mobilizable resources (education, skills, networks, political analyses) who need, yet are constrained in, access to the means of public representation. As with many other social movements, the impetus for system challenges derives neither from the very centre or the outermost margins but from the most privileged of the marginalized.

That said, we ought not to dismiss journalists as potential allies. Aspects of their material and cultural conditions militate against activism – e.g. their pursuit of 'professional' status, the 'regime of objectivity', the individualistic epistemology that inhibits them from endorsing structural solutions to journalism's democratic limitations (Baker 2002: 282–3). Still, journalists will mobilize under certain conditions: if they develop connections (ideological and/or personal) with social movements; if media owners threaten their material well-being via cutbacks and layoffs; if their professional status or ideals are blatantly violated.

The ambiguous position of journalists exposes a potential fault line in DMA, dividing relatively privileged and well resourced media professionals in the heart of the system, from marginalized groups excluded from or victimized by media. Hence the signal importance among media workers of progressive trade unionism, a vehicle for solidaristic relations and identities. Also marginalized are cultural needs that cannot be commodified and thus are under-rewarded by the system. On the other side of the fault line from media professionals, alternative media, the open source movement and the communications arms of progressive advocacy groups eke out a precarious existence dependent on volunteer labour, foundation funding and so forth.

DMA's inchoate character is in part due to *obstacles* peculiar to the media field and the project of media democratization, and distinct from those facing other social movements. To the detailed analysis of barriers to media activism that we presented in Chapter 7, we can add some closing reflections. Beyond the immediate reaches of groups like CPBF and Media Alliance, singularly devoted to the cause, DMA lacks a clear collective identity. On first glance, this diffuseness seems counterintuitive. If communications is not a mere superstructure but is constitutive of contemporary capitalism (through information and communication technologies, digital networks, massive investments in culture industries, saturation advertising, and so on) why have those struggling against the injustices of capitalism not identified media as a distinct site of struggle, and developed a movement so targeted? Part of the explanation may rest with the political inertia left over from the 'old Left's' totalizing critique of capitalism, which relegated DMA (at least in the US) to liberals who did not connect media reform to the broader contours of the social order and failed to inspire mass support. Among new social movements, as we discussed in Chapter 3, the tendency has been to deploy media strategies that strive for standing and sympathetic coverage or that produce alternative media for movement constituents. Neither of these instrumental strategies feeds into a collective effort to reform media.

The inchoate form is also a symptom of *low issue salience*. Media's democratic deficit is a 'process issue' that does not threaten material interests strongly and directly enough to inspire a primary 'old-style' movement similar to labour. Neither does it evoke identities distinct from other NSMs. Where media activists come closest to articulating a 'new' movement identity is in the lifeworld-focused alternative media, including IndyMedia centres. DMA's low salience is not necessarily a strategic weakness; it gives this activism an extraverted thrust, which can be a strength.

As a 'process issue', the struggle to democratize public communication focuses on transforming communicative relations themselves. In this, media reform faces a particularly strong 'free rider' problem. The costs of mobilizing are disproportionately borne by heavily engaged media activists, while the benefits would accrue to all progressive movements, regardless of whether a group contributes to the DMA cause. Locally, it may make sense for a group to focus its efforts on immediate initiatives using conventional media strategies, but if all groups embrace such 'local rationality' DMA gets relegated to the margins, despite its strategic centrality.

Yet another specific barrier is posed by media reform's target: a system specialized in the formation of consciousness. While environmental pollution is visible, the democratic deficit is obscured to many by corporate media themselves. Movements are typically driven by felt grievances. But if media consumers do not know they are not getting certain kinds of information, they may not feel aggrieved. The barrier here is not simply cognitive. Put crassly, environmental pollution attacks the body and provokes repugnance; cultural 'pollution' seduces the soul and induces compliance, even identification. Many consumers identify with the branded images, products, programmes and celebrities that constitute the corporate mediascape (Hackett 2000).

Complementing these seductions is the sense of *communicative empowerment* that some potential constituent groups derive from new information and communication technologies (ICTs). If people get too excited about new technology and simply adapt it for their own purposes, Aliza Dichter worries, policy advocacy, challenges to ownership, critiques of corporate media, and the like, will be abandoned. On the other hand, as we emphasized in Chapter 8, certain challenges can also be springboards to new forms of activism, and information technologies give one of the most compelling examples. The extensive use of internet and related communication technologies by media and other activists in Vancouver, San Francisco and other cities suggests that the ICTs, occupational groups and associated habitus generated by capitalism's own 'information revolution' create new skills and constituencies for addressing media's democratic deficit. The political implications of ICTs are thus mixed: 'Today, cyberspace is the scene within which the vectors of e-capital tangle and entwine with those of a molecular proliferation of activists, researchers, gamers, artists, hobbyists, and hackers' (Dyer-Witheford 2001: 179).

As a final reflection on the media field as a site of struggle, consider Habermas's (1987) famous claim that NSMs arise at the seam between system and lifeworld. What is striking is how the media field inhabits this very space. More than perhaps any other site in advanced capitalist formations, the media field is both *of the system* and *of the lifeworld*. It takes in corporate media and state organizations that produce and regulate public communication, and is organized around systemic norms of profit maximization and hierarchical power. Yet it also includes a mass-mediated public sphere (colonized but not eradicated by those systemic exigencies) and a host of subaltern counterpublics, alternative media, media education initiatives and the like. If all this gives media activism *prima facie* credentials as a new social movement (at least within a Habermasian optic), it also underlines the unique importance of the media field as a pivotal site for broader political and cultural struggles.

Our typology of democratic media activism in Chapter 3 attempts to capture this variegation, but we have only scratched the surface in this study. Future research could profitably look into the political *vectors* that emerge from different locations in and around the media field and that target different sites in and around the same field. Provisionally, we can distinguish a vector of state reformism that emanates from the reformist wings of the state and targets state-regulatory policy – as in the Royal Commissions that have probed media concentration and other issues in Canada and Britain. This vector has been weakened by the ascendance of neoliberalism, as business-friendly pressures within the state have left the Reports of such inquiries gathering dust. A second set of vectors has its point of origin in the dominant media system, as frustrated journalists have resisted management attacks on their working conditions and professional ideals, leading to internal reform movements, union militancy, and even (less commonly) coalitions with other, lifeworld-centred groups. For reasons we analysed in Chapter 7, these are also fairly weak vectors, apart from union action, which tends, however, to focus on bread-and-butter issues rather than broader questions of representation. Finally, social movements' communicative needs, and their frustration with (and dependence upon) dominant media, have spurred a set of vectors that originate in the lifeworld. These include (a) efforts by movements to reduce their dependence through creation of alternative media, (b) efforts to reduce the asymmetry of the movement/media relation by adopting public relations tactics to influence dominant media, and – more recently – (c) joining coalitions for structural media change. Presently, vectors *a* and *b* seem to have the most energy yet they also pose the most limited challenges to media's democratic deficit. Beyond suggesting that such political vectors may be a worthy focus for future empirical work, our typology of DMA identifies a strategic dilemma structured into the media field, between lifeworld- and system-focused strategies.

Democratic media activism and counterhegemony

As German social theorist Joachim Hirsch has argued, new social movements are ideologically and politically diverse. They comprise a 'contradictory battlefield in the struggle for a new hegemony' (1988: 51). How might DMA figure in this struggle? To pose this question presumes a conception of what the struggle entails. Among left intellectuals and activists today, there are actually two conceptions which, following Carroll and Ratner (1994) and Sanbonmatsu (2004), we term respectively counterhegemony and anti-hegemony. Counterhegemonic politics aspires to build consensus around an emancipatory project – to move beyond the fragments of resistant subcultures and movements, to forge 'political unity across cultural differences' (Sanbonmatsu 2004: 130), a unity-in-diversity supporting an alternative social vision. Anti-hegemony operates according to a different political logic. Informed by both postmodern social theory and the practice of identity politics (ibid.), anti-hegemony is sceptical of all attempts to construct a general interest, to build unity; it instead trumpets a politics of difference, of dispersed singularities, disavowing the need for consensus and coordinated political action (Carroll and Ratner 1994: 13). For anti-hegemonists, to struggle for a new order is simply to replicate the totalizing projects of Western modernity which have eventuated in such tragedies as fascism and Stalinism. The key to a different future lies not in amassing counterpower but in undoing the local and dispersed powers that routinely keep people in their places as disciplined subjects.

A counterhegemonic 'dual strategy' recognizes that power, including media power, is both concentrated within dominant institutions of state and capital and diffused across the terrain of civil society, where consent to the dominant order is secured in daily life; hence, the need to proceed on a multiplicity of fronts vis-à-vis system and lifeworld. It accepts the reality of an enduring system/lifeworld distinction[1] but argues that a diverse and inclusive public sphere can place the system under democratic control, and that the system itself can be democratized – that it need not privilege the prerogatives of private capital and bureaucratic hierarchy.

This perspective counsels coordinated counterhegemonic effort to counter the coordinated efforts by dominant groups and their functionaries to maintain hegemony.

When we look at media activism 'on the ground' – at the activists and organizations that strive to undo media's democratic deficit – we find in germinal form many of the rudiments of counterhegemonic politics. Activists often combine in their praxis a system focus and a lifeworld focus. Many realize that the struggle to democratize communication is hardly a single-issue campaign, that it needs to proceed simultaneously on multiple fronts. Media activists frame their politics in different ways, but most draw on a vision of media democratization that resonates with fairly conventional political ideas yet presses them in more radical directions – toward substantive claims for social justice and the right to communicate. The plurality of action frames we have found in play, centred on a multidimensional project of media democratization, can help collect a broad social base – liberals, middle-class consumers concerned with the cultural environment, media insiders and outsiders, subalterns and socialists seeking social justice.

Our case study of media activism in Vancouver allowed us to explore these emergent politics *in situ*, as a field of activism linked to other critical social movements, with media activists playing extraverted roles as cross-movement networkers. In Vancouver at least, media activism has become somewhat of a nexus, with a counterhegemonic potential to weave the strands of activism into a common project of democratizing communication. Not surprisingly, media activists tend to see their efforts as embedded in or ancillary to larger projects, rather than free standing. For the most part, they support efforts to form cross-movement coalitions (although they look with scepticism upon models of coalition-formation that entail hierarchical structures) – but then so do other activists on the Vancouver scene. And while lifeworld-centred initiatives to build independent media and foster critical audiences are viewed as the linchpin of democratization, many media activists recognize the importance of state-centred media reform, even if the hegemony of neoliberalism has induced a widespread pessimism about immediate results.

Contrary to some of the more extreme claims of New Social Movement theory, contemporary movements are interested not only in reconfiguring the daily culture of the lifeworld. Their 'four Rs of democratization' – rights, recognition, representation, redistribution of resources – imply demands on the system: the state, corporations, and supra-state institutions of governance, like the WTO. This is certainly the case for the two social movement organizations we have studied in depth. The British CPBF has held fast to a state-centred agenda for democratization, while broadening its scope over time to include broadcasting and internet. Media Alliance has also enlarged its agenda, gravitating in recent years to a politics of media reform that promotes independent media as well as the struggle for media justice.

In short, our investigations lead us to the inference that democratic media activism has become an integral and indispensable aspect of counterhegemonic politics. Media democracy comprises a social vision – an ethics – that has been missing on the left, and that is sorely needed. It points to a new paradigm of communication, beyond the liberal freedoms that critical movements, particularly in the US, have tended to endorse without reflection, namely individual freedom of expression and corporate freedom from the state. The new framework recognizes that communicative rights are not the possessions of abstract individuals; they are inherently collective rights, redeemable only within social relations. Communicative democracy requires equitable access to the means of communication, implying a pluralistic media system in which the powers of capital and of state authority are checked while the voices of citizens and communities carry into a vibrant and diverse public sphere. The new paradigm's break from liberal individualism is completed by a third facet, the obligation to listen – the recognition that communicative democracy is not simply a matter of exercising voice but of sustaining mutuality (cf. White 1995; Husband 1996). In pursuing this social vision on several fronts including those of the state, the corporate media and the lifeworld, and in conjunction with other critical movements, media democrats build a nexus among movements, a place where strategies might converge through dialogues across issue areas and movement identities. To the extent that it succeeds, DMA also unleashes forces for other social justice struggles.

This reading is somewhat at odds with the argument, made most cogently by Lance Bennett (2003), that contemporary media activism heralds what we earlier termed an anti-hegemonic politics. Bennett's argument, which we briefly considered in Chapter 3, is worth recalling here. For him, ICTs and the globalization of social and economic relations have enabled new activist networks, identities and strategies – a '*lifestyle politics* in which ideology, party loyalties, and elections are replaced with issue networks that offer more personal and often activist solutions for problems' (2003: 27). The new politics draws on the 'new media power' of the internet and a 'collective individualism … facilitated in part by discourses conceived less in ideological terms than in broad categories of threat, harm, and justice' (2003: 31). This 'liberation from ideology' finds its clearest expression in the electronic circulation of *memes* – readily imitated images that cross social networks as they resonate with shared experiences, as in the arresting subvertisements of culture jammers.

In contrast to reasoned analyses, dialogue, political education and consensus-building initiatives, memes do not presume or promote political literacy or counterhegemonic vision; instead they trigger cognitive, affective and behavioural associations. Just as decentralized networks lack any coherent organization, the memes that circulate across them do not add up to a coherent programme; rather, they fuel an anti-hegemonic 'counterculture'. But if in the view of culture-jam guru Kalle Lasn (1999) this anarchic chaos is cause for celebration, other commentators have pointed out that the lifestyle politics of counterculture dovetail nicely with corporate niche marketing strategies, a prime example being the Black Spot Sneaker that *Adbusters* introduced as its signature brand of 'subversive' footwear in September 2003. 'After that day', Joseph Heath and Andrew Potter claim, 'it became obvious to everyone that cultural rebellion, of the type epitomized by *Adbusters* magazine, is not a threat to the system – it *is* the system' (2004: 1). The rebellion and nonconformity, the 'uncooling' of established brands are more about the competitive pursuit of cultural distinction – a dynamic that does not subvert but that actually drives consumer capitalism – than they are challenges to hegemony:

> As a result, the proposed solution – individualistic sartorial and stylistic re-bellion – simply feeds the flames, by creating a whole new set of positional goods for these 'rebel consumers' to compete for. The struggle for status is replaced by the quest for cool, but the basic structure of competition remains unchanged.
>
> (Heath and Potter 2004: 322)

It is not that lifeworld-centred practices that jam the dominant culture or that create tiny, identity-confirming 'free spaces' shielded from state determination (as in the autonomous media centre studied by Atton: 2003a) make no contribution to the democratization of communication, although it is well to remember that our informants mainly viewed culture jamming as no more than a specialized tool. The problem is that real though modest contributions have been exaggerated and romanticized in academic literature that in the same breath dismisses both the 'old Left' (social democracy, state reforms, unions) and the idea of building counterhegemonic coalitions. Despite its radical pretence, the celebration of counterculture as an end in itself can be profoundly pessimistic, even conservative. Underneath its rhetoric of lifestyle politics, the anti-hegemonic alternative – the abstentionist refusal to take on 'the system' – amounts to a capitulation to the market liberals' mantra that There Is No (systemic) Alternative.

In our view, forms of media activism that aim to transform the lifeworld need to be pursued in conjunction with system-oriented initiatives. Struggles to democratize public communication are necessarily multiform; the key question is how to coordinate actions and campaigns to reap the benefits of synergy. Posing the question in this way invites us to retain the notion of a coherent political programme and ideological perspective, to recognize the strategic importance of organized campaigns as distinct from loose networks, to focus political efforts on the entire media field (not simply the internet), and to restore an emphasis on the state – not as the citadel of politics but as a weighty condensation of social power.

Recentring the state

Just as it is a mistake to reduce politics to all that revolves around the state, it is erroneous to pretend that politics can 'escape' or ignore the state. Indeed, in today's world the state is not only 'integral' in Gramsci's sense (it reaches into civil society in infinitesimal ways, e.g. though media regulatory policy, educational practices, public service broadcasting) but increasingly 'globalized', partly through supranational bodies such as the IMF and WTO (Gill 1995: 85–6). Although many media democrats are understandably drawn to lifeworld-centred politics, several of the groups and activists we have discussed here have over time re-centred their politics on the state – broadly conceived. Media Alliance's recent embrace of a grassroots politics of media reform presents the clearest example, but on a smaller scale the decision in the early 2000s by Guerrilla Media activists to put their culture jamming on hold while they engaged with local electoral politics is also worth pondering. By the same token, we have witnessed the growing importance of a transnational media activism within groups such as WACC and CRIS that is directed at globalized state practices – international regulations, standards and so on.

To recentre the state is not, in our view, to trade the self-limiting politics of the counterculture for a return to the self-limiting politics of liberal reformism and electoralism. Rather, it is to recognize counterhegemony as a 'war of position', a struggle to win space for democratic practice on various interconnected fronts in civil society and lifeworld, in the workplace *and* in and against the state. A full-scale media democratization project would need to work within and across all four of the quadrants of our typology from Chapter 3 – transforming/reforming the corporate media system, including its statist environing conditions, while also transforming the lifeworld through independent media, media education and the like. It would pose challenges to hegemony in everyday culture (delegitimizing corporate media, building democratic alternatives and so forth) but also in the long march through the institutions. Such a multiplex politics is by no means easily practised. The difficulties that the CPBF faced during the Thatcher years in reconciling its support for public broadcasting with its support for independent media, discussed in Chapter 6, give one of many examples of the fault lines that media democrats must work around in fashioning effective politics. Even so, recent efforts, particularly in the US, to build bridges across the strains of media activism – in the conferences of Free Press and the Union for Democratic Communication, in the coalition work of Media Alliance and other groups – point toward a more robust and comprehensive struggle.

Even so, as we concluded in Chapter 10, it is not enough for media activism to remain within the realm of media. To democratize public communication implies a broader social transformation. Bridges need to be built not only within the media field but also beyond it. If there is to be a 'deep media democracy movement', argues Dorothy Kidd, independent media and media activists need to follow the lead of social movements rather than vice versa. The point, observes Aliza Dichter, is to build a constituency for media reform by listening to other social movements (a principle embodied in 'The Listening Project') and figuring out how 'the media piece' fits into *their* agenda. The emerging media nexus must be a reflexive one, responsive to the concerns and needs of broad swathe of democratic movements.

In the years ahead, one of the challenges that will test media democrats' counterhegemonic potential is the question of hierarchy and inclusivity in the movement itself. Like other new social movements, democratic media activism has found its social base primarily in the new middle class. This sets up a possible tension, particularly in the US, between middle-class media democratization and movements of subaltern cultural resistance. Paul Baines, a Toronto-based activist using media literacy as a tool for organizing, has put his finger on the problem. Baines helped launch Media Democracy Day in 2001, but his satisfaction with the campaign began to fade as he considered who was speaking for whom, what issues were put into focus, and what issues were obscured. Baines's experiences and reflections led him to appreciate the 'interplay between democracy and justice' (2004: 93), and to prioritize the latter in framing his activism:

> I support media reform ... as long as it makes social justice its starting point and not de-contextualized red herrings such as de-regulation, commercialism, foreign ownership, public access, alternative media, and content diversity. These terms can be useful if used with precision and persistence towards justice and anti-oppression rather than the hollow ideals of Western democracy that never existed for the majority of people.
>
> (2004: 92)

In her plenary address to Free Press's National Conference on Media Reform in May 2005, Malkia Cyril, an activist with the Oakland-based Youth Media Alliance, noted the strategic implications of a media-justice frame. Given the media system's complicity in creating and sustaining structures of oppression, Cyril argued, 'if we want to bring about real change, the media reform movement must adopt a movement-building analysis, change model and vision that centers racial, economic and gender justice' (Cyril 2005).

For media democratization to become counterhegemonic it will need to broaden its social base to include subalterns and others on the outer circle of our Figure 3.1, which also implies a shift in strategic framing, toward social justice and radical democracy. If media reform fails to draw in the energies of the subordinated groups who are already mobilizing against the injustices of racial, class and gender hierarchies, if it does not foreground radically democratic demands for social, economic and environmental justice, its political impact will be limited to cooptative reforms that merely round off the system's rough edges. In that case, democratic media reform will join the ranks of the temperance movement, of business unionism and the like, as an avocation of the relatively privileged that reinforces social inequalities (such as educated/literate over the less 'articulate') and may even create new ones.

However, the struggle to democratize public communication contains an ethics that presses toward inclusivity, mutuality and justice. The dialectics of diversity, of mediating racial, generational and other social differences in a broad movement, may be a challenge, even an obstacle, to achieving ready consensus on strategies and priorities. But that challenge is also (as one of our students noted) a resource. It forces media democrats to adopt the dialogical and democratic consensus-building practices that they want to see institutionalized in the broader media system. These practices will, we sense, be crucial in any broader movement for social justice that might take shape in the foreseeable future.

Notes

1 Introduction

1   On the importance of the Anglo-American region as 'a relatively integrated "heartland"' providing a source of hegemonic leadership and economic/military pre-eminence for capitalism, see Van der Pijl (1998: 7, 92–7). In Van der Pijl's narrative, the heartland has expanded to include other regions of global capitalism, but its epicentre (and that of globalized commercial media) remains North Atlantic. Our focus on this 'central' region does not imply that struggles to democratize public communication elsewhere, or to reverse the profoundly undemocratic communicative relations between centre and periphery, are of any less strategic and ethical importance.

2   As John Downing (1996: x) reminds us, the UK and US have 'remarkably similar leitmotifs in their cultural, economic and political history that mark them out from most other nations on the planet', including their imperial status and their affluence. Moreover, their media systems enjoy a relatively stable relationship with a formally democratic state, and a longstanding hold on audience attention, however much the internet and channel multiplication may be eroding the dominance of any single outlet. These conditions, obviously, do not prevail throughout the planet.

3   A related project found similar blind spots in Canada's press during the 1990s (Hackett and Gruneau *et al.* 2000: 165–217).

4   Advertising's contribution to the democratic deficit deserves special consideration, since economically, the commercial media's bread is buttered not by audiences primarily, but by advertisers who pay for access to audiences of the right kind. Broadly speaking, affluent consumers have disproportionate influence regarding what kinds of media outlets and content will economically flourish, and which ones will die (Hackett 2001). Bagdikian (1997) and many others have noted the structural contribution of advertising to monopoly in the newspaper industry historically, as advertisers disproportionately favour papers that most efficiently meet their marketing needs. Baker (1994: 69–70) describes four negative consequences of advertising for journalism, including political blandness and minimal critical coverage of advertisers' products and interests.

2 What is at stake?

1   With thanks to University of Toronto Press, our discussion of canine metaphors draws from Hackett (2001:197–9).

2   Capitalism has historically created conflict across a range of social relations, but its information revolution and the distinct features of cultural industries arguably present new opportunities (Mosco, 1996: 233, 239; Miege 1989). Nick Dyer-Witheford (2001) holds that the digital information systems indispensable to globalized capital require new forms of intelligence – technical, cultural, linguistic, ethical – that are not easily

contained within the logic of capital;, moreover, informational capitalism generates new kinds of resistance, like cyberactivism (p. 180), that have the potential to democratize not only communication but the material production that is increasingly mediated, steered, shaped and indeed constituted by communication.

3   For an incisive technical critique of the neoliberals' 'consumer sovereignty' argument, using their own economic assumptions to demonstrate massive market failure in commercial media, see Baker (2002: Part I). For less technical accounts, see Curran (2002: 227–31) and McChesney (2004: 198–205).

4   Without wanting to carry all his political, biographical and conceptual baggage, this approach also owes something to Louis Althusser's structural Marxism. He argued that while political, economic, and cultural/ideological levels of practice had their own logics and were thus relatively autonomous from each other, the economic was determinant 'in the last instance' over the whole social formation, if only by 'selecting' which of the other levels would take the leading role in a particular social formation – for example, religion in Europe's feudal mode of production (Althusser and Balibar 1970).

3 Democratizing society

1   For example, in a 400-page collection of papers on social movements and globalization, bearing the subtitle 'Culture, power, and the transnational public sphere', there is virtually no mention of mass media as a factor in movement activism (Guidry *et al.* 2000)!

2   Such as (1) the conditions under which the 'media politics of protest' can place policy controversies in front of the public and lead to political changes (even if the changes do not coincide with core movement demands; Sampedro 1997) and (2) the contingent relationship between media coverage of mass protest and the use of repressive measures by police (Wisler and Giugni, 1999).

3   A third sort of activism around the internet is exemplified by Communication Rights in the Information Society (CRIS, www.crisinfo.org), which among other reforms calls for global democratic governance of cyberspace as an alternative to both arbitrary state surveillance/censorship and growing commercialization of the internet. The internet figures in this campaign both as a transnational communicative resource and as the evolving communications infrastructure which is the object of struggles over standards, financing, regulation, and so on. See Ó Siochrú (2005b).

4   Habermas's tendency in the 1970s to conceptualize 'newness' as a conflict-shift from the capital–labour relation to the 'seam' between system and lifeworld has been challenged by Gemma Edwards, who sees recent anti-corporate activism as a critical response to global capitalism's colonization of lifeworlds. Edwards goes on to argue that the labour movement is not passé, 'old' and coopted, but through community unionism and other recent initiatives is in the forefront of progressive politics. We agree. By recognizing the 'old' politics of the labour movement as part of the 'lifeworld battle against colonization' (Edwards 2004:128) we can appreciate the crucial importance of media workers' unions in the struggle to democratize public communication.

5   See for instance Florida State professor Andy Opel's (2004: 26–8) discussion of three main groupings involved in independent media creation and critique: individuals and grassroots organizations (GROs); institutions (NGOs); and academic discourses. See also activist and teacher Nan Rubin's threefold inventory of strategic approaches: confronting corporate media; owning our own media; and changing the media rules (www.nanrubin.com).

6   A search of websites reveals the proliferation and diversity of groups in each of the DMA sectors shown in Table 3.1. Space does not permit a listing of URLs, but most of the groups named in this book can be located through internet search engines. Also, good overviews and links (for the US and to some extent internationally) can be found at www.mediachannel.org, www.mediactioncenter.org (see the *Media Action Policy Directory*, 2003) and www.mediareform.net.

4 Visions and divisions

1 Notably, by insisting on the dispersal and ubiquity of power, and by rejecting as implicitly totalitarian the analysis and contestation of the social totality (e.g. capitalism), the 'French ideology' of poststructuralism and postmodernism calls into question the possibility, and desirability, of large-scale coalitions for the emancipatory transformation of the social order (Sanbonmatsu 2004: 122). And, especially in the US, right-wingers mask their anti-egalitarian political agendas, notably the redistribution of wealth from the poor to the rich, by a populist rhetoric directed against semi-fictional elites, like the 'left-liberal' media, or the 'politically correct' academic establishment.

2 With grateful acknowledgements to Open University Press/McGraw-Hill Education, and to Rowman & Littlefield, this section draws extensively from Hackett (2005) and from Zhao and Hackett (2005).

3 Conservatives may support coercive aspects of the state (law and order, military 'defence'), but typically they oppose the use of state power to promote social equality or collective well-being when those values conflict fundamentally with private capital.

4 In practice, conservatives' wrath at such government influence appears to be politically selective; they have sometimes been silent accomplices or active participants in state harassment of left-wing alternative media in the US and Canada (Hackett and Zhao 1998: 79). More often, market liberals direct their fire against public service broadcasters, like the CBC and BBC, that receive licence fees or taxes. Why? Such broadcasters, market liberal doctrine holds, 'distort' market outcomes, provide 'unfair competition' to private broadcasters, and are too vulnerable to pressure from the governments which fund them (even though historically, the BBC has established a global reputation for its independence). Market liberals regard commercial, privately-owned media as more democratic, shaped as they allegedly are by audience preferences. This is the 'consumer sovereignty' argument which we critiqued in Chapter 2 and below.

5 In one laudable (albeit pre-internet) attempt to offer such a working model, James Curran (2002: 240–6) proposes a system of structured pluralism, starting from the premise that no single type of medium can serve all democratic purposes. At the centre of his model is a reformed public broadcaster to function as a mass-mediated public sphere, surrounded by social market, civic (interest group), professional journalist and private enterprise media – each serving distinct functions and counterbalancing the structural biases of the others. Such democratic alternatives would almost necessarily involve a challenge to corporate political power and 'free market' policies, one entailing new taxes or fees on commercial users of public resources like the broadcast spectrum, and conversely, subsidies to public service modes of communication.

6 The text of the Charter analysed here is from the WACC's website; another version can be found in Duncan (1999: 177–81).

5 The long revolution and the Media Alliance

1 This section draws upon Zhao and Hackett (2005). We thank Rowman & Littlefield for copyright clearance

2 We are indebted to Arthur-Martins Aginam for an extended working paper on Media Alliance.

6 Campaigning for press and broadcasting freedom in the UK

1 This chapter draws from an unpublished working paper by Scott Uzelman (2002), as well as the CPBF journal *Free Press*, and Hackett's interviews with CPBF members and others.

7 Challenges for media activism

1   We are indebted to Helga Hallgrimsdottir (personal communication) for this concept.

2   Evidence from the environmental movement, however, suggests that this age profile may be more an American than European phenomenon, perhaps related to the 'materialism' of American culture (Dale 1996). Amongst our respondents, activists over forty were rare in the US, but the norm in the British CPBF.

3   Sometimes discord is due to appearances rather than real antagonisms: Lee expresses frustration that WACC is sometimes 'dismissed out of hand' because people assume from the word 'Christian' in its title that it is an evangelical association.

4   This seems to be a particularly American phenomenon; the oft-noted entrepreneurial spirit of its culture is strongly evident within even left-wing groups.

5   The CEM had other problems as well. On paper, it had many affiliated organizations, but no clear action orientation or campaign focus, argued Peter Franck. It was more 'a highly effective public education campaign' than an organizing campaign or movement, notes John Anner. Consensus around priorities was difficult to achieve in such a diverse coalition. The Board was too large and unwieldy to function effectively. The organization failed to develop a support staff with continuity and appropriate skills. The organization's style, such as the 'Robert's Rules' formality of its proceedings, was probably unappealing to younger activists. The need to incite enthusiasm and creativity from the membership was difficult to reconcile with Gerbner's ultimate veto over decisions. Gerbner saw the CEM as analogous to the Popular Front, the coalition of democratic forces confronting fascism in inter-war Europe; but this was probably the wrong historical metaphor for the task at hand. The CEM coalition was probably too diverse to be effective within a single organization. All told, the CEM was a welcome harbinger of the range of groups which could be attracted to media reform, and it left a legacy of media education and a network of activist-scholars which has helped to catalogue other groups (Dichter 2005: 4–5) But it was also a lesson on how not to build a sustainable organization.

6   Part of the problem, argued one activist, is that the alternative press is less unionized than the commercial press.

7   As Mike Davis (1986: 8) observed two decades ago, the American working class has been exceptionally integrated into corporate capitalism through its 'internal stratification [particularly by race], its privatization in consumption, and its disorganization vis-à-vis political and trade-union bureaucracies'. Davis proposed a distinction between a reformist working class in western Europe (and, we might add, Canada) and '*a "disorganized" and increasingly "depoliticized" working class in the United States*' (ibid., emphasis in the original).

8   Five of the seven Canadian journalists interviewed mentioned 'objectivity' as an inhibition (whether internalized, or enforced by management) against joining political organizations.

9   British Labour MP Clive Soley, a supporter of press reform who chaired a parliamentary enquiry on press responsibility, was the butt of negative (and inaccurate) news stories about his private life: the Murdoch-owned *Sun* portrayed him as gay and altered his photograph 'to elongate my teeth to make them look slightly more like Dracula'. Ian Morrison asserts that his personal life was investigated by media corporations that the Friends of Canadian Broadcasting had challenged at CRTC hearings.

10   With 60 employees and an annual budget of about $15 million, the right-wing Media Research Center alone probably has more resources than all the progressive media-focused institutes discussed in this book combined (McChesney 2004: 111).

11   By contrast, the left-liberal thesis has had relatively little purchase in the UK. Colin Leys (personal communication) suggests three possible reasons. First, the Conservatives during the 1970s to 1990s felt secure with a large section of the daily press behind them; it may not have been in their interests to highlight the issue of media bias. Second, the

BBC has been politically astute, and enjoys wide support even among Conservative MPs, many of whom declined to back their own Prime Minister, Margaret Thatcher, when she did try to attack the BBC. Third, progressive academics like the Glasgow University Media Group (1976) have successfully popularized a left-wing critique of Establishment bias at BBC as well as other media.

8 Springboards for media activism

1 For instance, in San Francisco, the desperation of people who cannot afford housing, their victimization by police brutality, the frequent harassment of Food not Bombs activists feeding the homeless in public parks, and the indifference of the local media (including the relatively well-established alternative media) could easily have produced despair. Instead, it sparked rage and the creation in 1993 of one of America's first and most dynamic microradio stations, *San Francisco Liberation Radio* (Edmondson 2000). The city's housing crisis also provided a bridge-building entry point for the Bay Area Alternative Media Network. Through initiatives like a 'top 10' list of slum landlords, the network helped mobilize and draw attention to the housing movement.

9 Movement formation and counterhegemony in a global city

1 Men outnumber women in the sample by a margin of 32 to 22, and the mean age of respondents is 43. Although half of the sample had lived in Vancouver for 20 or more years, our informants reported various geographical origin points: only eight were born in Vancouver; another 19 were born in Canada west of Ontario; 14 were born outside of Canada. The sample is ethnically quite diverse. When asked an entirely open-ended question on their ethnic background, only 11 respondents offered descriptions consistent with the imagery of Canada's dominant ethnic group (white European, WASP, British-Canadian, English). Consistent with the typical sociological profile of new social movement activists, our respondents were on the whole well educated. Only three of them lacked post-secondary education, and 23 had had postgraduate training of some sort, with 19 holding master's or doctoral degrees.

2 This approach to selecting our cases suited our research objectives. 'The logic and power of purposeful sampling lies in selecting information-rich cases for study in depth. Information-rich cases are those from which one can learn a great deal about issues of central importance to the purpose of the research' (Patton 1990: 169).

3 Our use of 'field' in discussing the local Vancouver scene is inspired by Crossley's analysis of social movements as 'fields of contention' and of the broader social movement sector as a larger field comprising the intersecting fields of contention. Such a conceptualization invites us 'to explore the interpenetration of these fields with the economic, political and media (etc.) fields' (Crossley 2003: 62).

4 The tabulations are based on the following questions. Column B respondents were asked, 'Which are the key activist groups active around mass media issues in Vancouver today?' Column C respondents were asked, 'Which of these groups [i.e., groups nominated by the respondent as 'key'], if any, are you in touch with as part of your own activism?'

10 Identity, vision, strategies

1 One, active in PCAJ, described her affiliation to 'partly the anti-capitalist globalization movement, and partly an alternative media movement'; another, active in AdBusters, stated that 'rather than media democracy, I actually feel like talking about the mental environmental movement', a movement to 'transform the mindscape'. An activist at the Vancouver Community Network described himself as a 'community media activist', but

noted that besides this 'area of specialty', 'I definitely see myself as anti-poverty, anti-war currently.'

2   The classic study of the (problematical) role of mass media in creating a collective representation for a movement is Gitlin's (1980) post-mortem on the 1960s student movement. As mentioned earlier, our respondents noted problems in the way that mainstream media had represented the resistant politics of Seattle 1999 and its spin-offs as simply 'anti-globalization', an identity that implies parochialism. For aspiring movements, gaining standing in the mainstream media tends to be a mixed blessing (Gamson and Wolfsfeld 1993).

3   These images included an end to business dominance of life (three respondents), an egalitarian society (two), a society based on cooperation and sharing (two), a social democracy featuring equality, the expansion of autonomous spaces for creativity and participation, and the flourishing of democracy and self-determination.

4   These included visions of a society based on dignity and universal welfare, a sharing of power and wealth, a participatory democracy, a 'triple bottom line' – social, environmental and economic, a sustainable society, a fair-trade world economy, and a 'new Jerusalem' based in the social gospel tradition.

5   'We don't have enough staff and financial resources to do the things that we set ourselves out to do every year as it is,' stated an activist with the feminist monitoring group Media Watch; 'the greatest obstacle is that everyone is overworked and burned out', noted an activist with CPBF; 'I think where the real problems [lie], and this goes probably with every single movement, is the lack of resources – we struggle to pay the rent on our office all the time, so just to exist in a physical space, which is important, is really difficult,' claimed an IndyMedia activist.

6   The question involved a card on which were printed four strategies for change, rendering our simplified typology in non-theoretical terminology. We asked: 'Arguably there are four main ways in which activists might reform or transform the media.' We then handed the respondent the card, which read:

(1) influencing content and practices of mainstream media – e.g. promoting fair and accurate news coverage;
(2) building independent media – e.g. print, radio, television, internet;
(3) promoting more critical audiences – e.g. through media education or culture jamming;
(4) advocating for reform of government policy/regulation of the media.

Respondents were then asked, 'Would you agree?' They were allowed to reframe or add to the list.

11 Conclusion

1   Through a Habermasian optic, Calhoun (1992: 31) has pointed out that large-scale modern society would be impossible without some kind of system integration, 'and dreams of doing away with such large-scale societal integration are not only romantic but dangerous because reduction in scale can only come about in catastrophic ways …'. Anti-hegemonic strategies generally ignore this constraint, which is one reason why their 'prefigurative' initiatives tend to fail. It is not clear, for instance, that an anarchist infoshop (Atton 2003a) barely subsisting on self-exploited labour and donated left-overs prefigures anything more promising than the rejection of modernity and complex society. Alternatively, system-focused initiatives such as Sweden's press subsidies, the UK's Channel Four, France's laws on right of reply and Holland's segmented broadcasting system do illustrate how communications can be organized more democratically within existing societies.

Bibliography

Abbs, M. (2000) 'Charting the path to sustainability for the Pacific Centre for Alternative Journalists, an Alternative Media Collective', online manuscript (accessed 18 April 2005).

Adamson, N. L., Briskin, L. and McPhail, M. (1988) *Feminist Organizing for Change*, Toronto: University of Toronto Press.

Allan, S. (2004) *News Culture*, 2nd edn, Buckingham and Philadelphia, Maidenhead: Open University Press.

Alterman, E. (2003) *What Liberal Media? The Truth about Bias and the News*, New York: Basic Books.

Althusser, L. and Balibar, E. (1970) *Reading Capital*, trans. B. Brewster, London: NLB [Paris: Francois Maspero, 1968].

Angus, I. (2001) *Emergent Publics: An Essay on Social Movements and Democracy*, Winnipeg: Arbeiter Ring.

Ash Garner, R. and Zald, M. N. (1987) 'The political economy of social movement sectors', in M. N. Zald and J. D. McCarthy (eds), *Social Movements in an Organizational Society*, New Brunswick, NJ: Transaction Books.

Atton, C. (2002) *Alternative Media*, London, Thousand Oaks, New Delhi: Sage.

—— (2003a) 'Infoshops in the shadow of the state', in N. Couldry and J. Curran (eds), *Contesting Media Power: Alternative Media in a Networked World*, Lanham: Rowman & Littlefield, pp. 57–69.

—— (2003b) 'Reshaping social movement media for a new millennium', *Social Movement Studies* 2(1): 3–15.

Aubin, B. (2005) 'Les X Revolt', *Maclean's* (10 January): 8–30.

Aufderheide, P. (1999) *Communications Policy and the Public Interest: The Telecommunications Act of 1996*, New York: Guilford Press.

Bagdikian, B. H. (1997) *The Media Monopoly*, 5th edn, Boston: Beacon Press.

Baines, P. (2004) 'Media Democracy Day', *Democratic Communique* 19: 90–4.

Baker, E. C. (1994) *Advertising and a Democratic Press*, Princeton, NJ: Princeton University Press.

—— (2002) *Media, Markets and Democracy*, Cambridge: Cambridge University Press.

Barker-Plummer, B. (1995) 'News as a political resource: media strategies and political identity in the US women's movement, 1966–1975', *Critical Studies in Mass Communication* 12: 306–24.

Bennett, L. W. (2003) 'New media power: the Internet and global activism', in N. Couldry and J. Curran (eds), *Contesting Media Power: Alternative Media in a Networked World*, Lanham: Rowman & Littlefield.

Benson, R. (2003) 'Commercialism and critique: California's alternative weeklies', in N. Couldry and J. Curran (eds), *Contesting Media Power: Alternative Media in a Networked World*, Lanham: Rowman & Littlefield, pp. 111–27.

Bleyer, P. (1997) 'Coalitions of social movements as agencies for social change: the Action Canada network', in W. K. Carroll (ed.), *Organizing Dissent: Contemporary Social Movements in Theory and Practice*, Toronto: Garamond Press, pp. 134–50.

Blumler, J. G. and Gurevitch, M. (1995) *The Crisis of Public Communication*, London: Routledge.

Boggs, C. (1976) *Gramsci's Marxism*, London: Pluto Press.

—— (1995) 'Rethinking the sixties legacy: from new left to new social movements', in S. M. Lyman (ed.), *Social Movements: Critiques, Concepts, Case-Studies*, London: Macmillan, pp. 331–55.

Bohman, J. (2004) 'Expanding dialogue: the Internet, the public sphere and prospects for transnational democracy', in N. Crossley and J. M. Roberts (eds), *After Habermas*, Oxford: Blackwell, pp. 131–55.

Bourdieu, P. (1993) *The Field of Cultural Production: Essays on Art and Literature*, (ed. and intro. by R. Johnson), Cambridge: Polity Press.

Boyte, H. C. (1992) 'The pragmatic ends of popular politics', in C. Calhoun (ed.), *Habermas and the Public Sphere*, Cambridge, MA, and London: MIT Press, pp. 340–55.

Brecher, J., Costello, T. and Smith, B. (2000) *Globalization from Below: The Power of Solidarity*, Cambridge, MA: South End Press.

Buechler, S. M. (2000) *Social Movements in Advanced Capitalism*, New York: Oxford University Press.

Calhoun, C. (ed.) (1992) *Habermas and the Public Sphere*, Cambridge, MA: MIT Press.

Carroll, W. K. and Ratner, R. S. (1989) 'Social democracy, neo-conservatism and hegemonic crisis in British Columbia', *Critical Sociology* 16(1): 29–53.

—— (1994) 'Between Leninism and radical pluralism: Gramscian reflections on counter-hegemony and the new social movements', *Critical Sociology* 20(2): 3–26.

—— (1995) 'Old unions and new social movements', *Labour/Le Travail*, 35: 195–221.

—— (1996) 'Master framing and cross-movement networking in contemporary social movements', *Sociological Quarterly* 37: 601–25.

—— (1999) 'Media strategies and political projects: a comparative study of social movements', *Canadian Journal of Sociology* 24(1): 1–34.

—— (2001) 'Sustaining oppositional culture in "post-socialist" times: a comparative study of three social movement organizations', *Sociology* 35: 605–29.

Carty, V. (2002) 'Technology and counter-hegemonic movements: the case of Nike Corporation', *Social Movement Studies* 1(2): 129–46.

Castells, M. (1997) *The Information Age: Economy, Society, Culture, vol. 2: The Power of Identity*, Malden, MA: Blackwell.

Center for International Media Action (2003) *The Media Policy Action Directory*, New York: CIMA.

Chester, J. and Larson, G. O. (2002) 'Something old, something new', *The Nation* (7/14 January). Also at www.thenation.com/docprint.mhtml?i=20020107&s=chester (accessed 29 March 2005).

Christians, C. (1995) 'Communication ethics as the basis of genuine democracy', in P. Lee (ed.), *The Democratization of Communication*, Cardiff: University of Wales Press, pp. 75–91.

Clement, W. (1975) *The Canadian Corporate Elite*, Toronto: McClelland & Stewart.

Cohen, J. and Arato, A. (1992) *Civil Society and Political Theory*, Cambridge, MA: MIT Press.

Cormier, J. (2004) *The Canadianization Movement: Emergence, Survival, and Success*, Toronto: University of Toronto Press.

Couldry, N. (2003) 'Beyond the hall of mirrors? Some theoretical reflections on the global contestation of media power', in N. Couldry and J. Curran (eds), *Contesting Media Power: Alternative Media in a Networked World*, Lanham: Rowman & Littlefield, pp. 39–54.

Couldry, N. and Curran, J. (eds) (2003a) *Contesting Media Power: Alternative Media in a Networked World*, Lanham: Rowman & Littlefield.

—— (2003b) 'The paradox of media power', in N. Couldry and J. Curran (eds), *Contesting Media Power: Alternative Media in a Networked World*, Lanham: Rowman & Littlefield, pp. 3–15.

CRIS (2002) 'Why should intellectual property rights matter to civil society?', CRIS Campaign Issue Paper No. 2, *Media Development* 4: 6–8.

Crossley, N. (2003) 'From reproduction to transformation: social movement fields and the radical habitus', *Theory, Culture & Society* 20(6): 43–68.

Croteau, D. (1998) 'Challenging the "liberal media" claim', *Extra!* 11(4): 4–9.

Curran, J. (2000) 'Press reformism 1918–98: a study of failure', in H. Tumber (ed.), *Media Power, Professionals and Policies*, London: Routledge.

—— (2002) *Media and Power*, London: Routledge.

—— (2003) 'Global journalism: a case study of the internet', in N. Couldry and J. Curran (eds), *Contesting Media Power: Alternative Media in a Networked World*, Lanham: Rowman & Littlefield, pp. 227–41.

Curran, J., with Ecclestone, J., Oakley, J. and Richardson, A. (eds) (1986) *Bending Reality: The State of the Media*, London: Pluto Press.

Dahlgren, P. (1995) *Television and the Public Sphere: Citizenship, Democracy and the Media*, London: Sage.

Dale, S. (1996) *McLuhan's Children: The Greenpeace Message and the Media*, Toronto: Between the Lines.

Davis, M. (1986) *Prisoners of the American Dream*, London: Verso.

DeLuca, K. M. and Peeple, J. (2002) 'From public sphere to public screen: democracy, activism, and the "violence" of Seattle', *Critical Studies in Mass Communication* 19: 125–51.

Dichter, A. (2005) 'Together, we know more: networks and coalitions to advance media democracy, communication rights and the public sphere 1990–2005', unpublished paper presented to Social Science Research Council 'Necessary Knowledge Workshop', New York (April). Contact: cima@mediaactioncenter.org.

Downing, J. D. H. (1996) *Internationalizing Media Theory: Transition, Power, Culture*, London, Thousand Oaks, New Delhi: Sage.

—— (2003) 'The Independent Media Center movement and the anarchist socialist tradition', in N. Couldry and J. Curran (eds), *Contesting Media Power: Alternative Media in a Networked World*, Lanham: Rowman & Littlefield, pp. 243–58.

Downing, J. D. H., with Ford, T. V., Gil, G. and Stein, L. (2001) *Radical Media: Rebellious Communication and Social Movements*, Thousand Oaks: Sage.

Dreier, P. (1982) 'Capitalists vs. the media: an analysis of an ideological mobilization among business leaders', *Media, Culture and Society* 4: 111–32.

Duncan, K. (ed.) (1999) *Liberating Alternatives: The Founding Convention of the Cultural Environment Movement*, Cresskill, NJ: Hampton Press.

Dyer-Witheford, N. (2001) 'The new combinations: revolt of the global value-subjects', *New Centennial Review* 1(3): 155–200.

Edmondson, R. (2000) *Rising Up: Class Warfare in America from the Streets to the Airwaves*, San Francisco: Librad Press.

Edwards, G. (2004) 'Habermas and social movements: what's "new"?', in N. Crossley and J. M. Roberts (eds), *After Habermas*, Oxford: Blackwell, pp. 113–30.

Egan, D. (2001) 'The limits of internationalization: a neo-Gramscian analysis of the multilateral agreement on investment', *Critical Sociology* 27, 3: 74–97.

Emirbayer, M. and Sheller, M. (1999) 'Publics in history', *Theory and Society* 28: 145–97.

Eschle, C. (2001) *Global Democracy, Social Movements, and Feminism*, Boulder, CO: Westview.

Eyerman, R. and Jamison, A. (1991) *Social Movements: A Cognitive Approach*, University Park: Pennsylvania State University Press.

Fallows, J. (1996) *Breaking the News: How the Media Undermine American Democracy*, New York: Pantheon.

Fiske, J. (1987) *Television Culture*, London and New York: Methuen.

Ford, T. V. and Gil, G. (2001) 'Radical internet use', in J. D. H. Downing with T. V. Ford, G. Gil and L. Stein, *Radical Media: Rebellious Communication and Social Movements*, Thousand Oaks, London, New Delhi: Sage, pp. 201–34.

Forsyth, S. (2004) 'Hollywood reloaded: the film as imperial commodity', *Socialist Register 2005*, London: The Merlin Press, pp. 108–23.

Foucault, M. (1984) 'Truth/power', in P. Rabinow (ed.), *The Foucault Reader*, New York: Pantheon Books.

Franken, A. (2003) *Lies and the Lying Liars Who Tell Them: A Fair and Balanced Look at the Right*, New York: Plume.

Fraser, N. (1997) *Justice Interruptus*, New York: Routledge.

Gallagher, M. (2001) *Gender Setting: New Agendas for Media Monitoring and Advocacy*, London and New York: Zed Books, with WACC.

Gamble, A. (1988) *The Free Economy and the Strong State: The Politics of Thatcherism*, London: Macmillan.

Gamson, W. (1987) 'Introduction', in M. Zald and J. D. McCarthy (eds), *Social Movements in an Organizational Society*, New Brunswick, NJ: Transaction Books.

Gamson, W. A. and Wolfsfeld, G. (1993) 'Movements and media as interacting systems', *Annals of the American Academy of Political and Social Science* 528: 114–25.

Gandy, O. H., Jr. (1982) *Beyond Agenda Setting: Information Subsidies and Information Policy*, Norwood, NJ: Ablex.

Gaventa, J. (1980) *Power and Powerlessness: Quiescence and Rebellion in an Appalachian Valley*, Oxford: Clarendon Press.

Gerbner, G. (1969) 'Toward "cultural indicators": the analysis of mass mediated public message systems', in G. Gerbner, O. R. Holsti, K. Krippendorff, W. J. Paisley and P. J. Stone (eds), *The Analysis of Communication Content*, New York: John Wiley, pp. 121–32.

—— (1999) 'Introduction', in K. Duncan (ed.), *Liberating Alternatives: The Founding Convention of the Cultural Environment Movement*, Cresskill, NJ: Hampton, pp. 1–12.

—— (2002) *Against the Mainstream: The Selected Works of George Gerbner*, ed. Michael Morgan, New York: Peter Lang.

Giddens, A. (1991) *Modernity and Self-Identity*, Cambridge: Polity Press.

Gill, S. (1995) 'Theorizing the interregnum: the double movement of global politics in the 1990s', in B. Hettne (ed.), *International Political Economy: Understanding Global Disorder*, Halifax: Fernwood Books, pp. 65–99.

Gitlin, T. (1980) *The Whole World is Watching: Mass Media and the Unmaking of the New Left*, Berkeley: University of California Press.

—— (1995) *The Twilight of Common Dreams: Why America is Wracked by Culture Wars*, New York: Metropolitan Books.

Glasgow University Media Group (1976) *Bad News*, London: Routledge & Kegan Paul.

Gramsci, A. (1971) *Selections from the Prison Notebooks*, ed. and trans. Q. Hoare and G. Nowell-Smith, New York: International Publishers.

Guidry, J. A., Kennedy, M. D. and Zald, M. N. (2000) 'Globalization and social movements', in J. A. Guidry, M. D. Kennedy and M. N. Zald (eds), *Globalization and Social Movements*, Ann Arbor: University of Michigan Press, pp. 1–32.

Habermas, J. (1987) *The Theory of Communicative Action*, Boston, MA: Beacon Press.
—— (1989) [1962] *The Structural Transformation of the Public Sphere*, Cambridge, MA: MIT Press.
—— (1992) 'Further reflections on the public sphere', in C. Calhoun (ed.), *Habermas and the Public Sphere*, Cambridge, MA, and London: MIT Press, pp. 421–61.
Hackett, R. A. (1991) *News and Dissent: The Press and the Politics of Peace in Canada*, Norwood, NJ: Ablex.
—— (2000) 'Taking back the media: notes on the potential for a communicative democracy movement', *Studies in Political Economy* 63: 61–86.
—— (2001) 'News media and civic equality: watch dogs, mad dogs, or lap dogs?', in E. Broadbent (ed.), *Democratic Equality: What Went Wrong?*, Toronto: University of Toronto Press, pp. 197–212.
—— (2004) 'Dissent may not need to be disciplined: corporate influence in the news media', in W. Bruneau and J. L. Turk (eds), *Disciplining Dissent*, Toronto: James Lorimer, pp. 143–61.
Hackett, R. A. and Carroll, W. K. (2004) 'Critical social movements and media reform', *Media Development* 51(1): 14–19.
Hackett, R. A. and Gruneau, R., with D. Gutstein, T. A. Gibson and NewsWatch Canada (2000) *The Missing News: Filters and Blind Spots in Canada's Press*, Toronto and Ottawa: Garamond Press/Canadian Centre for Policy Alternatives.
Hackett, R. A. and Uzelman, S. (2003) 'Tracing corporate influences on press content: a summary of recent NewsWatch Canada research', *Journalism Studies* 4(3): 331–46.
Hackett, R. A. and Zhao, Y. (1998) *Sustaining Democracy? Journalism and the Politics of Objectivity*, Toronto: Garamond.
Hall, S. (1982) 'The rediscovery of "ideology": return of the repressed in media studies', in M. Gurevitch, T. Bennett, J. Curran and J. Woollacott (eds), *Culture, Society and the Media*, London: Methuen, pp. 56–90.
—— (1986) 'Media power and class power', in J. Curran, J. Ecclestone, G. Oakley and A. Richardson (eds), *Bending Reality: The State of the Media*, London: Pluto Press, pp. 5–14.
Hall, S., Critchner, C., Jefferson, T., Clarke, J. and Roberts, B. (1978) *Policing the Crisis*, London: Macmillan.
Halleck, D. (2002) *Hand-Held Visions: The Impossible Possibilities of Community Media*, New York: Fordham University Press.
Hallin, D. C. (2000) 'Commercialism and professionalism in the American news media', in J. Curran and M. Gurevitch (eds), *Mass Media and Society*, 3rd edn, London: Arnold, pp. 218–37.
Hamelink, C. (1995) 'The democratic ideal and its enemies', in P. Lee (ed.), *The Democratization of Communication*, Cardiff: University of Wales, pp. 15–37.
Harcup, T. and O'Neill, D. (2001) 'What is news? Galtung and Ruge revisited', *Journalism Studies* 2(2): 261–80.
Hazen, D. and Winokur, J. (eds) (1997) *We the Media: A Citizen's Guide to Fighting for Media Democracy*, New York: The New Press.
Heath, J. and Potter, A. (2004) *The Rebel Sell: Why the Culture Can't be Jammed*, Toronto: HarperCollins.
Held, D. (1987) *Models of Democracy*, Stanford, CA: Stanford University Press.
Henaut, D. (1991) 'The "Challenge for Change/Société nouvelle" experience', in N. Thede and A. Ambrosi (eds), *Video the Changing World*, Montreal and New York: Black Rose, pp. 48–53.
Henry, F. and Tator, C. (2002) *Discourses of Domination: Racial Bias in the Canadian English-language Press*, Toronto: University of Toronto Press.

Herman, E. S. and Chomsky, N. (1988) *Manufacturing Consent: The Political Economy of the Mass Media*, New York: Pantheon.

Herman, E. S. and McChesney, R. W. (1997) *The Global Media: The New Missionaries of Global Capitalism*, London: Cassell.

Hertsgaard, M. (1989) [1988] *On Bended Knee: The Press and the Reagan Presidency*, New York: Schocken Books.

Hewitt, M. (1993) 'Social movements and social need: problems with postmodern political theory', *Critical Social Policy* 13(1): 52–74.

Hirsch, J. (1988) 'The crisis of Fordism, transformations of the "Keynesian" security state, and new social movements', *Research in Social Movements, Conflicts and Change* 10: 43–55.

Holub, R. (1992) *Antonio Gramsci: Beyond Marxism and Postmodernism*, New York: Routledge.

Hourigan, N. (2001) 'New social movement theory and minority language television campaigns', *European Journal of Communication* 16(1): 77–100.

Husband, C. (1996) 'The right to be understood: conceiving the multi-ethnic public sphere', *Innovation: The European Journal of Special Sciences* 9(2): 205–15.

Hyman, R. (1999) 'European industrial relations observatory on-line', online at www.eiro.eurofound.eu.int/1999/07/feature/uk9907215f.html (accessed 18 Jan. 2006).

Innis, H. A. (1951) *The Bias of Communication*, Toronto: University of Toronto Press.

International Commission for the Study of Communication Problems (MacBride Report) (1988) [1980] *Many Voices, One World: Communication Today and Tomorrow; Towards a New More Just and More Efficient World Information and Communication Order*, London, New York, Paris: Kogan Page, Unipub, Unesco, World Association for Christian Communication.

Jakubowicz, K. (1993) 'Stuck in a groove: why the 1960s approach to communication democratization will no longer do', in S. Splichal and J. Wasko (eds), *Communication and Democracy*, Norwood: Ablex, pp. 33–54.

Johnson, R. (1993) 'Editor's Introduction: Pierre Bourdieu on art, literature and culture', in P. Bourdieu, *The Field of Cultural Production: Essays on Art and Literature*, ed. and intro. R. Johnson, Cambridge: Polity Press.

Karim, K. H. (2000) *Islamic Peril: Media and global violence*, Montreal: Black Rose.

Keck, M. E. and Sikkink, K. (eds) (1998) *Activists Beyond Borders: Advocacy Networks in International Politics*, Ithaca, NY: Cornell University Press.

Kidd, D. (2005a) 'Public lecture at Dialogue on Democracy', Bob Everton Memorial Colloquium, Vancouver, B.C. (6 May).

—— (2005b) 'Afterword: linking back, looking forward', in A. Langlois and F. Dubois (eds), *Autonomous Media: Activating Resistance and Dissent*, Montreal: Cumulus Press, pp. 151–61.

Kielbowicz, R. B. and Scherer, C. (1986) 'The role of the press in the dynamics of social movements', *Research in Social Movements, Conflict and Change* 9: 71–96.

Klandermans, B. (1992) 'The social construction of protest and multiorganizational fields', in A. D. Morris and C. M. Mueller (eds), *Frontiers in Social Movement Theory*, New Haven: Yale University Press, pp. 77–103.

—— (2001) 'Why social movements come into being and why people join them', in J. Blau (ed.), *Blackwell Companion to Sociology*, Malden, MA: Blackwell, pp. 268–81.

Klein, N. (2000) *No Logo*, Toronto: Vintage.

Knightley, P. (2002) 'Journalism, conflict and war: an introduction', *Journalism Studies* 3(2) (May): 167–71.

Lapham, L. (2004) 'Tentacles of rage: the Republican propaganda mill, a brief history', *Harper's* (September): 31–41.

Lasn, K. (1999) *Culture Jam: The Uncooling of America*, New York: Eagle Brook.

Leys, C. (2001) *Market-Driven Politics: Neoliberal Democracy and the Public Interest*, London and New York: Verso.

Lichter, R. S., Rothman, S. and Lichter, L. S. (1986) *The Media Elite: America's New Powerbrokers*, New York: Hastings House.

Lippman, W. (1963) *The Essential Lippmann: A Political Philosophy for Liberal Democracy*, ed. C. Rossiter and J. Lare, New York: Random House.

Lukes, S. (1974) *Power: A Radical View*, London: Macmillan.

Lynch, J. and McGoldrick, A. (2005a) 'Peace journalism: a global dialogue for democracy and democratic media', in R. A. Hackett and Y. Zhao (eds), *Democratizing Global Media: One World, Many Struggles*, Lanham: Rowman & Littlefield.

—— (2005b) *Peace Journalism*, Stroud, UK: Hawthorn Press.

McChesney, R. W. (1997) *Corporate Media and the Threat to Democracy*, New York: Seven Stories.

—— (1999) *Rich Media, Poor Democracy: Communication Politics in Dubious Times*, Urbana and Chicago: University of Illinois Press.

—— (2002) 'September 11 and the structural limitations of US journalism', in B. Zelizer and S. Allan (eds), *Journalism after September 11*, London and New York: Routledge, pp. 91–100.

—— (2004) *The Problem of the Media: US Communication Politics in the Twenty-First Century*, New York: Monthly Review Press.

McChesney, R. W. and Hackett, R. A. (2005) 'Beyond wiggle room: the democratic deficit of US corporate media, its global implications, and prospects for reform', in R. A. Hackett and Y. Zhao (eds), *Democratizing Global Media: One World, Many Struggles*, Lanham: Rowman & Littlefield.

McChesney, R. W. and Nichols, J. (2002a) *Our Media, Not Theirs: The Democratic Struggle against Corporate Media*, New York: Seven Stories.

—— (2002b) 'The making of a movement: getting serious about media reform', *The Nation* 7/14 January: 11–17

Macey, D. (2000) *The Penguin Dictionary of Critical Theory*, London: Penguin Books.

McGuigan, J. (1992) *Cultural Populism*, London and New York: Routledge.

McKibben, B. (1999) 'Living second hand: an environmental view of the mass media', in K. Duncan (ed.), *Liberating Alternatives: The Founding Convention of the Cultural Environment Movement*, Cresskill, NJ: Hampton, pp. 43–47.

—— (2003) 'Small world: why one town stays unplugged', *Harper's* (December): 46–54.

McNair, B. (2000) 'Journalism and democracy: a millennial audit', *Journalism Studies* 1(2): 197–211.

Macpherson, C. B. (1977) *The Life and Times of Liberal Democracy*, Oxford: Oxford University Press.

McQuail, D. (1992) *Media Performance: Mass Communication and the Public Interest*, London, Newbury Park, New Delhi: Sage.

—— (1994) *Mass Communication Theory: An Introduction*, 3rd edn, London: Sage.

Marliere, P. (1998) 'The rules of the journalistic field: Pierre Bourdieu's contribution to the sociology of the media', *European Journal of Communication* 13(2): 219–34.

Media Development (1999) 'First public hearing on languages and human rights', *Media Development* 46(4): 8–13.

Melucci, A. (1989) *Nomads of the Present*, London: Hutchinson Radius.

—— (1996) *Challenging Codes: Collective Action in the Information Age*, New York: Cambridge University Press.

Meyer, D. S. and Tarrow, S. (1998) *The Social Movement Society: Contentious Politics for a New Century*, Lanham, MD: Rowman & Littlefield.

Miege, B. (1989) *The Capitalization of Cultural Production*, New York: International General.

Miljan, L. and Cooper, B. (2003) *Hidden Agendas: How Journalists Influence the News*, Vancouver and Toronto: UBC Press.

Minogue, K. (n.d.) 'The Resurgence of Trade Unionism in the United Kingdom 1979 to 89', online at www.hrnicholls.com.au/nicholls/nichvol7/vol71the.htm (accessed 18 Jan. 2006).

Molotch, H. (1979) 'Media and movements', in M. N. Zald and J. D. McCarthy (eds), *The Dynamics of Social Movements*, Cambridge, MA: Winthrop Publishing Inc, pp. 71–93.

Montgomery, K. C. (1989) *Target: Prime Time*, New York: Oxford University Press.

Mosco, V. (1996) *The Political Economy of Communication*, London, Thousand Oaks, New Delhi: Sage.

Mouffe, C. (1988) 'Hegemony and new political subjects: toward a new conception of democracy', in C. Nelson and L. Grossberg (eds), *Marxism and the Interpretation of Culture*, Chicago: University of Illinois Press, pp. 89–101.

Mueller, M., Kuerbis, B. and Page, C. (2004) *Reinventing Media Activism: Public Interest Advocacy in the Making of US Communication-Information Policy, 1960–2002*, Syracuse, NY: The Convergence Center School of Information Studies, Syracuse University (www.digitalconvergence.org), 15 July.

Mulgan, G. and Worpole, K. (1986) 'Selling the paper: socialism and cultural diversity', in J. Curran, J. Ecclestone, G. Oakley and A. Richardson (eds), *Bending Reality: The State of the Media*, London: Pluto Press, pp. 136–48.

Mythen, G. (2004) *Ulrich Beck: A Critical Introduction to the Risk Society*, London: Pluto Press.

Navasky, V. (2002) 'Foreword', in B. Zelizer and S. Allan (eds), *Journalism after September 11*, London and New York: Routledge, pp. 13–18.

Nichols, J. and McChesney, R. W. (2000) *It's the Media, Stupid*, New York: Seven Stories Press.

Norris, P. (2000) *A Virtuous Circle: Political Communications in Postindustrial Societies*,, Cambridge: Cambridge University Press.

Oakley, G. (1986) 'The aims of the campaign', in J. Curran, J. Ecclestone, G. Oakley and A. Richardson (eds), *Bending Reality: The State of the Media*, London: Pluto Press, pp. 212–20.

Oberg, J. (2005) 'The Iraq conflict and the media: embedded with war rather than with peace and democracy', in R. Hackett and Y. Zhao (eds), *Democratizing Global Media: One World, Many Struggles*, Lanham: Rowman & Littlefield, pp. 185–203.

O'Malley, T. and Soley, C. (2000) *Regulating the Press*, London: Pluto Press.

Opel, A. (2004) *Micro Radio and the FCC: Media Activism and the Struggle over Broadcast Policy*, Westport, CN, and London: Praeger.

Ó Siochrú, S. (2005a) 'Global media governance as a potential site of civil society intervention', in R. A. Hackett and Y. Zhao (eds), *Democratizing Global Media: One World, Many Struggles*, Lanham: Rowman & Littlefield, pp. 205–21.

—— (2005b) 'Finding a frame: towards a transnational advocacy campaign to democratize communication', in R. A. Hackett and Y. Zhao (eds), *Democratizing Global Media: One World, Many Struggles*, Lanham: Rowman & Littlefield, pp. 289–311.

Ó Siochrú, S. and Girard, B. (2003) 'Introduction', in B. Girard and S. Ó Siochrú (eds), *Communicating in the Information Society*, Geneva: United Nations Research Institute for Social Development, pp. 1–10.

O'Sullivan, T., Hartley, J., Saunders, D., Montgomery, M. and Fiske, J. (1994) *Key Concepts in Communication and Cultural Studies*, 2nd edn, London and New York: Routledge.

Owens, L. and Palmer, L. K. (2003) 'Making the news: anarchist counter-public relations on the world-wide web', *Critical Studies in Mass Communication*, 20: 335–61.

Palmer, B. D. (1987) *Solidarity: The Rise and Fall of an Opposition in British Columbia*, Vancouver: New Star Books.

Patelis, K. (2000) 'The political economy of the Internet', in J. Curran (ed.), *Media Organisations in Society*, London: Arnold, pp. 83–106.

Patton, M. Q. (1990) *Qualitative Evaluation and Research Methods*, Newbury Park, CA: Sage.

Phillips, P. (1999) 'Building a media democracy movement', in P. Phillips and Project Censored (ed.), *Censored 1999*, New York: Seven Stories, pp. 129–35.

Phillips, P. and Project Censored. (2004) *Censored 2004: The Top 25 Censored Stories*, New York: Seven Stories Press.

Phillips, P. A. (1967) *No Power Greater: A Century of Labour in British Columbia*, Vancouver: B.C. Federation of Labour and Boag Foundation.

Pijl, K. van der (1998) *Transnational Classes and International Relations*, London: Routledge.

Poulantzas, N. (1975) [1968] *Political Power and Social Classes*, ed. and trans. T. O'Hagan, London: NLB.

Power, M. (1986) 'Right of reply', in J. Curran, J. Ecclestone, G. Oakley and A. Richardson (eds), *Bending Reality: The State of the Media*, London: Pluto Press, pp. 221–8.

Press, A. L. and Liebes, T. (2003) 'Has feminism caused a wrinkle on the face of Hollywood cinema? A tentative appraisal of the '90s', in N. Couldry and J. Curran (eds), *Contesting Media Power: Alternative Media in a Networked World*, Lanham: Rowman & Littlefield, pp. 129–46.

Price, M. E. and Rozumilowicz, B. (2002) 'Conclusion', in M. E. Price, B. Rozumilowicz and S. G. Verhulst (eds), *Media Reform: Democratizing the Media, Democratizing the State*, London and New York: Routledge, pp. 254–68.

Rampton, S. and Stauber, J. (2003) *Weapons of Mass Deception: The Uses of Propaganda in Bush's War on Iraq*, New York: Jeremy P. Tarcher/Penguin.

Ray, L. (1993) *Rethinking Critical Theory*, London: Sage.

Reese, S. D. (2001) 'Understanding the global journalist: a hierarchy-of-influences approach', *Journalism Studies* (May) 2(2): 173–88.

Richardson, A. and Power, M. (1986) 'Media freedom and the CPBF', in J. Curran, J. Ecclestone, G. Oakley and A. Richardson (eds), *Bending Reality: The State of the Media*, London: Pluto Press, pp. 195–211.

Riordan, E. (2002) 'Intersections and new directions: on feminism and political economy', in E. Meehan and E. Riordan (eds), *Sex and Money: Feminism and Political Economy in the Media*, Minneapolis: University of Minnesota Press, pp. 3–15.

Rodgers, J. (2004) 'Online media: Franchising the alternative?', unpublished paper presented to International Association for Media & Communication Research, Porto Alegre, Brazil, 25–30 July.

Rodriguez, C. (2003) 'The bishop and his star: citizens' communication in southern Chile', in N. Couldry and J. Curran (eds), *Contesting Media Power: Alternative Media in a Networked World*, Lanham: Rowman & Littlefield, pp. 177–94.

Ruggiero, G. (1999) *Microradio and Democracy: (Low) Power to the People*, New York: Seven Stories.

Ryan, C. (1991) *Prime-time Activism: Media Strategies for Grassroots Organizing*, Boston: South End Press.

Sabato, L. (1991) *Feeding Frenzy: How Attack Journalism Has Transformed American Politics*, New York: Free Press.

Sampedro, V. (1997) 'The media politics of social protest', *Mobilization*, 2: 185–205.

Sanbonmatsu, J. (2004) *The Postmodern Prince: Critical Theory, Left Strategy, and the Making of a New Political Subject*, New York: Monthly Review Press.

Schudson, M. (1978) *Discovering the News: A Social History of American Newspapers*, New York: Basic Books.

Schulz, W. (1997) 'Changes of mass media and the public sphere', *Javnost – The Public* 4(2): 57–69.

Schumpeter, J. (1976) [1942] *Capitalism, Socialism and Democracy*, New York: Harper & Row.

Shoemaker, P. and Reese, S. (1996) *Mediating the Message: Theories of Influences on Mass Media Content*, 2nd edn, White Plains, NY: Longman.

Smelser, N. (1962) *The Theory of Collective Behavior*, New York: Free Press.

Smith, J. (2001) 'Globalizing resistance: the battle of Seattle and the future of social movements', *Mobilization* 6: 1–19.

Smythe, D. W. (1981) *Dependency Road: Communications, Capitalism, Consciousness and Canada*, Norwood, NJ: Ablex.

Snow, D. A. and Benford, R. D. (1988) 'Ideology, frame resonance, and participant mobilization', *International Social Movement Research* 1: 197–217.

Snow, D. A., Rochford, Jr., E. B., Worden, S. K. and Benford, R. D. (1986) 'Frame alignment process, micromobilization, and movement participation', *American Sociological Review* 51: 464–81.

Sreberny, A. (2005) 'Globalization, communication, democratization: toward gender equality', in R. A. Hackett and Y. Zhao (eds), *Democratizing Global Media: One World, Many Struggles*, Lanham: Rowman & Littlefield, pp. 256–67.

Stanfield, D. W. and Lemert, J. B. (1987) 'Alternative newspapers and mobilizing information', *Journalism Quarterly* 64(2/3): 604–7.

Starr, J. M. (2000) *Air Wars: The Fight to Reclaim Public Broadcasting*, Boston: Beacon Press.

Stone, S. D. (1993) 'Getting the message out: feminists, the press and violence against women', *Canadian Review of Sociology and Anthropology* 30: 377–400.

Taras, D. (2001) *Power and Betrayal in the Canadian Media*, 2nd edn, Peterborough: Broadview Press.

Tarrow, S. (1989) *Struggle, Politics, and Reform: Collective Action, Social Movements, and Cycles of Protest*, Western Societies Program Occasional Paper No. 21, Ithaca, NY: Center for International Studies, Cornell University.

Tarrow, S. (1998) *Power in Movement*, 2nd edn, Cambridge: Cambridge University Press.

Tehranian, M. and Tehranian, K. K. (1995) 'That recurrent suspicion: democratization in a global perspective', in P. Lee (ed.), *The Democratization of Communication*, Cardiff: University of Wales, pp. 38–74.

Tetzlaff, D. (1991) 'Divide and conquer: popular culture and social control in late capitalism', *Media, Culture and Society* 13: 9–33.

Thompson, J. B. (1984) *Studies in the Theory of Ideology*, Berkeley: University of California Press.

Tilly, C. (1978) *From Mobilization to Revolution*, Reading, MA: Addison-Wesley.

Tomaselli, K. (1999) 'The United States and the West: What about the rest? The internationalization of struggle and the need for global solidarity', in K. Duncan (ed.), *Liberating Alternatives: The Founding Convention of the Cultural Environment Movement*, Cresskill, NJ: Hampton Press, pp. 107–15.

Traber, M. (1993) 'Changes of communication needs and rights in social revolutions', in S. Splichal and J. Wasko (eds), *Communication and Democracy*, Norwood, NJ: Ablex, pp. 19–31.

Turow, J. (1997) *Breaking up America: Advertisers and the New Media World*, Chicago and London: University of Chicago Press.

Underwood, D. (1995) [1993] *When MBAs Rule the Newsroom*, New York: Columbia University Press.

Uzelman, S. (2002) *Catalyzing Participatory Communication: Independent Media Centre and the Politics of Direct Action*, unpublished Master's thesis: School of Communication, Simon Fraser University.

Valle, C. A. (1995) 'Communication: international debate and community-based initiatives', in P. Lee (ed.), *The Democratization of Communication*, Cardiff: University of Wales Press, pp. 199–216.

Van Aelst, P. and Walgrave, S. (2002) 'New media, new movements? The role of the internet in shaping the "anti-globalization" movement', *Information, Communication and Society* 5: 465–93.

Vogel, D. (2003) *Challenging Politics: COPE, Electoral Politics and Social Movements*, Halifax: Fernwood Books.

Wallerstein, I. (1989) '1968, revolution in the world-system', *Theory and Society* 18: 431–49.

White, A. (2004) 'Dissent and collective action in oppressive times', in W. Bruneau and J. L. Turk (eds), *Disciplining Dissent*, Toronto: James Lorimer, pp. 171–81.

White, R. A. (1988) 'NWICO has become a people's movement', *Media Development* 35(1): 20–5.

—— (1995) 'Democratization of communication as a social movement process', in P. Lee (ed.), *The Democratization of Communication*, Cardiff: University of Wales Press, pp. 92–113.

Williams, R. (1961) *The Long Revolution*, London: Chatto and Windus.

Winter, J. (1997) *Democracy's Oxygen: How Corporations Control the News*, Montreal: Black Rose.

Wisler, D. and Giugni, M. (1999) 'Under the spotlight: the impact of media attention on protest policing', *Mobilization* 4: 171–87.

Wolschon, E. (1996) 'History of Media Alliance', at www.media-alliance.org/history.html (accessed February 2003).

Young, R. J. C. (2003) *Postcolonialism: A Very Short Introduction*, Oxford: Oxford University Press.

Zhao, Y. (2005) 'Who wants democracy and does it deliver food? Communication and power in globally integrated China', in R. A. Hackett and Y. Zhao (eds), *Democratizing Global Media: One World, Many Struggles*, Lanham, Boulder, New York, Toronto, Oxford: Rowman & Littlefield, pp. 57–79.

Zhao, Y. and Hackett, R. A. (2005) 'Media globalization, media democratization: challenges, issues, and paradoxes', in R. A. Hackett and Y. Zhao (eds), *Democratizing Global Media*, New York: Rowman & Littlefield, pp. 1–33.

Index

challenges 129–42; changing lifeworld
as media environment 59–62;
counterhegemony and 204–7;
embedded identities 186–9; internet
activism 45–50, 96–7; location 86–8;
Media Alliance 97–109, 138; media
field as site of struggle 199–204; missed
and blocked opportunities 135–42;
missing partners and cultural divides
136–9; mobilization challenges 130–5;
mobilization on multiple fronts 50–4;
as nascent movement 65–6; network
analysis 179–85; New World
Information and Communication
Order (NWICO) 94–5, 200; opponents
of media democratization 139–41;
positive springboards 145–56; post 9/11
political climate 141–2; post-
communist media reform 95–6; prods
to activism 143–5; reforming public
communication systems 62–5; resource
shortages 130–1; resources 148–51;
right-wing reaction 95; self-
marginalization 131–5; 'Sixties' 92–4;
sociopolitical visions 189–92; strategy
156–63, 192–8; structural
conduciveness 145–7; typology 54–7,
203; Vancouver 165–7
democratic socialism 74
democratization of media 18, 37–9, 62–3,
65–6, 90, 200; contending frames
78–82; long-term view 77; opponents
139–41; People's Communication
Charter 82–6; *see also* democratic media
activism (DMA)
dependency: asymmetrical 44
Deterline, Kim 80, 130, 133
Dichter, Aliza 79, 132, 139, 147, 162, 203
direct action media critique 60
diversity 38, 82, 85; reduction in 6–7
Downing, J. D. H. 19, 48, 69, 76, 106
Dunifer, Stephen 76
Dyson, Rose 132

Edmondson, Richard 132
education: media 60, 62, 119, 146, 157–8,
194
Ehrenreich, Barbara 144
elitism: model of democracy 69–71; moral
leadership 76
embedded identities 186–9
Enlightenment 77
environment of media 25, 79; changing
lifeworld as media environment 59–62

environmental issues 120
equality 85
European Convention on Human Rights
116

Fairness and Accuracy in Reporting
(FAIR) 63, 120, 135, 149, 150, 155–6,
159, 160, 162
Fallows, James 72
feminism 75
field 15; media as 17, 31–5; as site of
struggle 199–204
focus: lack of 133–5
Foucault, Michel 32
Fox News Channel 5, 8, 35
Franck, Peter 80
Fraser, Nancy 15, 72
Free Press (US) 67, 97
Freedman, Des 124
freedom 78; freedom versus moral order
77; of information 115
Fry, Hedy 142
functionalism 15
funding *see* resources

Gamson, W. A. 44, 135
gay rights movement 62, 98, 155, 159
gender: feminism 75; gender justice 61;
under-representation of women in
media 6, 113
General Electric 3
Gerbner, George 8
ghettoization 59
Global Exchange 46, 102
Global Media Monitoring Project 60
globalization 1, 8, 147; internet activism
and 45–6
government and state 25, 27; alliances with
152–3; grants from 131, 148; Left and
76; market liberalism/conservatism and
70; recentring 207–9; regulation by 64
Gramsci, Antonio 15, 65, 207
Greenpeace 26, 28, 164
grievances: shared 50
Guerrilla Media 173–4, 179, 182, 208
Gunther, Herbert Chao 129
Gutstein, Donald 196

Habermas, Jürgen 2, 15, 40, 52–3, 55, 203
Hackett, R. A. 30, 33, 34
Hall, Stuart 16, 28, 31
Hamelink, Cees 86, 129, 135, 140, 152
Hart, Peter 163
Hazen, Don 134

Power without Responsibility

Sixth Edition

James Curran and Jean Seaton

'This is a useful and timely book'
Richard Hoggart, Times Educational Supplement

'In a fast-changing media scene this book is nothing less than indispensable'
Julian Petley, Brunel University

'*Power without Responsibility*, the best guide to the British media'
Nick Cohen, The New Statesman

Power without Responsibility is a classic, authoritative and engaged introduction to the history, sociology, theory and politics of media and communication studies. Written in a lively and accessible style, it is regarded as the standard book on the British media. This new edition has been substantially revised to bring it up-to-date with new developments in the media industry. Its three new chapters describe the battle for the soul of the internet, the impact of the internet on society and the rise of new media in Britain. In addition, it examines the recuperation of the BBC, how international and European regulation is changing the British media and why Britain has the least trusted press in Europe.

ISBN10: 0-415-24389-0 (hbk)
ISBN10: 0-415-24390-4 (pbk)

ISBN13: 978-0-415-24389-6 (hbk)
ISBN13: 978-0-415-24390-2 (pbk)

Available at all good bookshops
For ordering and further information please visit:
www.routledge.com

Media and Power

James Curran

Media and Power addresses three key questions about the relationship between media and society.

- How much power do the media have?
- Who really controls the media?
- What is the relationship between media and power in society?

In this major new book, James Curran reviews the different answers which have been given, before advancing original interpretations in a series of ground-breaking essays.

Media and Power also provides a guided tour of the major debates in media studies. What part did the media play in the making of modern society? How did 'new media' change society in the past? Will radical media research recover from its mid-life crisis? What are the limitations of the US-based model of 'communications' research? Is globalization disempowering national electorates or bringing into being a new, progressive global politics? Is public service television the dying product of the nation in an age of globalization? What can be learned from the 'third way' tradition of European media policy?

Curran's response to these questions provides both a clear introduction to media research and an innovative analysis of media power, written by one of the field's leading scholars.

ISBN10: 0-415-07739-7 (hbk)
ISBN10: 0-415-07740-0 (pbk)

ISBN13: 978-0-415-07739-2 (hbk)
ISBN13: 978-0-415-07740-8 (pbk)

Related titles from Routledge

Media, Technology and Society
Brian Winston

Media Technology and Society offers a comprehensive account of the history of communications technologies, from the printing press to the internet.

Winston argues that the development of new media forms, from the telegraph and the telephone to computers, satellite and virtual reality, is the product of a constant play-off between social necessity and suppression: the unwritten law by which new technologies are introduced into society only insofar as their disruptive potential is limited.

Winston's fascinating account examines the role played by individuals such as Alexander Graham Bell, Gugliemo Marconi, and John Logie Baird and Boris Rozing, in the development of the telephone, radio and television, and Charles Babbage, whose design for a 'universal analytic engine' was a forerunner of the modern computer. He examines why some prototypes are abandoned, and why many 'inventions' are created simultaneously by innovators unaware of each other's existence, and shows how new industries develop around these inventions, providing media products to a mass audience.

Challenging the popular myth of a present-day 'information revolution' *Media Technology and Society is* essential reading for anyone interested in the social impact of technological change.

ISBN10: 0-415-14229-6 (hbk)
ISBN10: 0-415-14230-X (pbk)

ISBN13: 978-0-415-14229-8 (hbk)
ISBN13: 978-0-415-14230-4 (pbk)

Available at all good bookshops
For ordering and further information please visit:
www.routledge.com